Jewish Insights on Death and Mourning

Jewish Insights on Death and Mourning

Edited with introductions by *Jack Riemer*

Foreword by Sherwin B. Nuland

Formerly
WRESTLING WITH THE ANGEL

SCHOCKEN BOOKS   NEW YORK

Permissions acknowledgments appear on pp. 369-374.

Library of Congress Cataloging-in-Publication Data

Jewish insights on death and mourning / edited by Jack Riemer.
p. cm.
Previously published under the title: Wrestling with the angel. New York :
Schocken Books, © 1995.
ISBN 0-8052-1035-0
1. Death—Religious aspects—Judaism. 2. Bereavement—Religious
aspects—Judaism. 3. Mourning customs, Jewish. 4. Consolation (Judaism)
I. Reimer, Jack. II. Title.
BM635.4.W73 1996
296.3'3—dc20   95-53115
CIP

Book design by Maura Fadden Rosenthal

Manufactured in the United States of America
First paperback edition
2 4 6 8 9 7 5 3

In loving memory of my parents,
and of Poppa, Sammie, and Hermina,
who taught us how to wrestle with the angel of life by their example,
to Sue, to whom my debt is inexpressible,
and to Yosef, Tina, and Adena, Nathan and Naomi,
who make the wrestling so worthwhile

Contents

Acknowledgments

To Evelyn Lowe, my faithful secretary, who brings a measure of
    order out of chaos
To Susanne Nunez and David Weinberg, who know how to deal
    with the machines of this world
To Bonnie Rothschild, my link to the library
To Congregation Beth David with gratitude
And to my editor, Bonny Fetterman, who argued with me so
    many times and who was almost always right.

And an angel wrestled with Jacob until the break of dawn. . . .
And he said: "Let me go for dawn is breaking." And Jacob
answered him: "I will not let you go, unless you bless me."

—Genesis 32:25, 27

God is in the answers . . . and in the questions too.

—Elie Wiesel

Foreword

The derivation of a term sometimes speaks volumes about the history and values of the culture in which it is being used. *Livayah,* the Hebrew word for funeral, means "to accompany"—and in this simple truth lies the entire significance of the remarkable book you are about to read. In much the same way that we accompany our loved ones through the voyages that are their lives, the Jewish tradition teaches us how we may travel with them to their final rest, and beyond.

The closing sentence of Thornton Wilder's Pulitzer Prize classic, *The Bridge of San Luis Rey,* is one of the most beautiful prose statements I have ever encountered in a long lifetime of reading: "There is a land of the living and a land of the dead and the bridge is love, the only survivor, the only meaning." Love can express itself in many ways when a life has ended, and we seek comfort in all of them. The years may diminish the force of memory's details, but they do not diminish the force of love. As Wilder wrote in his penultimate line, "Even memory is not necessary for love." The multitude of us who still feel its power many decades after a loss know exactly what is meant by those words.

The grief of death is ultimately one of the most personal of emotions, not transferable and sometimes not capable of being understood by anyone other than the individual mourner. In a sense, every one of us mourns alone. And yet, not only individuals but communities too sustain painful losses when a death occurs. The Jewish tradition teaches us ways in which we may join our singular grieving into pathways that are as communal as they are private, and thereby find the sustenance to carry ourselves—and to allow ourselves to be carried—forward. Jewish mourning customs function to transform the chaos of internalized grief into a pattern of responsible order, so that fearful introversions may be replaced with an open acknowledgment of shared loss; they bring their very structure to the turbulence of a distraught mind.

In his recent book *To Life!* Rabbi Harold Kushner makes the point that, unlike Christianity, which is a religion centered in faith—specifically faith in the divinity of Jesus—Judaism finds its center in its history and sense of community. Nowhere is this more clear than in the customs that unite Jews around the death of one of us. These customs enfold us closer into the nurturing company of our Jewish fellowship; for many they have served as an introduction to the strengths of our heritage. *Jewish Insights on Death and Mourning* is Rabbi Jack Riemer's skillful weaving together of a group of personal testimonies to the spiritually and psychologically enhancing value of our ways. These writings contain not only the wisdom of modern rabbinic thought but also the essence of that emotional fulfillment which can come when we observe the rituals that our people follow when we mourn.

We read here of the experiences of men and women like ourselves as they have discovered reassurance and renewal through the ancient duties of visiting the dying, participating in a burial society, preparing the body for interment, watching over it as a *shomer,* planning the funeral service, carrying out the burial, tearing one's garment, sitting shivah, saying the Kaddish, observing the month of *shloshim* and the eleven months of mourning as part of a regular minyan, and, finally, recalling memories at yahrzeit. These are all obligations we perform as members of a group, and in this book we hear from people who tell us how they found in each of them a specialized meaning that far transcended the mere carrying-out of a prescribed formula.

Some of the contributors to *Jewish Insights on Death and Mourning* had never carried out these duties before the death of which they write—in some cases they had no previous knowledge of them—and yet they discovered in their fulfillment a reality that permitted expressions of love that would otherwise not have been possible, or that might have been channeled into disappointing or even harmful directions. Centuries of shivah and Kaddish should have taught us the psychological and communal value of Jewish mourning customs, but still we seem to need to learn it anew in each generation and perhaps even with each death. In this book, Rabbi Riemer sets it down for all to see, and wonder at.

Rabbi Riemer has called on representatives of all facets of American Jewish life; contributors range across the spectrum from Orthodox to what might be called innovative Reform. It is obvious, not only from these essays but by witnessing our society in general, that there must be almost as many reasons for traditional observance as there are men and women who observe traditionally. The one criterion that unites us all is personal fulfillment, and here I will carry Rabbi Kushner's words beyond his intention. More than most of us think, there are observant Jews (although admittedly their degree of observance varies widely) who cannot bring themselves to believe in any power beyond what can be proven by rational, or scientific, thought. A priori, this excludes a belief in God, and yet such people are sometimes paradoxically adherent to the customs of their ancestors and find gratification and a vital strength in Judaism that enriches their life in ways that would seem to defy possibility. I would argue that, for many of those individuals, such a stance is neither hypocritical nor even inconsistent.

For some of us, it is necessary only to believe in the continuity of the Jewish people and to understand that the ultimate source of Jewish survival is the millennia-old certainty by the faithful that God exists and that God will redeem humankind. Even should one not share that certainty, it is impossible not to be awed by its bountiful influence in the history of Judaism. When one has been nurtured by generations of the truly faithful, adherence to observance sometimes becomes synonymous with adherence to the generations, to one's parents and grandparents and the centuries of those who came before. Those generations comprise a continuity of love and a sense of belonging, not only to family but to the worldwide community of Jews, *klal Yisrael*. It is the history and the human spirit of Judaism, our need to be at one with *klal Yisrael*, that lead to our observance. Clearly, this is not religious belief in the usual

sense, but it is a form of spirituality that has no doubt existed
among us for thousands of years. In Rabbi Riemer's extraordinary
book, we find reassurance that in following the precepts of our
forebears, we—believers and nonbelievers alike—bring wisdom
and honor to our lives, and the gratification of remaining joined to
our beloved dead and to all the living of our ancient people.

                                        —SHERWIN B. NULAND, M.D.

New Haven
October 1994

Preface

This book is a sequel to *Jewish Reflections on Death*, which was published by Schocken Books in 1974. When the publisher first asked me to do a second volume I was reluctant, for the questions of how to find strength and meaning in time of loss are eternal and I did not think that there was anything new or different to say today that had not been said already in the first book. But as I set about the task, I learned something about how Jewish life has changed in these last two decades. A comparison of the two books teaches us something about the difference between the way we were in Jewish life and the way we are now.

The good news is that there is a new generation of young Jewish writers and teachers, people who care and study and teach with much talent and insight. More good news is that there are now many women teachers. The first volume had only a few; this one has many. The bad news is that some of the people who wrote in the first book—such as Rabbis Joseph B. Soloveitchik, Abraham Joshua Heschel, and Milton Steinberg, and some of the others, *zichronam livrachah*—of blessed memory, were the giants of their generation and of any generation, and we have no replacements for them in our time.

A significant difference between the mood of those who write in the two books lies in their starting points. Some of those teachers who wrote in the first volume were so totally imbued with Jewishness that it was the fulcrum of their thinking, whereas many of the teachers in this volume begin with the world—with the pain of their own encounter with loss and their own experience of mourning—and then work their way back to the Jewish sources in search of a resource in their time of loss. Whereas the teachers who came out of a traditional Jewish world sought to explain the contemporary meaning of the old practices, the new teachers are imbued with a sense of discovery as they seek out forms and rituals that will bring healing, whether from the tradition or ones invented in our time.

Three issues take on special focus in this book, and each is a sign of the times. The first is the agonizing question of whether we are permitted to hasten the process of dying. Because of the medical technology that makes it possible to keep a patient technically alive indefinitely, people must now struggle with the question of whether we should or not. Hospitals now have "ethicists" on staff to help their doctors deal with this dilemma. In a relatively short time, nearly every state legislature in the country has passed a law formulating the precise language of what are euphemistically called "living" wills, which lawyers now give to their clients and hospitals provide to their patients automatically. Does the Jewish tradition have any insights to offer into this complex question? We bring together a number of statements by committed Jews who have had to face this issue, not only in classrooms but in waiting rooms, not only in theory but in their lives. Their answers range from "Yes—it is a mitzvah" to "No—it's forbidden" to "Maybe—but not yet."

A second issue that is given more scrutiny in this book than in the first is the question of what we mean by afterlife and what we can hope for and yearn for after this life is done. Only Dr. Heschel addressed this issue in the first book; here, a number of people do. They remind us that this was once a premise of Jewish thought and that there is a long and serious literature on the theme within our tradition. But somehow, during the nineteenth and twentieth centuries, as rationalism came to dominate the Western world, Jewish teachers became apologetic about all the spiritual dimensions of Judaism, including this one. It was repressed, considered nonnormative, and ignored. But now, as the borders between Eastern and Western civilizations become more porous and as the search for spirituality becomes worldwide, young Jews are returning to ask spiritual questions of their own tradition. There is a new openness on the part of contemporary Jews to the nearly lost body of thought within Judaism concerning an afterlife. The essays in this book are not dogmatic or prescriptive. They do not claim to be able to describe the furniture of heaven or the geography of hell, but they do give us permission to believe. These essays are remarkable because they weave together insights out of Judaism, computer science, astrophysics, and the hopes of the human heart.

The third issue that emerges prominently in this book is the determination of this generation to *take back our lives and our deaths* from the hands of the experts and the professionals. It is a trend that is manifest throughout our culture. People today are no longer content to sit docilely in impressive sanctuaries ("Ours sleeps eight hundred," one rabbi once said about his) and listen politely to a rabbi who speaks from "six feet above contradiction," and they no longer want to come to services to "watch their employees pray." Instead, they want a share in the service. They feel the need and the right to add words, to choose melodies, and to be part of the planning of the prayers. And so it is in medicine. People now see themselves as partners with their physicians in the decision-making process, instead of simply being under their control. Two striking illustrations of this new determination to wrest the conduct of our lives back from the professionals are the Vidui and the Hevra Kadisha.

The Vidui is the confessional prayer in which a person tries to sum up and then let go of his or her life. In a death-denying culture, there was no place for such a prayer. If patients are kept out of sight in the intensive-care unit, tranquilized so that the pain will be less but with the result that consciousness will be less too, if relatives are kept away or if they see their task as "cheering up the patient" and not letting him or her find out the true nature of the illness, the Vidui is not possible. But in this book we see a return to an appreciation of the place of honesty and openness at the end of life. We read of how peace was made and reconciliation achieved within one family at the end, and of the blessings that resulted from another family's decision to keep their loved one at home till the very end. Who would have imagined a generation ago that the Vidui would come back?

And even more amazing is the current new interest in the Hevra Kadisha, which this book manifests. It was hardly mentioned in the last volume because hands-on contact with the dead, actually performing the purification ceremonies that the tradition requires before burial—surely this was something to be left to the professionals and the experts. The rest of us felt far too squeamish for such a task. And yet—who would have believed it?—all around the country young people are now learning how to carry out this difficult mitzvah. They testify that they come out of the experience with a deeper awe for the holiness of life and for the mystery of death. And they testify that the shared experience has brought about a new and deeper sense of community for those who participate. As Rabbi Margaret Holub puts it in her description of what the Hevra Kadisha has meant in her shtetl of Mendocino, California:

> When my husband and I married last year, our Jewish community was present for us in ways that still overwhelm us when we recall them. I don't think that this would be true were it not for the experiences we have had struggling to be present when someone here has died. The traditions that surround death have brought us Jewishly to life.

This book is in two parts, called "Answers" and "Questions." "Answers" is composed of writings in which we have tried to show how the resources of the Jewish tradition can help us through the end of life and provide healing for those who mourn. "Questions" is composed of writings that show that after all our answers, questions still remain; that after all the explanations, pain still remains; that after all the words of comfort, silence still remains; that after all the theologies, God still remains. That is the reason why, after all the pages of wisdom that were put together in the first book, a second one was needed, and that is the reason why, after this book is read and absorbed, there will still be room for and need for more search, more study, more wisdom.

This is not a book for thanatologists or for any other kind of *ist;*

it is meant only for those who are mortal and who know it. Some of the essays provide basic information about the Jewish way in death and dying and explain some of the main rituals and traditions. But most are testimonies, not histories. They speak not so much about how these rituals developed down through the centuries, but of what they can mean to us here and now. The people in this book write of how they themselves went through loss, of what they have learned out of their pain, and of the ways in which the resources of the Jewish tradition spoke to them in their time of greatest need. This explains why we have included the insights of poets as well as historians, of ordinary people as well as scholars and rabbis, of storytellers as well as halakhic experts and therapists. For when we face our end, those who speak from the heart have as much to teach us as those who speak from the mind.

I invite you to listen to the voices that speak here. All have wrestled with the angel of death and all have paid the price in loss, which is the price of love. They speak out of their own experience to others who are companions on the same road of life. May they speak for—and to—all who yearn for solace and for strength.

—JACK RIEMER

Jewish Insights on Death and Mourning

Introduction: Jewish Insights on Death

Jack Riemer

When I was a child, our attitude toward death was like that of the Victorians toward sex: we knew it was there but we didn't talk about it. Now, everyone is talking about it. You hear it in the lyrics of the hit songs; you see it as the theme of many movies. There are now classes in death and dying in high schools and colleges, at conventions of teenagers and in the Elderhostels. And a book with the title *How We Die* becomes a bestseller!

Why this new interest in the topic? No one can say for sure, but I have a number of guesses. One is that the baby boomers are now reaching maturity and are being confronted for the first time with the reality that they are mortal too. I think they thought that doctors had found a cure for so many other diseases that they would surely have found a cure for death by now, but they haven't. Or it may be because the turn of the millenium is drawing near. Such a time has occasioned anxiety and speculation about the end of the world before in history, and perhaps it will again. Or it may be because of all the violence that permeates our culture. We always knew that we were mortal, but now we are aware that the planet itself may be mortal. Ever since the invention of the atomic bomb, we and all future generations are destined to live under its shadow, forever conscious of the vulnerability of the earth itself. The ecologists, with their concern for the ozone layer, overpopulation, the rain forest, and all the other ominous terms that they have brought into our awareness, have made us understand that the earth itself is in danger of dying. Or again, this generation goes to the funerals of its heroes through television and so is beginning to understand that death is a constant traveling companion all during life.

Another reason for the new interest may be the new medical

achievements and the moral questions they raise. Science has produced new technologies for preserving life that were not available to previous generations. But as a result, we must now deal with new ethical dilemmas. We can now keep someone technically alive indefinitely by means of machinery. Should we? Is that life? Or is that just vegetative existence? We can now transplant organs from a dead person's body into a living person. Should we hurry a death along in order to obtain an organ that can save a life? Is that murder or not? We used to know the definition of death: it was when the heart stopped beating. But I have a friend whose heart stopped beating thirty-seven times, and they started it up again thirty-seven times! So now the definition of death is not as clear as it once was. Is it when the heart stops beating or is it when the brain stops making waves, or do we need another definition? Questions that once seemed simple need to be rethought today.

Or it may be that the interest in this topic is in large part the work of one woman, Elisabeth Kübler-Ross. Her book *On Death and Dying* single-handedly created the field. She tells of how, when she first started her studies, she went to doctors and nurses in a Chicago hospital and asked if she could interview their dying patients. "We don't have any," they said. Or, "You can't talk to them because you'll upset them if you ask them any questions." Then she realized that doctors and nurses have a problem in dealing with death. When she finally got to the patients, over the opposition of the doctors, she found that they were hungry for someone to talk to and for someone who would listen to them. And so now she goes around the country holding seminars at which the dying speak to the not-yet-dying and help them understand what they are going through.

For whatever reason, whether it is because of the violence that surrounds us or the new medical technology and the questions it raises or the work of Elisabeth Kübler-Ross and others in this field—for whatever reason, the topic is "in" nowadays. I think that there ought to be a Jewish voice in the discussion. Judaism is a religion that claims to speak to all of life. Death is surely a part of life, and I wanted to investigate what Judaism has to say about it. For we all stand before the very same darkness and we all hunger for whatever wisdom and guidance we can find. If Judaism has any insights that can guide us, we surely want to know what they are.

Let me begin by making one thing clear. *I am no expert; no one is.* No one knows anything at all about death. No one has ever come back to tell us what it is like to die. People have been dying ever since the beginning of time, and yet everyone believes—not in his head but in his heart—that it will happen to others but not to him. I am no different, no less anxious, no less apprehensive than anyone else. This book is not intended for experts or for professional thanatologists. It is intended only for those people who are mortal—and who know it.

What I have done in this book very simply is go to my teachers and to my fellow seekers and ask them: *What do you know? What has helped you get through grief? What has helped you cope with mortality?* And I have listened to their answers and set them down.

What they tell me is that, just as the Jewish way of life is different from that of contemporary culture, so it is with the Jewish way of death. They tell me that it goes directly against the grain of much of contemporary culture in at least five ways.

I had a friend whose father died on the seventh day of Passover. He once reminisced with me about the way his father died. The father did what he did every Passover: he recited the Hallel, the psalms of thanksgiving and rejoicing that are said on this holiday. Then, sometime later, he sensed that he was nearing his end. And so he reopened the prayer book and recited the Vidui, the prayer you are supposed to say at the end of your life. A little while later, he died.

When I heard that story, I had two reactions. One was: What a way to go! To go connected to King David and to the Psalms and to his children—what a wonderful memory to leave behind! And the second thought that occurred to me was a question. He must have said the Hallel a thousand times in his life; which were the words in the Hallel that meant the most to him when he said them for the last time? Was it perhaps the phrase "I am Your servant, the son of Your handmaiden, undo my chains"? Or was it "Grievous in the sight of the Lord is the death of His loved ones"?

I am willing to wager that most of us will not go that way. Most of us will probably go heavily sedated by tranquilizers which, thank God, will lower the pain but which will also blur the consciousness. Many of us will go in intensive-care units where visitors are allowed in for only a few minutes every few hours and where children are not allowed in at all—as if children were a contagious disease. We will go connected to tubes and wires and all kinds of complicated machinery. And if you juxtapose those two images— of the man who died connected to King David and the Psalms and his children, and the man who dies in sterile, antiseptic isolation— you have the difference between the way it was and the way it is in contemporary culture.

There are, as I have said, five Jewish insights into death and dying that I have learned from my teachers. The first is *realism and honesty*. It is bad enough to fool others; it is worse to fool yourself. And so Jewish tradition is honest. When it came time for Father Jacob to die, he gathered his children around his bedside and said to them: "Behold, I am now about to die." *He said the word*—no euphemisms, no cosmetics, no artificial grass carpets, none of the many devices that we use nowadays in the futile and ultimately unsuccessful effort to deceive ourselves. In the prophetic portion that is read in the synagogue on the same Sabbath when we read the story of Jacob's death from the Torah, we read how King David died. He too speaks to his child and says: "Behold I am now about to go the way of all flesh." There is no effort to deceive his child; there is no effort to deceive himself. He faces the truth.

This is so different from contemporary culture, with all its denials and coverups. The poet Charles Reznikoff has written a satire of modern funerals:

A well-phrased eulogy, a low-pitched dirge,
faces politely sad
before the expensive, well-polished coffin;

a thick green cloth about the deep grave
to keep loose earth
from the sod:

a funeral
punctual, well-mannered, neat.

I see that from the rude young man you were
you have gone far.

There is a double entendre in that last line. At one level it means that from the plain, untutored young man you once were, you have gone far up the social ladder and so you now have a fancy, formal, dignified funeral. And the other meaning is, of course, that from all the distinctions of class and status that matter so much while we are alive, you have gone far—down into the earth, as all human beings must eventually go.

In Jewish thought, death is not only the inevitable end of life; it is a constant companion and possibility within life. That is why you are never supposed to say, "I'll see you tomorrow." For no one owns tomorrow. Instead, one is supposed to say, "I'll see you tomorrow, *God willing*," or "I'll see you tomorrow *but that is not a promise.*"

This is not a morbid way to live. On the contrary, the fact that life is fragile and precarious, the fact that each new day is a gift and not an entitlement, makes it even more precious, more to be appreciated, more to be savored.

Thus one of the sages in the Talmud taught his disciples that "a person should repent one day before he dies" *and* a person should know that every day might be that day. So Jews would buy plots and have their shrouds and make their final arrangements, not out of morbidity but simply in order to be ready.

I love the story that is told about the tourist from America who came to visit the Chafetz Chayim, who was one of the great sages of eastern Europe. The tourist came in and looked around. He saw a table, a desk, a bookcase, a closet, a bed, and a chair.

"Where are your possessions?" he asked.

"Where are *your* possessions?" was the rabbi's reply.

"What do you mean, 'Where are my possessions?' " asked the tourist. "I am just a visitor here."

"So am I," said the Chafetz Chayim.

We are all just visitors upon this earth. As the psalmist put it, "I am a sojourner upon this earth."

Yom Kippur, the Day of Atonement, has many meanings. But surely one of the most important is that it is an annual rehearsal for and confrontation with death. So we fast on this day and carry no possessions, as if we need no things. We bless our children before it begins, as if in farewell. And the whole focus of the prayers on this day is on the preciousness and the fragility of life. One of the things that brought the lesson home most effectively was what the Jew used to wear on this day. He wore, and in many congregations he still wears, a simple white linen garment called a *kittel*. A *kittel* is a shroud. It is the same plain white garment—*with no pockets*—that he will wear when he is buried. It is a powerful educational experience to put on your shroud once a year. Do you see that person over there that you have been meaning to make up with one of these days? He is wearing a *kittel*—which means that "one of these days" may be too late. And I am wearing one too—which means that I am mortal. It is a humbling experience to put on a *kittel*. It makes you realize, more effectively than words can, that one more year of your life has disappeared, and that you are now one year closer to your end.

My favorite headline of the year comes from the *Vail Trail* newspaper of Vail, Colorado. It seems that the community is divided over whether to change the zoning laws in order to allow for a cemetery to be established in this posh ski resort. One side feels that real communities make room for those who live and work in them, even when they die. The view of the other side is expressed by the cofounder of the newspaper:

"A cemetery in Vail is against what Vail is all about.

"People come here in order to have a good time and ski and enjoy the atmosphere. It would be bad for business if we did anything that would depress them."

I didn't make that up—honest.

In our synagogue we have the custom of a book burial once every couple of years. We do it for two reasons. One is to teach people respect for books. You don't just throw a holy book away. When it is worn out and can no longer be used, you bury it. And the second reason is to provide our children with an opportunity to visit a cemetery. I give them a walking tour and show the children some of the tombstones and explain to them the American Jewish history inscribed on those stones. There is one stone, for example, that reads: SHE BROUGHT OVER MANY, which means that the person who rests there vouched for and helped a good number of relatives to come to this country.

Every time we schedule a book burial, some parent calls me up in great agitation and says, "I don't want you to take my child along. I don't want my child traumatized. My child is only eighteen." I say to that parent, "It's up to you. You don't have to send him if you don't want to," but I think that such parents make a mistake. If we had a contract with the world whereby the world would not expose our children to any experience until we felt they were ready for it, that would be nice, but we don't have such a contract. *It is better to know before you need than to need before you know.* Those parents who try to shield their children by keeping them from Zaide's hospital bed or from Bubbe's funeral or from visiting a cemetery may mean well, but they are doing their children a disservice.

Look at the traditional Jewish prayer books and the ones we have today, and you will see at least one significant contrast. The traditional prayer book was intended to cover all of life. There was a prayer for going on a trip or for having a baby or for opening your store or for blessing your children. Most modern prayer books are intended only for synagogue services, as if Jews pray only in public. There is no prayer for putting up a mezuzah or for starting school or for going on a trip or for any of the other luminous moments in life. And there is one page that was found in all the old prayer books that is missing from almost all the modern ones. It is the Vidui, the prayer to be said when dying: *Dear God, I want to live. But if this is Your decree, then I accept it from Your hand. Take care of my loved ones, with whom my soul is bound. Into Your hand I commit my soul. Hear, O Israel, the Lord our God, the Lord is One.*

Why is that prayer not found in most of the modern prayer books? Is it because we don't expect ever to need it, because we don't expect ever to die? We spend weeks and months preparing our children to become bar and bat mitzvah, but we never teach them that page, as if they are never going to need to say it. There is something radically wrong with our curriculum if we never tell our children of the existence of this prayer. We cheat our children of a vital dimension of life that ought to be a part of their education.

So the first Jewish insight into death, as it is into life, is *realism and honesty.* We are all born to die: that is what wearing the *kittel* on the Day of Atonement teaches; that is what studying the stories of the last days of Jacob and of David teaches, that is what going to a book burial teaches, and that is what studying the Vidui teaches.

The second Jewish insight is *equality and simplicity.* We spoil, we strain, we shorten, we warp, we waste so much of our lives keeping up with each other and getting ahead of each other. We are so envious of what the other person has that we can't enjoy what we have. We are involved all our lives in a frantic never-ending race to do more, to have more, to be more than our rivals.

The Jewish tradition teaches that *it has to stop somewhere!* If not before, then at least at the end, at least before God, let all people be equal and let the competition stop! And so the tradition provides that everyone should be buried in the same plain white linen shroud, the gown that has no pockets, because you can't take your possessions with you. And the tradition provides that everyone should be buried in the same simple wooden box. Let at least the end of life, if not before, be a time when you don't have to keep up with the Joneses or the Cohens and when everyone is equal.

Mourners are emotionally vulnerable. It is easy to take advantage of their grief and to persuade them to buy fancy bronze or mahogany caskets, caskets with art on the inside, caskets that are a way of putting good money into the ground. It is a free country, and no one can force a person to do what the tradition teaches is right. But what some congregations do is to keep a cover, which is put over every single coffin. No one can tell what kind of coffin is underneath the cover; no one knows whether it is bronze or mahogany or pine. And that takes off the mourners some of the pressure to keep up with others.

The third Jewish insight is *community*. Ours is *not* an I–Thou religion; ours is a We–Thou religion. To be a Jew means to be a cousin of the Jew in Cairo and the Jew in Calcutta, the Jew in Berlin and the Jew in Baghdad, the Jew in New York and the Jew in New Delhi. To be a Jew means to be connected, horizontally and vertically, to all the Jews around the world and to all the Jews of the past, the present, and the future. To be a Jew means to be a great-great-great-great-grandchild of Abraham our father and to be a great-great-great-great-ancestor of the Messiah. We come before God not by our own merits but as part of a people. A Jew by himself is impossible. And so, at the time of our bereavement, at the time of our greatest confusion and helplessness and isolation and bewilderment, the community reaches out and embraces us and says, "You are not alone, we care about you."

The community says that, not just in words, but by deeds. When the mourner comes back from the funeral, the law is that he must eat. The reason is that you really don't want to eat at such a time. To eat means to live, and you don't really want to live, so the law makes you eat. The law further requires that you do not prepare the food yourself. Others—relatives and friends—have to make the meal for you. That means that relatives and friends have to come into the house and have to be with you, and by their presence make you realize that you are not alone. And then, for the seven days of shivah, the minyan is held and the prayers are said, not in the synagogue but in the home. That means that twice a day ten people come into the house and thereby send you the message that you are not alone. And then for the rest of the year you join a club. You join what Joseph Zashin calls "the fraternity of mourners," a fraternity that has now been integrated. At first you are clumsy; you don't know your way around and someone has to show you the ropes. But soon you become a regular, and you are the one who helps newcomers. A sense of camaraderie and community develops.

There are a number of different terms for dying in the Jewish tradition. One of them is *to be gathered to your people*. That means "to become an ancestor, to become a part of history." When you stand with a mourner at a grave, what should you say? Whatever you say seems glib, inadequate. Should you say, "I know how you feel"? You *don't* know how I feel! Should you say, "How old was she?" What difference does it make how old she was? Should you say, "Time will heal"? Time *won't* heal! Whatever you say seems superficial, stupid, insufficient. What then are you supposed to say, according to the tradition? You are supposed to say, *"Hamakom yinachem etchem bitoch shaar aveyley Tsiyon viyirushalayim,"* which means: May God comfort you—since we don't know how—together with all those who are mourning for Zion and Jerusalem.

But don't I have enough troubles of my own? Do I need to be reminded of the loss of Zion and Jerusalem at such a time? The answer is that it *is* a comfort to know that we are not the only ones in mourning, that there are others in pain, that the world is in exile, and that we are needed to help assuage the grief of others. At the time of our loss we are all self-absorbed. And so it is good to be reminded that there are others in pain and that we are needed. Those words of comfort give us perspective and remind us that we are a part of the community, a community that needs us and cares about us.

The fourth Jewish insight into death as into life is Halakhah, which, for want of a better name, we translate as "the way in which to walk." It is the term for Jewish law. Ours is a legal religion. It is more than just a legal religion, but it is based on law. I learned this when I was working on this book. I went to psychology books on death and dying. There I found that the focus was on how to mourn in a therapeutically beneficial way. I went to Christian books on death and dying. There I found that the focus was on what we must do in order to be saved. I went to Jewish books, and there I found that the focus was on what our duties are in time of loss. The Shulhan Arukh, the great code of Jewish law, has page after page of technical, detailed regulations. How do you visit a sick person? Do you visit in the morning or in the afternoon? Do you pray or do you not? And then it goes on to regulate all the rest of the experience of mourning. You are supposed to sit home for a week. What constitutes a week? Does the first day count? Does the last day? You are supposed to tear a garment. What kind? What size tear? Which side of the garment? Can it ever be mended? And so on. Page after page of complicated, technical, detailed exposition of the law is found in the classic Jewish books on mourning.

Why so much law? For two reasons. First, it gives form and shape to our grief. It prevents excess and it prevents anarchy. Left to ourselves, who knows what we would do in time of loss? The law comes and regulates our mourning. Two thousand years before Freud, the sages said: "Whoever wants to mourn more than the law requires must be mourning for something else." You are not allowed to mourn more than the law requires or less than the law requires. When the seventh day ends, you have to move on to the next stage—ready or not. And you cannot mourn less than the law requires either. I have seen people who sloughed off loss as if nothing had happened. And I have seen people who said that they didn't have time to sit for seven days end up sitting seven times seven days on a therapist's couch afterward, working out the grief that they didn't have time to work out then.

Why do we sit shivah for seven days? Because the world was made in seven days and each person is a world, a world that never was before and that will never be again. If death is not something to be marked for a week because it is so awesome an event, if death is nothing, if death is cheap, then life is cheap. So the tradition says: Stop whatever you are doing and take notice, mourn, work it out, talk it out, for seven days. No more and no less.

The second reason the law is so detailed and explicit is that life is very complicated. We are an ancient people, and whatever can happen in this world has happened. What to do when it happens has been thought through by wise people, by people who were thinking calmly and not responding in time of crisis. When we have a problem, we can look up what those who came before us think we should do.

I remember studying in rabbinical school the question of what you do when a funeral procession meets a bridal procession at a crossroads. Which one has the right of way? And I remember thinking: How often could such a thing ever happen? You know what? It has happened twice already in my personal experience. Twice I have been involved in situations where the mother of the bride dropped dead on the day of the wedding. The family was stunned and bewildered, and I was stunned and bewildered, and no one could think clearly or figure out what to do. Do you know what you do in such a situation? *You look it up,* because it has happened before, and wise people, in calm deliberation, have thought through what you should do. That is the benefit of having a legal system.

The fifth Jewish insight into death as into life is *God.* It is very hard to talk about God in our time. The word has been cheapened and misused so often that perhaps we ought to declare a moratorium on its use for a while. If every politician is called a "prophet," if every movie star is called "divine," if even a pipe tobacco can be called "revelation," then how can we use any religious vocabulary without embarrassment?

The real question is not whether there is life after death but whether there is life after birth. If a human being is only a collection of chemicals which are worth a few dollars on the market, or if humans are only a species of the animal world, then we have no reason and no right to hope for anything more after this life. But if life is a gift, if life is a loan, if life is a wonder and a trust, then we have reason and right to hope and yearn and pray for something more after life. So the real question, when we want to talk about God, is What is man, or, to use Dr. Heschel's formulation, *Who* is man?

The keys to a culture lie in its language. There are a number of terms for death and dying in the Jewish tradition. One is "to be gathered to his people," which means to become an ancestor. Another is "to surrender life to the living," which suggests that there is a divine economy in which each generation has its turn and then must let go for the sake of the generation that comes next. And there is *niftar*, the term that is most usually used or abreviated on tombstones. *Niftar* means to be released from duty, to be summoned back after service.

There is a world of meaning in that term, *niftar*. What it means is that this is the world of work, and the next world is the world of rest. This is the world where you can do things for God. There is the world where you can be rewarded and sustained by God. And this world is better than the world-to-come because here you can serve; there you can only be sustained.

Let us look at our society by the light of these five insights. Honesty and realism? There is so little in this world. There is a multimillion-dollar industry by which we try to disguise and deny the coming of old age. Nowadays, it is less rude to ask a person how much money he has or the intimate details of his love life than it is to ask how old he is. Equality and simplicity? There is so much envy and competition in our culture. Community? There is very little sense of community in our lives. We live either in huge suburban developments or in large apartment houses in which no one really knows his neighbor. I remember when I lived in one of those apartment houses. I was riding up in the elevator one day and I noticed that the person going up with me was wearing a black ribbon, a sign of mourning. I uttered some cliché of sympathy and found out that he lived in the apartment directly above mine. I not only did not know that someone had died just above me; I did not even know that he lived just above me.

We live in a world in which, if you want to move up, you have to move out, and so we move constantly but pay a fearful spiritual price for our mobility. Very few people nowadays live in either the same state or the same state of mind as either their parents or their children. When I was a child, if I misbehaved and my mother was busy, the neighbor would hit me for her. But now I hardly know my neighbor, for I moved in yesterday and he is moving out tomorrow.

Kurt Vonnegut describes our culture in this way: "I am a great admirer of Alcoholics Anonymous, Gamblers Anonymous, Shoppers Anonymous, and all the rest of those anonymouses that are springing up. For they give to Americans something as indispensable to health as vitamins, something most of us no longer have: namely—an extended family. Human beings have almost always been supported, comforted and disciplined by stable lattices of relatives until the Great American Experiment, which is an experiment not only with liberty but also with rootlessness, mobility, and tough-minded loneliness" (Fates Worse than Death).

Vonnegut is right. How do you have a *simhah,* a celebration, when there are no relatives? And how do you sit shivah by yourself? There has been a trade-off. In exchange for the successes we achieve through mobility has come a breakdown in the sense of community, and I am not sure the trade-off is worth the price.

Law? There is very little sense of law in our religious life. We make our spiritual and moral decisions in terms of popular or unpopular, fashionable or unfashionable, relevant or irrelevant, not in terms of permitted or forbidden. As a result, our decisions change as fast as the fads, and "What are you into this year?" becomes the question with which we greet each other when we try to catch up on one another's spiritual situation.

And God? There is very little sense of God in our society. We have replaced God with ourself, and by ourself we mean our body, and so when the body wears out or breaks down, we have nothing to depend on. I remember how, during the period when "God is dead" was a fashionable slogan, Dr. Heschel said that we are like a patient crying out in his delirium that the doctor is dead.

Realism and honesty, equality and simplicity, community, law, and a sense of reverence for God—these are the central insights that the Jewish tradition offers to contemporary culture. They are basic to how Judaism would teach us how to live and how Judaism would teach us how to die.

There is a phrase that means a great deal to me. It is: "Attention must be paid." This whole book and all its insights can be summarized in these four words. They come from Arthur Miller's *Death of a Salesman,* which I believe is a deeply Jewish play, even though there is not a single explicit Jewish reference in it. It was written at a time when, if you wanted to make it on Broadway, you had to perform a lobotomy on your memory and deny your Jewish roots.

It is the story of Willie Loman—*low man*—an unsuccessful, insecure salesman who trudges from city to city, from store to store, carrying his satchels. Willie is getting old and lives in fear that his boss's son, who has now taken over the business, will fire him. He is lonely and full of anxiety as he faces old age and eventual death. One night he picks up a floozie in a bar and takes her up to his hotel room. His son, Biff, comes in unexpectedly and discovers them. He calls his father all kinds of names and refuses to listen to Willie's desperate attempts to justify himself. Biff storms out of the room, slamming the door behind him, and leaves Willie standing there, arms outstretched, trying to find the words with which to defend himself to a door that has been shut.

Willie Loman is a pathetic, worn-out wreck of a human being, and no one cares. No one pays any attention to him—no one that is except his wife. With all his faults and all his shortcomings, she still loves him. And so, at one point in the play, she comes center stage forward and says:

"Willie Loman is having a breakdown. *Attention must be paid!*"

And it is as if she hasn't said anything. No one hears. No one pays attention. Everyone else on the stage is too busy with his own concerns to hear what she has said. But those four words have haunted me ever since I first heard them. And if I had to summarize all the Jewish wisdom that I know about death and dying, it would be in those four words: *attention must be paid.*

The doctor has to understand that it is not the heart patient in room 407; it is a *person* who lies in that bed. The undertaker has to understand that it is not a booking he is arranging; it is a *person* he is burying. The hospital chaplain has to understand that it is not a name on a list that can now be deleted; it is a *person* who has died. *Up to, at, and after the end of life—attention must be paid.*

I have two striking illustrations of this truth, one from Israel, one from a certain hospital in America.

America is a big country and it has many people. When a soldier dies in an American war, the family receives a standard telegram: "The Department of Defense regrets to inform you that . . ." Israel is a very small country with far fewer people, and therefore every person in the country counts. When a soldier dies in an Israeli war, they do not send a standard telegram. Instead, two soldiers from that unit come to the house to break the news. *Attention must be paid.*

Elisabeth Kübler-Ross found that the nurses visit the rooms of terminal patients, or of patients whom they think are terminal, much less often than they visit the rooms of other patients. You can't blame them. After all, these patients don't smile and they don't respond to the nurses' ministrations. They make you feel helpless because there is so little you can do for them. You see your own mortality reflected when you visit them. It is understandable that nurses avoid them. I sometimes do too. I remember the first time I had to make a pastoral visit to a dying patient. I drove around the hospital parking lot and "couldn't" find a parking space, so I came home. I have done that, I am embarrassed to admit, so I understand when nurses and doctors do it and when family and friends do it.

But it isn't right—not right to the patient and not right to ourself. If we avoid them, we treat them as if they were already dead when they are still alive. If we come in and talk small talk and lie and pretend, we do them no favor. By avoiding them or treating them as children, we cheat them and we cheat ourself of what could be a precious and sacred experience. We miss what could be a profound moment with people who are not really different from us, with people *who are us,* just a bit further along the road that everyone in this life has to travel.

And so the central lesson that the Jewish tradition has to teach us—the point of this whole book—is: *up to, at, and after the end of life—attention must be paid.*

PART ONE

Answers

Chapter One

What I Have Learned from Illness

When you look back over the death of someone whom you loved or if you try to think about your own end, it is not so much the death but the dying that you remember with the most resentment or anticipate with the most dread. It is the long period of illness, the gradual wearing away of the body and the spirit, the debilitating effects of the illness that you resent—and rightly so.

And yet illness can sometimes be a time of genuine spiritual healing and of real inner growth for the patient and for those around him or her. There is a remarkable midrash that says that up until the time of Father Jacob there was no illness. People simply died one day. But Jacob prayed to God for the *gift of illness*, and God, in His goodness, granted the request. What this midrash means is that we have work to do at the end and therefore we need to have notice. We need to arrange our affairs and set our house in order. We need to make an accounting of our life. And we need to bless and bid farewell to those whom we love. Then we can "turn our face to the wall," which is the biblical term for surrendering our attachments and letting go of life.

Not all illnesses end in death. Here are some testimonies by a poet, a teacher, and three rabbis of how illnesses were transforming experiences for them. The Israeli poet Rachel tells of how illness was for her an emotional roller coaster, bringing hope and despair and hope again in the course of a single day. Harold Schulweis and Lawrence Kushner tell of how their own encounters with illness taught them truths that they knew from books but never really knew. Marcia Moskowitz tells of how she did something that is very seldom done anymore: she took her father-in-law into her home so that he could die amidst his family. The experience was both an ordeal and an inspiration that continues to shape their lives.

To Wake Up in the Hospital Early in the Morning

Rachel

To wake up in hospital early in the morning
To the prospect of a pointless day, and feel
Set in the flesh of your heart
The teeth of despair gnaw and pierce,
Through the eye of the minutes with weary hand
To feed the rotten thread of life
Over and over again,
What do the healthy know of such an hour?

In the hospital now the day grows dark,
Already night rules;
Softly in its wake descend
Reconcilement and peace.
The doctor's footsteps are heard in the hall,
Gently the comforting hand
touches yours,
What do the healthy know of such an hour?

Coronary Connections: From a Hospital, Some Secrets of the Heart Revealed

Harold M. Schulweis

Some attribute the statement to Santayana, others to Einstein. "We cannot know who first discovered water, but we can be sure it was not the fish." Why not the fish? Because water is all about them; they breathe it, taste it, swim in it. For them, water is too obvious to be noticed. Could it be that only when they are caught in the fisherman's net, trembling, gasping for air, the revelation occurs to them?

Water is life. Water is our life.

We humans are born into life. It is in us, in our being. It pulsates in our veins. We sleep and rise up into life; and often we are late, sometimes too late, to discover it. In our infantile omnipotence, we take our immortality as given. To those who, like the fish, take their life-support system for granted, the powerful biblical reminder—"therefore, choose life, that you shall live" (Deuteronomy 30:19)—is addressed.

When we are removed from the vital source of our energy, when we tremble, gasp for air, flail about wildly to grab at a straw of life, then it is that we catch a glimpse of the miracle of breathing, seeing, touching, hearing, smelling, feeling. *In extremis* old sayings, clichéed greetings—*"zei gezunt," "l'chayim"*—sound profound truths.

Surrounded by catheters and monitors and masks and needles, faced with the real possibility of my incapacitation and my death, I am jolted by transforming revelations. Fear and trembling are fierce instructors of the human spirit. "Do you not know that there comes a midnight hour when we must unmask? Do you suppose that life will forever suffer itself to be treated as a joke? Do you suppose that one can slip out a little before the midnight hour?" (Søren Kierkegaard).

"Every man is a child and pain is his teacher" (Alfred de Musset). Out of sickness and pain and fear, prayers once mechanically recited, benedictions mindlessly changed take on a new pertinence.

"Make you a new heart and a new spirit, for why will you die?" (Ezekiel 18:31). I hear with new ears. I see with new eyes this prayer I have recited from my childhood: "Blessed art Thou who has formed the human being in wisdom and created in him a system of veins and arteries. It is well known before Thy glorious throne that if but one of these openings be closed, it would be impossible to exist in Thy presence." Once I thought this a primitive prayer—not of dreams or refined petitions—but of openings and closings, orifices, apertures, cavities of my own flesh. How unseemly a prayer, how lacking in esthetics, how out of place within the covers of our majestic liturgy. But now I read it with new amazement and respect for its penetrating candor and concreteness.

Real prayer is with your body and your soul, with your bones and your flesh, and about your whole being. "The soul is Thine and the body is Thine. Blessed art Thou, O Lord, who healest all flesh and doest wonders."

Doest wonders. That is what prayer is about, to dissolve the boredom that dulls our senses, to open our eyes to the miracles that are daily with us—evening, morn, and noon. Prayer is not boring. We are boring. Prayer is the antidote to yawning. Prayer means to overcome the pedestrian perspective. Menachem Mendel of Kotzk chastised those who walk through life "with honey smeared on the soles of our shoes."

Pay attention. The sand beneath our sandals is holy. We walk on sacred soil, this amazing earth on which we tread.

I have been shaken by the shoulders of my being, awakened to life-and-death options. As one of T. S. Eliot's characters put it, "I have seen the moment of my greatness flicker, and I have seen the Eternal Footman hold my coat and snicker—and, in short, I was afraid."

But fear has its wisdom. Out of real fear, the fear of life and death, a thousand petty anxieties and dangers evaporate. Out of fear comes lucidity and out of lucidity a different understanding. When I have seen the shadow of death, and have lived to remember its face, how am I so readily frustrated with the myriad irritations, brooding over imperfections, failures, flaws?

"The Lord is my light and my healing; whom shall I fear? The Lord is the stronghold of my life; of whom shall I be afraid?" (Psalm 27).

Out of real fear, the glimpse of a new consciousness, a new gratitude is born.

Knowing mortality, what ambitions do I seek, what achievements, what acquisitions, what thrills, what childish fantasies of the rich and the famous? Why so full of complaints and demands? "I want, I want . . ."

Do you want what you want?

What do you crave with your insatiable neediness?

And where do you look for transcendence? Is there not wonder enough in your world? Will you forget the ecstasies of life, those postoperative marvels, the wonders, the signs, the miracles—to turn freely in your own bed from side to side, to cough, to sneeze, to walk, to wash without pain and fatigue?

Nissim, miracles—not in mountains moving or seas splitting, or people walking on the surface of waters—but in the rapture of breathing and sighing, in understanding a word spoken or a paragraph read, in following an argument, in recognizing a face, in waking to the ecstasy of ordinariness, the extraordinary ordinariness:

> A solitary stroll through the streets; windows, tastes, colors, a dark climb up the stairs, broken, crooked, a good *shabbos* greeting to uncle and aunt. Hallah dunked in red wine, pepper-sprinkled fish with white horseradish, green–red Sabbath fruit cherries, currants, gooseberries, the sourest of gooseberries between tart teeth.
>
> —Yaakov Glatstein

I wonder at the restless searchers, the voyagers for spirituality, looking for mystic signs, special mantras, séances, levitations, transmigration, trance-channeling communications with the dead, flirtations with extraterrestrials. Not that I am unmoved by the yearning for the transcendent, by the hunger for communion with another dimension beyond the flat surface of a material world that might offer this planet greater meaning. But they seek for God and wonder and spirituality in outlandish places, climbing the mountains, plumbing the depths of oceans.

Where else should they seek spirituality? Reb Eizek, son of Yekel of Cracow, dreamed that he was to look for a treasure beneath the bridge in Prague. He trusted the dream and set off to Prague. But the bridge was guarded by soldiers and he dared not dig. One day, the captain of the guard asked him what he was doing, standing day after day at the bridge. Reb Eizek told him he was following the mandates of a dream. "And so to please a dream you have traveled from Cracow to Prague. I too had a dream, that there is a treasure beneath the oven of a Jew in Cracow. The Jew's name was Eizek, son of Yekel." The captain laughed. Eizek bowed and returned to Cracow and dug up the treasure.

The treasure is not elsewhere. It is close to you, in your neighborhood, within your people, all about you.

It is not far off in the heavens above or the depths beneath, but in you. "In thy mouth and in thy heart."

Consider the heart, the soul of life. One-half pound, the size of a closed fist, pumping blood through vessels more than one hundred thousand miles long, pumping blood ten thousand times a day. This heart, now wounded, scarred, occluded, atrophied, is deliberately stilled, the patient anesthetized, marsupialized, heparinized, intubated, cannulated. The patient prepared, subject to hypothermia, cardioplegia, oxygen pumped to allow skillful courageous hands to sever sternum bone and muscle, to penetrate the heart itself so that it can be given life.

Who now dares take life for granted? Who can yawn in the face of this . . . worldly resurrection? Whose tongue can remain locked, whose lips sealed before such awesome wonder? Who cannot but offer benediction before the surgeon and his team and declare: "Blessed art Thou, O Lord our God, who shares His wisdom with flesh and blood."

Who can rant against science and technology, as if they stood in opposition to faith and religion? Are these marvelously contrived machines not instruments of divinity? Blessed is the human mind who can put together fragmented parts, make strong fragile organs, circumvent dead parts, and connect life with life. Look where for miracles? We carry them in our flesh and blood.

Blessed is the curative wisdom of the body.

We pray wrong. To pray is not to pay off your debt to some celestial creditor. It is not some unnatural act of piety. To pray is to notice, to pay attention, to overcome the apathy of entitlement. I look with new eyes at the opening prayers of our daily service, bursting with gratitude for opening the eyes to the blind, for raising up those bowed down, for guiding the step, for strengthening the weary.

I am not the only one who has been afflicted by illness, not the only one frightened by death and to life, but I now have a knowledge different from that drawn from texts. Knowledge by acquaintance is different from knowledge by description. It is one thing to read about it or to hear about it from another, and something else to offer testimony out of your own flesh. I have come out of this, not with revelations, but with the testimony of old truths renewed.

For Judaism, life is holy—not life in another time or another place, not life in heaven among angelic forms—but this one here and now with all its human agonies and frustrations. There is basic to Judaism an intense thirst for life.

Life is the major attribute of God—He is *chai ha-olamim,* life of the universe. To desire life is to desire God. To destroy life in oneself or another is to loathe God. We are bidden to fall in love with life again, to seize hold of this day and rejoice in its marvel.

The rabbinic tradition reminds us that laws and ordinances are for life, "that man shall live by them and not die by them" (Leviticus 18:5, Sanhedrin 74a). And in one of the major rabbinic codes we read that whoever asks whether or not it is permissible to desecrate the Sabbath in order to save life is "as if he sheds blood" (Jerusalem Talmud), and whichever scholar is asked that question is reprehensible because diligent religious teachers should have taught clearly so that the question would never have been raised.

Life is holy and life is plural—as it is grammatically plural in the Hebrew term *chayim.* What a conceit to think of myself as a self-sufficient biosystem, a portable set of plumbing, a self bounded by my outer skin. What a deceit is played upon us by the false intimacy of "me" or "I." There is no solitary life. There is no I without Thou, no "me" without "us." For our life, we are profoundly dependent upon each other.

The evidence stares me in the face. A call went out for blood contributions and was answered with quiet, anonymous dignity.

But consider, in our biblical tradition, "blood is life." We are warned not to shed the other's blood, not to stand idly by the spilled blood of the victim and to spill the blood of the slaughtered animal upon the ground so as not to drink of its life. But you are not mandated to transfuse your blood into another's veins, to put your God-given vitality into another. What, then, does it mean voluntarily, out of care and concern and love, to share of your life with another, save to enact an imitation of God?

I stare at the intravenous vessel. Am I indeed a solitary, discrete, self-sufficient, independent creature? How foolishly tragic is Narcissus gazing at his own reflection. Your vitality courses through my veins. My energy is derived from yours. Can we ignore our interdependence? We need one another. We are each other's life—in sickness and in health.

In the Jewish prayer for healing we pray not "Heal me, O Lord, and I will be healed," but "Heal us, O Lord, and we shall be healed. Blessed art Thou, O Lord, who heals the sick of Thy people."

No postoperative praise of illness and suffering is intended. I do not mean that illness and pain are somehow good, that because they can sensitize us, fear and suffering are somehow justified. Sickness, pain, anguish, torment, and death are neither rewards nor punishments from God. In our tradition, it is not piety but blasphemy to pursue martyrdom for its own sake. But how and what we learn from adversity, how we raise private trauma into public morale is the way we add dignity to God's name. Not the suffering, but the refusal to let it subdue our will to live; not the pain, but the courage and hope that enable us to overcome despondency are the signs of God's goodness and reality. No one struck me down from above to punish me for my transgressions—God is no sadist. No one struck me down from above to reward me with new insight—God is no clumsy instructor. But God gave me mind and heart to learn divine matters from natural events.

I have learned that God's language is in human behavior; that we are God's alphabet from *alef* to *tay*. We are God's vocabulary.

Consider the story based on the ambiguous biblical verse "Charity averts death." Whose death? His mother is ill. The son quickly calls for an ambulance to take her to the hospital. In the midst of the turmoil his father whispers to him that it is Friday and that he should not forget to bring home a stranger for the Sabbath meal. The young man is disturbed that his father would think of poor strangers when his mother is in such dire straits.

But days later he says to his father: "Now I understand, Father, about the stranger. You wanted to save Mother's life. 'Charity averts death.' " "No," says the father. "What I asked you to do I did not because I thought it would avert Mother's death, but because 'charity averts God's death.' "

Without charity, without love, God dies in this world. We are God's witnesses. If we are alive to each other, God is alive. If we live and love and help and heal, God is confirmed. God's name is exalted.

We prove God's goodness not by philosophic argument, but through the demonstration of our relationship with His world. In our behavior we argue God into existence on earth as He is in heaven.

I have learned from this experience that friendship in family and in community is sacred, and that it is a foolish canard to declare that "words are cheap." A letter, a card, a prayer are life transfusions of the human spirit. A call or a visit is as therapeutic as the cleverest of medicines; our ancient sages did not exaggerate when they wrote, "He who visits the sick causes him to live" (Nedarim).

Do not diminish the mitzvah (commandment) of *bikkur cholim,* visiting the sick. There is an ethics, an esthetics, an art in visiting the sick. In the Shulhan Arukh (Yoreh Deah 335:4, 5, 8), the visitor is counseled to "speak with discretion and tact, so as neither to revive him (with false hopes) nor depress him (with words of despair); not to visit a patient whose condition is an embarrassment to him or for whom conversation is difficult."

Why are friendship and family so vital? Because the fear we experience is not simply of physical death and dying. There are deaths in abandonment, deaths in friendlessness, deaths in living without love, without passion, without purpose. Death and dying wear many disguises; life and recovery must call upon many allies.

There is a profound correlation between illness and isolation, and between health and community.

In a Jewish tale the angels band together to conspire against God's intent to form Adam and Eve in His own image. They are jealous that ordinary men and women should inherit such spiritual treasure. The angels plot to hide goodness and truth from the human being. One angel proposes to hide God's mystery in the highest mountains; another suggests concealing it beneath the deepest seas. But the shrewdest angel counsels, "Men will search for godliness in the remotest of places. Hide it within them. It is the last place they will search for the miracles of godliness."

I received gifts of books in the hospital and during my recuperation. But I have come to learn what Buber concluded when he grew older. When in his youth he was asked which he preferred, Buber thought he preferred books to people. Books are easy to handle, easy to open and to close, to remove or place back on the shelves. Books are manna from heaven, while humans are like hard, brown bread on whose crust he breaks his teeth. But as he grew older, Buber changed his mind.

> I knew nothing of books when I came forth from the womb of my mother, and I shall die without books; I shall die with another human hand in my own.

What I fear, now that the energy returns and the scars fade, is that I will forget the dark caverns of fear and those bright illuminations of love. There is, of course, a natural comfort in the mind's capacity to forget the fearful past; but the consolation would be questionable if loss of memory led to loss of gratitude. I now understand better the biblical imperatives to remember: to remember not only the Sabbath and the triumphs of the past, but the violations and defeats of our history; to remember the bondage in Egypt and villainy of the Amalekites so as to rejoice in our freedom and our strength. "Out of my depths, I have called unto God" (Psalm 130:1).

A Wake-up Call

Lawrence Kushner

Last winter, during a board meeting, I realized that I was wiping my eyeglasses every few minutes. It was a good meeting; people argued fairly and about important religious matters, and even I managed not to say anything too stupid. So it wasn't until well into the meeting that I realized that the smudge I was trying to wipe off my glasses wasn't on my glasses; it was on my left eye. It appeared almost imperceptibly, painlessly, quickly.

When it didn't go away after a few days, naturally I called my ophthalmologist who, to my concern, wanted me to come in right away. "It's probably just a 'floater,' " said my wife. "Don't worry, I'm sure it's nothing." And, since as an adult (except for the time in rabbinic school when I demolished a TR-4 on I-75 and wound up in the hospital for a few days) I've never been hospitalized, I figured she must be right.

But my physician, after a very thorough examination, told me that there was something going on with my optic nerve which he could not explain and that he therefore wanted me to see an ophthalmic neurologist in the city. "What's wrong?" I asked. It's probably nothing; just a precaution. "Against what?" I pushed. He listed several maladies, but none of them was grave enough to warrant the urgency I thought I detected in his voice. I won't bore you with the details. After some very frontal and direct questions like, "Give me the worst possible scenario," he confessed that my symptoms could be the early signs of a brain lesion.

I tried to act matter-of-fact. You know: "Oh, sure, doc, brain tumor. I'll cut down on fried foods and it'll go away." But I also was aware of what I can only call "a trembling deep inside me." And I remember thinking clearly: So this is how it happens. One day you're well, then suddenly and almost gracefully you are in possession of an all-consuming new piece of information—the probable cause of your imminent death. One minute I am preoccupied by a thousand daily tasks, and the next it's as if some hand from out of nowhere had swept everything off the game board onto the floor and replaced all the papers, diversions, tasks, problems, toys, and assignments with one paragraph of medical information.

When I was growing up in Detroit, the rabbi assigned to the youth group was a man named Harold Hahn. He was a good rabbi. He went on to assume a major pulpit. One morning, while shaving, he noticed that the razor kept slipping from his hand. Within a short time he was dead of a brain tumor. I saw him at a convention just before he was taken, and he shared with me a passage from Kierkegaard: "A tiger can jump out of the forest at any moment." So this is how it happens. Now I was scheduled for a CAT scan in two days. And for two days I felt like Woody Allen in *Hannah and Her Sisters.*

I also felt like it was a Yom Kippur marathon. Everything I did was supercharged and overdetermined with meaning. I was unable to take anything for granted. The most trivial sensations were gifts. The smell of my children's hair. The sound of the dog barking. My wife's kiss. The morning coffee. Each one of them was too precious to let go of. What can I say? I went for the CAT scan. They couldn't find anything. After two decades of Kabbalah, it was a miracle they could even detect a brain.

The next weeks brought more tests. All negative. I learned a new word, "idiopathic," which means that the doctors don't exactly know the cause but that you shouldn't worry. "If you want," one of my physicians said, "you can call it 'optic neuritis,' an inflamed optic nerve." I got a reprieve. Whoever it was who pulled my file must have put it back in the "life" cabinet. Or, as one of my congregants said, "Kushner, think of it as a wake-up call— God's way of saying, 'Gottcha!' "

Life, you are so sweet. Would that there be some way of getting to that heightened gratitude for life without the terror. Well, it occurs to me that there is. It's called Judaism.

In the last few weeks of Deuteronomy we read about the death of Moses. For not even Moses, *eyed Adonai,* servant of the Lord, could live forever. According to rabbinic tradition, Moses was just like us.

When he realized that he was going to die, even he coaxed for more time. "Consider," he begged, "what a devoted leader of your people I have been." But it was no use. "Give me just a tiny reprieve so that my feet can at least splash in the Jordan." Still it was no use. "Then maybe," he pleaded, "You would permit me to be a bird and fly over the promised land." And again it was no use. Not for Moses and not for us. "You can see it from a distance, but you cannot go in." Not so different from Woody Allen, who says: "I'm not afraid of death. I just don't want to be there when it happens."

You treasure life most when you keep the certainty and the imminent possibility of your death constantly before you. Not only will you die, but you could die at any moment. This is not a pitch for life insurance; it is a religious truth. All you have is the fact that you are alive right now. Beyond that, there simply are no guarantees. No promises about anything six years from now, or six months, or six days, or even six hours.

Be grateful for the mystery and wonder of simply being able to experience anything for even one more moment. It is not sad. In a holy way, it is very beautiful. Only the certainty of our death and the possibility that it can come at any time make life precious.

And should, God willing, we all live for even a few more minutes, then our life will be filled with renewed meaning and purpose. Each moment will be precious. The smell of our children's hair, the words of a friend, the touch of our parent's hand, the smile of our brother and sister, the embrace of our spouse, watching the leaves turn, the first chill of autumn air.

Rabbi Simha Bunam as he lay dying took his wife's hand and said, "Why are you crying? My whole life was only that I might learn how to die."

In Praise of Denial

Chava Freud

I recall a question raised in the novel *Zorba the Greek* by the pensive, introspective foil to the colorful, exuberant Zorba: "Shall we live each day as if it were our last, or as if we would never die?"

Several decades of lived life have taught me to choose the latter. Although it cuts against the grain of the confrontation baby-boomer generation, with its no-frills approach to honesty and realism, I think there is a lot to be said in favor of denial.

When my mother was diagnosed with cancer, and when we discovered it had spread beyond its original site, I felt myself swallowed by a sea of fear, panic, and rage. My anger was largely directed at doctors, many of whom deserved it, but also at the punchline of their ineptly delivered conclusions: that this was a terminal illness, which we would not fight but would treat to control its pace and its symptoms. Some of these medical men were infuriated by me as well, for refusing to accept what they regarded as inevitable; one asked me quite hostilely, "How much more do you want for someone born in 1912?" My answer is: More. And I'm willing to fight for it.

It astounds me that these doctors don't realize what most patients and their families do: that to fight is to live. The challenge is to give death a run for the money. For what is terminality, other than knowing the name of the calamity that may, in the end, possibly cause one's death? Disease is no more a terminal condition than life itself.

Whenever I get my nose rubbed in "medical facts," I sink into black degrees of anticipatory mourning, which does nothing to enhance living for either for us. I'm not at all sure that the consciousness of death helps one to "savor" life, and would in fact argue against it. It certainly would have destroyed the joy in living the past seven years that we have been blessed with thus far!

I remember that first big vacation we took after Mom's illness was discovered. I could not shake the thought that it might be our last trip together. Weepy, sentimental sensations overwhelmed me—thankfully only after she retired for the night—which certainly detracted from the pleasures to be experienced in the present. When I think of the half-dozen or so vacation trips we've enjoyed together since then, I must conclude that an obsession with death and dying produces a morbidity that must be transcended if one is to live at all.

I am guided by the courage and optimism of my mother, who simply believes that she will live as long as God wants her to live. She leaves it to Him and continues her life as she has always lived it.

I cannot transcend fear of loss completely, but in the midst of happiness, I say the blessing *Sheheheyanu,* thanking God for sustaining us in life to see this day, instead of envisioning its converse in a time of loss. Once a death has occurred, there is all the time in the world to face its reality. While there is life, there should only be blessings.

And here is what I've learned in the years of wrestling and denying the angel: living in the present requires faith and hope in the future—faith and hope that there will be time, to start new projects, to plan reunions, to plant lilac trees and hope to see them bloom. Because there may well be time and to withdraw prematurely is to cheat oneself.

Life in the valley of the shadow of death is also life, if we can ignore the shadows long enough to till the valley—and this applies to all of us. None of us knows when our hour will come; what a shame it would be to refrain from starting things and wait for it. I think of the midrash of the old man whom Rabbi Yohanan met planting a carob tree. Did he expect to see its fruit? It's not clear from his answer that he had given up all hope of seeing it, but he trusted that his children would.

I can never fully evade the consciousness that these good days will not last forever, that every month, every year is a gift. But memories last forever and the time to make good memories is now. And if denial helps you to do that, you have my blessing.

A Small Miracle Happened Here

Rex D. Perlmeter

A kind and loving woman has died. That is the first reality. But she died well, and at peace. That is the second reality. And the little miracle as well. The third reality: in dying well and at peace, she ennobled my life and taught me much.

This gentle soul had been a part of my life within our congrega-tion for most of the time I have been there. We first met at the time of her sister's death, when her need was great and her pain deep. Francie (as we shall call her) had known difficult days through much of her life. While she was yet young, her mother abandoned Francie and her father in their Midwest community and went to seek a new life, settling eventually in Florida. Francie's father was unable to cope with the responsibility of single parent-hood and eventually sent his daughter to a series of foster homes. The constant displacement and alienation of affections marked Francie for life. She emerged needy and unwilling to trust in oth-ers' love—an insecurity not surprising in one raised amidst so lit-tle constancy of affection and concern.

In her early twenties, Francie came to join her mother in Florida, where she was taken into the mother's new life and fam-ily. She grew particularly close to the half-sister she had never known and eventually shaped a life for herself, a life that ultimately included a loving, very protective husband and two daughters, now grown. It was when Francie's half-sister died that we first became acquainted. Her need was apparent, as was her kindness and sweetness. I warmed to her immediately.

We grew very fond of one another, and she began to share with me some of the other concerns of her life. Over the years, we were there for one another and shared of the joys and sorrows of life. In those years, among other things, she struggled valiantly with an illness which she knew would most likely ultimately take her life.

As Francie approached her final days, one particular concern over-rode all others in her life. For years, she and one of her children—a daughter whom we shall call Lorene—had had a difficult and tempestuous relationship, not because either was evil (as each would rapidly reassure you), but because of what pop psycholo-gists today call "static."

In that sadly cyclical way of family life, Lorene was scarred by the lacks in her childhood—particularly, she felt, by the lack of a strong and reassuring maternal presence. Francie's need was such that she constantly demanded demonstration of love and encouraged an atmosphere in which she was the one given care, rather than the caregiver. Lorene's own unfulfilled needs left her angry and embittered, with a near-complete absence of patience for her mother and her demands. And yet, within the darkness of this tense and needy environment, in strange and oft-confused ways, there was light as well.

For Francie and Lorene had important messages they longed to communicate to one another—messages of love and appreciation. But that communication was impeded by the other messages—tensions, old baggage, present responsibilities, and anxieties over immediate problems, including Francie's illness. All of these were much closer to the surface in their relationship, and more easily (perhaps less painfully) focused upon and voiced. It was old hat to carp and kvetch at one another and avoid communicating the far more essential messages: "I love you and I'm scared of losing you." And so both were sad, at times angry, and ultimately ill at ease.

And then the miracle occurred. Somehow, in the final days, the other stuff—the baggage and conflicting messages—seemed suddenly less important. Francie sat in my office and committed herself to having it out with her daughter, to letting her know of her love and of her appreciation for all Lorene had done for her in these years of illness. Lorene sat in my office and gave herself permission to let go of lingering resentments and disappointments. She allowed herself finally to accept the unconditional love that underlay all of her mother's other messages.

And in the final days they came together. And the love flowed, and with it the forgiveness. The static no longer mattered. The signal of the true message was transmitted with strength and clarity, and the miracle was fulfilled. And when her mother was gone, Lorene told me, "Rabbi, these past few days changed my life—literally. I've always been afraid that after Mom was gone, I'd carry this burden of guilt and frustration around for the rest of my life. But now, not only does she have peace—so do I. It was our last gift to one another." Truly, with the profound change in two lives, a little miracle happened here.

Charlie and the Angel of Death

Marcia Moskowitz

I came into the kitchen early in the morning to find my elder son, Steven, then twelve and a half years old, already eating his breakfast. I asked him where his younger brother, Michael, was, because it struck me as strange that Mike was not with him. Michael, two months shy of his ninth birthday, was always the earliest one to awake. Steven's answer startled me. "He's praying at the guinea pig's grave." Yesterday morning one of the baby guinea pigs (born just two days before) had died. My suggestion that we put the dead guinea pig in a bag and then in the garbage was rejected immediately as disrespectful. Instead, Mike dug a grave in the middle of the garden and buried the guinea pig. He placed a rock on the grave and wrote on it R.I.P. He explained that he had refrained from placing a Jewish star on the rock because the animal might be considered a form of pig. "Pigs can't be Jewish," he told me. A cross, he had decided, was simply inappropriate in our garden. Logically, he had come up with "Rest in Peace." It was at this grave that Mike was now praying.

The whole incident, so important to Mike, was bothersome to me. I despaired that he should have to deal with so unimportant a death when we were in the midst of facing death in a much larger framework. Downstairs in the children's playroom lay my father-in-law. The hospital bed had been rented. The homemaker spent each morning with him to bathe his helpless body and cleanse his bedsores; the wheelchair needed when he first came to us three weeks before now stood unused. My mother-in-law slept in a bed next to his, and the various medicines lay neatly displayed on what was the children's old dressing table. Before he had arrived, the boys had tried to brighten the room with things to cheer him and so college banners, a Sesame Street poster, and a scientific one explaining the sky, sea, and land hung on the walls.

My father-in-law had come to spend the last weeks of his life with us as we all waited for the cancer which had begun its work years before to win finally, completely. Medical science had borrowed years for him, but the beginning of this last phase had started Memorial Day weekend. Now it was November. How he came to spend these last days with us was a circuitous route. From that hospital stay in the spring, he went to a nursing home. Unable to walk or care for himself, he looked forward to my mother-in-law's visits each day. But he missed his children, and so each of us, during the course of that hot summer, made pilgrimages to Florida. My visit was in August. His manner during his life was to avoid painful issues; my mother-in-law's was to deny. So they never discussed his cancer or his eventual death. He cried when I sat with him, and when I kissed him goodbye, he said, "Take me home to my children to die. Take me to New Jersey." I decided to make his wish my task. Somehow this wish would be mine and I would find a way to achieve it. When I suggested to my mother-in-law that she and Dad come to stay with our family, she vetoed the idea as too difficult. "No one does that anymore." Suffering and waiting for death occur in hospitals and nursing homes in the modern age. For many years now, I had felt this was not only wrong; it was unnatural. It was a violation of man's basic need: the support and care of loved ones. The need is double-edged. Not only does the dying man need love and care, but those who love him need to do something to comfort and support.

In mid-October my husband, Carl, went to Florida, and he and his mother brought my father-in-law to Passaic, New Jersey, the town he considered his home. The arrangements for his stay at the hospital were facilitated by my husband's older brother, who is a cardiologist. We brought our sons to see Grandpa Charlie, and they cried and held his hand. It was difficult for him to remember many things of his life, but his love for his grandchildren was apparent in his tears. I dutifully explained to the children that Grandpa's death was imminent. Uncle Bob and the other physicians had already explained that to us. At our nephew Richard's bar mitzvah the last week in October, the rabbi's prayer was that Charles Moskowitz should soon be with his family again. It was an empty prayer, because we all knew it was never to be. All we did know was that Charlie was not with us at his eldest grandson's bar mitzvah. But Charlie did live on, and the rabbi's prayer came to be.

My father-in-law didn't die when the doctors said he would. The hospital could no longer keep him, and everyone investigated local nursing homes. I appealed to the family and asked that my father-in-law be brought to our home. Family and friends seemed to think I had lost my usual clear thinking ability. My husband was overwhelmed that I felt so strongly about caring for his father. My own parents questioned the wisdom of my decision to expose their grandchildren to suffering and death. I answered my father's query "Why?" with "Would I do any less for you, Father?" His embrace was his approval. Carl and I asked the children for their support in what we wished to do. We explained that we saw this as an opportunity to do something for Grandpa Charlie. That his death was inevitable we never sought to deny. Instead we were in the unique position of granting his last wish—to be with his family as he faced his death. We assured the children that it would be difficult but that we would have each other for comfort.

Grandpa Charlie arrived at our house the first week in November. He was wheeled from the ambulance and looked small and cold under the gray blankets. His face, so ashen, seemed in stark contrast to the crisp fall day. He was crying and saying it was a miracle that he was "home." He was more lucid than we had seen him in months. I had cooked his favorite soup; the boys served him lunch. We didn't stay death's hand; we made the waiting for him bearable.

Our life in those first two weeks developed a pattern and a coherence. Luckily, I was not working and so I handled the management of the house. Carl went to work; Mike and Steve went to school. My mother-in-law cared for Charlie. Medicare sent a homemaker who came each morning to bathe him, change the linens of his bed, tidy his room. Twice a week a nurse from a Hackensack hospital came to cleanse the catheter and treat the advancing bedsores. Bob came three to four times a week in his dual role as physician and eldest son. The children would visit Charlie before they left for school and when they came home. They fixed his pillows, straightened his blankets, fetched drinks for him, but most of all they talked with him.

The second Sunday after my in-laws were with us, a psychiatrist friend came to visit. He, as one would expect, was eager to understand how I was coping. I turned to the ancient symbols of my people to interpret metaphorically what I was experiencing. As a child I had heard the stories of the Malach Hamavis, the angel of death. He stopped at the houses of the Egyptians and passed over the houses of the Israelites. Now the angel of death had taken up residence in my house. I had met him before in the lonely corridors of hospitals, and he always frightened me. But in my home, he seemed less threatening, more natural. He had his work to do and I had mine. I had agreed to accept his presence and his task, and as his initial quarry the angel of death had taken the baby guinea pig.

The angel of death sat in the corner of Charlie's room, and I would nod respectfully in his direction when I entered. But his hold on the Moskowitz family was even greater than I suspected. Charlie's older sister, Sophie, also lay dying of cancer. Neither knew of the other's plight. During the third week of his stay with us, he began to call for his mother (dead now some thirty years) and for his younger brother Moe, who was killed in France in World War II. My father-in-law was seventy-two years old; he had a wife whom he had loved for forty-nine years, two sons in their forties, a daughter of thirty, two daughters-in-law, one granddaughter, and three grandsons. But he called to his mother to ease his pain and stop his suffering. Sophie died the last week in November, and, the day of her funeral, Charlie rambled incoherently of a procession walking in the cemetery, of a fresh grave, of his sister Sophie. He then called for his mother, his brother, and his sister. It seemed to me his dead were calling to him. They were waiting for him.

It was at this time that I had a dream. The angel of death appeared to me like someone from a 1930s gangster movie. He wore a trench coat with its collar turned up; his hat covered his eyes so that his face was indiscernible. Like a thief, he was trying to enter our house by prying open one of the windows. Somehow he made it into the house and was walking down the long hallway to the children's bedrooms. I ran out of my room, blocked his path, and screamed, "No, not one of us, not the children. Charlie's waiting for you in the downstairs bedroom. You're supposed to take him, not us. Don't make a mistake!" My screams awakened both Carl and me.

Charlie's mental and physical condition deteriorated, and we marveled at how long life could go on. He ceased to recognize Carl and Steve. He prayed for the pain to cease. It was impossible to touch or move his body because the bones of his back and legs were riddled with cancer. The bedsores, in spite of constant care, had exposed the flesh on his legs. They bled and festered. All quality of life had been destroyed.

When we first started out on this mission, Bob had assured me that he would have Dad moved to the hospital for the final days. We were obviously at this point now. Bob, my mother-in-law, and Carl all felt this decision was mine. If I did not want the children exposed to death, if I did not want the death to occur in our house, Charlie would be moved. I know I have never felt such determination and resolve; Charlie would spend his last days at home.

Charlie spoke his last words Friday afternoon and then slipped into a coma. The pain had finally stopped; his breathing became shallow; all the muscles relaxed. We began the ancient death vigil. We took turns sitting with him. Saturday, Ruth and I potted plants that I had been rooting from the summer. Saturday evening Bob and Bernice and their children, Lisa and Richard, arrived to have dinner with us and stay late into the night. They went home after midnight; Carl canceled his trip to St. Louis and asked his older brother, "How long?" Bob confessed his inadequacy and said, "I don't know but it can't be much more."

Sunday, December 12, was a bright and bitterly cold day. Bob arrived early in the morning and sat by his father's bedside. During the many years of his illness, Charlie had looked to Bob to make him well. Bob sat now with his eyes filled with tears. He went home at midday. Mike spent the day with our cousins. Carl paced the house; Steve wandered after him. Ruth and I drank endless cups of coffee.

The rabbi came and we sat and talked together. He asked if we had any unanswered questions about what we still had to face. Steve said yes, he did indeed have a question. "What is the purpose, what is the meaning of life?" Hesitantly the rabbi went to Ecclesiastes for his answer. He spoke of life as a gift that is given to each of us, of the mysteries and complexities of life, of life as it continues from generation to generation. He asked if he might say the ancient prayers of our people by Charlie's bedside. Carl asked to stand by his father's bed for the prayers; Steve asked to stand by his father's side.

As the afternoon came to its close, the moment we wished for, we longed for, arrived. In spite of all the preparation, we were still unprepared. Ruth sat by Charlie's bed crying that she had lost her best friend. I held his still-warm hand and spoke of my love. Carl began to cry; Steven's eyes filled with tears. As I went to comfort my husband, I heard my cousin's voice at the door. Mike was returning home. I ran out the front door to stop my young son before he could enter. As I held Mike in my arms, I explained that Grandpa had just died. Mike and I entered the house to find Steve, his arms barely long enough to reach around Carl's shoulders, holding his father, seeking to comfort him. Life moves from generation to generation.

Bob, Bernice, and their children arrived within the hour. The men from the funeral home came and did their necessary work behind the closed playroom door. When Charlie's body, now shrouded in the gray leather case, was wheeled out to the waiting station wagon, his wife, his sons, his daughters-in-law, his grandchildren stood silently. Bob and his family stayed a bit longer as we made the necessary plans together. Ruth would stay with us for this night.

Late that evening, after the friends who had come to offer

solace had left, my mother-in-law came to me with two gifts. Earlier she had sent Charlie's prayer shawl with his body. After the ritual cleansing, his body would be wrapped in a shroud and then the shawl placed around it. The round silver clips he used to wear to hold the prayer shawl in place, Ruth offered to me for Steven. The blue velvet case with its gold embroidery, in which Charlie carried his prayer shawl to and from the synagogue, she offered to put aside for Michael.

We had completed our task and I felt a sense of relief. Throughout the five weeks Charlie had been with us, the words of the Twenty-third Psalm echoed and reechoed through my head as a form of prayer. I felt as if I were journeying through the valley of the shadow of death. Tuesday morning when we gathered at the funeral home, the rabbi opened the service with King David's words, "Yea, though I walk through the valley of the shadow of death . . ." and I felt the end of the valley was near.

On a bitterly cold day—so cold I wondered how the grave had been dug in the frozen earth—we buried my father-in-law under the skeletal branches of a dogwood tree.

We returned to Bob and Bernice's house to begin the period of mourning and ate the hard-boiled eggs, symbols of life, which neighbors had prepared for us. Friday evening, we entered the synagogue, sat in the front pew, and were greeted with "May you be comforted among the mourners of Zion and Jerusalem." The service ended as it always had with the memorial prayer for the dead. The rabbi asked for "those who mourn and those who would stand with them" to rise. Carl stood; the children and I stood with him so he would not mourn alone.

Our lives slowly returned to normal. The hospital bed was gone; the children's paraphernalia reappeared in the playroom. Ruth went home to Florida; I started teaching again. The pain began to lessen, and I found I measured time by Friday services. I could see from each Friday to the next that we were better. The winter was long and cold, and snow lay on the ground until late in March. By April, the new season seemed to reflect our greater commitment to life.

Steven's bar mitzvah was the end of April. Ruth arrived from Florida, and again our family assembled. Steve had worked many hours in preparation for this day. He agonized over the injustice of life: his grandfather would not see his accomplishment. He asked if he could talk about Grandpa Charlie in his bar mitzvah speech and we agreed.

Charlie's silver prayer-shawl clips, which Steve had refused to accept until the morning of the bar mitzvah, the rabbi lovingly placed on the new prayer shawl. Steve led the congregation in prayer. He read from the Torah the passage from Leviticus describing the code for holiness. In ancient melodies he chanted verses from the prophet Amos. He spoke to the congregation of what he had learned of life, of sorrow, of suffering. He spoke of being able to bear life's pain when one has the support of others. He spoke of Ecclesiastes and of the rabbi's words three months before. He spoke of the obligation he felt to do something with his life. He spoke of his memories of his grandfather, and to him that was how his grandfather would live on.

That summer Carl, the children, and I moved to St. Louis. We took the plants Ruth and I potted with us. The following year Bob and Bernice moved to another town in New Jersey, but Bob returns to Passaic regularly to tend the white heather he planted on Charlie's grave. Each spring the dogwood blooms by the gravesite; each winter on December 12 we light a memorial candle. The blue velvet prayer-shawl case waits for Mike's bar mitzvah.

Chapter Two

When Death Arrives

The moment when the body and the soul separate is a moment filled with awe. No doctor, nurse, or health care giver should ever become so inured, so accustomed to this moment that its sacredness is no longer felt.

And yet in contemporary culture it is possible to live one's entire life and never once be present at the time of someone's death. Now the dying are put into intensive-care units, behind screens and curtains, where visitors are allowed to come in for just a few minutes every few hours. We do it partly for the patient's sake, partly for our own. We do it for the patient's sake because it makes it easier for the doctors and the nurses to control the environment, to do their work, and to protect the patient from contagion. We do it for our sake because in this way we can shield ourself from having to confront the reality of death.

Deathbed scenes occur nowadays mainly in movies and novels. In real life the consciousness of the patient is often blurred. He may not be able to speak or even to hear, so it is seldom a time for poignant leavetakings. And if we are with them at the end, what should we say? What should we do? What do you say at a time when there are no words? What do you do at a time when there is nothing more to do? We all sit mute at such a time.

The Jewish tradition does contain a prayer, the Vidui, that is supposed to be said by or for the person who is dying. We include it here, and then we include a different version, one that was written by a woman whose feelings could not be adequately expressed in the traditional words.

Rabbi Nancy Flam offers a prayer for doctors and nurses to say when a patient dies. It is intended to help them appreciate the limits of their own powers and to enable them to move on to the work of comforting the mourners and caring for the patients they still have, who depend on them. It is intended to remind them that *curing* is not always possible but that *caring* always is.

Like Removing a Hair from Milk

Rava, while seated at the bedside of Rabbi Nachman, saw that he was dying. Said Rabbi Nachman to him, "Please tell the angel of death not to torment me." Said Rava, "Are you not a person of importance [i.e., why not appeal to the angel of death yourself?]" Rabbi Nachman replied, "Who is esteemed, who is regarded, who is distinguished before the angel of death?"

Rava said, "I will appeal for you, but promise me that you will show yourself to me in a dream after you die." He did so. Rava asked him, "Did you suffer much while you died?" Rabbi Nachman replied, "As little as when you remove a hair from milk. And yet, if God were to say to me, 'Go back again to the world as you were,' I would not wish to do so because the fear of death is so great."

—The Talmud, Moed Katan 28a

Rabbi Salanter's Last Night

Rabbi Israel Salanter, renowned thinker and the founder of the Mussar movement, died in a foreign country, away from his numerous admirers and disciples. Only a very plain and simple man, who took care of him when he was sick, was present when he passed away. Eager to learn what legacy of profound spiritual truths or philosophical ideas the great scholar had expounded in his last hours, the disciples rushed to question the attendant. "Tell us, what philosophical truths or metaphysical concepts did the master teach you in his last hours?" they asked.

The simple man replied: "All evening he tried to convince me that I should not be afraid to be alone all night with the body of a dead man."*

—Abraham Joshua Heschel, *The Earth Is the Lord's*

Prelude

Abba Kovner

Thus,
Without a knock the door opened
A shadow
Pushing aside the straw screen
In its wake the man with a mane
Of dark hair
Young, with big eyes

At once
They stood at his head
(The shadow crouching quietly between
The drain and the vials of secretions)
A taciturn mask announced:
"The time has come."
"My time has come?" he shuddered.
"That's it," he muttered.
"Where are we going? Do you know the way?"
"We've come to take you." No details.
"May I ask a question?"
"Too late."

(Bastard!) "Will you let me take a towel,
Soap. A book?"

---

*The body of a dead person was never left alone until interment, but simple people were often afraid to be alone with a body all night. This episode was told to Professor Saul Lieberman by Rabbi N. N. Frankel, who heard it directly from the attendant.

"Superfluous. He who enters
Goes there as he came."

At once he turned
To leave. Behind him trudged
His smell, his shadow
And his dread.

The Power of Music at the End

Jeff Friedman

I have two skills. Here in Jerusalem, I have learned to integrate them. I am a family and a bereavement counselor; I am also a musician, a guitarist. This essay explains what I have learned from doing the two together.

But first, a word about the power of music. The Bible abounds with stories about the power of song to express more than words can. When the Israelites were rescued at the Red Sea, Moses and the people of Israel sang out their gratitude to God in a song, and Miriam and the women danced out their praise to God in a dance. The whole Book of Psalms is filled with songs, some of them meant to be accompanied by instruments, through which people gave voice to the whole gamut of human emotions. The Talmud speaks of the use of flutes as standard in funeral processions. And the biblical tale that means the most to me is the one about how David played the harp before King Saul when he was suffering from melancholia and the music healed his spirit. That story has long stayed with me, and my goal is to achieve for the people I work with some portion of what David did for Saul: "And it came to pass that when David took his harp and played before him, the evil mood lifted from Saul and a good spirit came into him" (1 Samuel 16:23).

The secret of music for me is in the contact it can make between the person playing and the person listening. Music has the power of reaching deep into the soul of the listener and calling forth responses that mere words by themselves cannot do.

Death and dying, grief and loss are awesome moments and experiences. It is for this reason that most of us are filled with fear and dread when we think of them, and I am no different in this respect from anyone else. I can sometimes feel my own anxiety rising when I come into the room of a dying person. But that very anxiety is what enables me to empathize with the families I work with. I cannot say that I can empathize equally well every time, and I cannot claim that I do my work equally well every time. There are times when I feel numb, times when I cannot focus as fully as I should, and times when I simply have no words to say to those who are grieving that are at all adequate. But I try, and sometimes my very inability to speak is a contact with those I wish I could help.

My own education in loss and grief, as well as my own education in the healing power of music, comes from my childhood. My parents went through the Holocaust. My father lost his first wife and his three children. And he kept the pain of those immense losses inside himself. I never knew about these losses until years later. My mother lost her parents, a number of her brothers, her sister, and a large extended family. I realize now that their grief must have been almost overwhelming, but very little was ever said about their experience when I was growing up.

Each person deals with loss in his or her own way. My father was raised in the hasidic tradition. He came from a village in the Carpathian mountains, in what was then Czechoslovakia. As a child I remember how he would become absorbed in the niggunim and the chants of his childhood. Those melodies were the means by which he somehow transformed the loss and pain into yearnings. I am convinced that it was those melodies that gave him solace and a measure of healing. My father, unfortunately, died when I was only fifteen and so I too had to experience the loss of a parent in my youth, as he did. He was buried in Israel, where he had planned to retire.

It is no mystery to me how I ended up being involved with

music as a tool of healing and why I came to Israel to live. I had a role model, even though my father never directly told me of his losses. I only found out about his first wife and his other children after he died, and yet the sense of loss with which he lived was tangible. I sensed it even though I did not know the details, and I also sensed that music was for him a response to that pain.

Irena, a new Russian immigrant to Israel, in her early seventies, was dying of cancer. Her last couple of months were spent at the hospice of Hadassah Hospital on Mount Scopus. Irena was unmarried; her only living relative was a nephew. When I came into her room for the first time I had no idea what I could say or do that would help her, but she told me what it was that she needed.

She asked if I could find a recording of Tchaikovsky's Piano Concerto No. 3 for her. Nobody had ever made a request like this to me before. I was used to people asking for tranquilizers or pain killers or prescriptions; no one had ever asked for a piano concerto. But I honored the request, at first simply out of courtesy. And then I came to understand that she knew what her soul needed, better than I and better than all the doctors and nurses and nutritionists around her.

We sat together and listened to the recording each time I came. Often she would break into tears. Tchaikovsky's music was a precious part of her childhood memories. And so it was her life as a child, her memories, her very being that the music recalled for her. After listening to the work, she would begin to reminisce about her childhood, and color and animation would appear on her face. Gradually she found a way to deal with her cut-off future by coming into contact with her past. She even said goodbye to her parents, who had died long ago, as the recording ended one day. She died with the music on, and with a smile of contentment on her face.

And I, who sat at her bedside and listened with her, began to comprehend the power of music to elicit memories and to help us understand the very essence of who we were and are.

I do not think that there are any specific "techniques" that work in going through grief. But I think that the sages of old were right in understanding the importance of grieving, the importance of giving external expression to grief, and the importance of sharing one's grief with others. We in Israel have learned these three lessons very well, because unfortunately we have gone to grief school many, many times. If you watch Israeli television after a terrorist incident, you will see how grief is shared collectively. The entire community identifies with and shares in the grief of every loss, together with the family. And the grief is expressed openly. There is no stiff upper lip here; instead, people weep and wail in public. And it helps—it brings solace—to know that your grief is shared by the community.

Recently I had the privilege of being witness to another kind of collective sharing. A friend called me and asked if I would bring my guitar to the hospital where his father was. The family gathered and went through with him the songs that they loved most. Grandchildren, children, the relatives, and the closest friends were all there. The old man sat in a wheelchair, upright but coughing, as he and they sang "Yankele," a lovely Yiddish lullaby, together. In the song a mother gently soothes her sleeping child. As they sang, I had the sense that the children and the grandchildren were gently lulling the father to his last sleep. Occasionally they laughed; sometimes they cried; from time to time one of them would have to leave the room because it was too difficult to control his feelings. But there was a power to that experience, a power to those songs and lullabies they sang with him and for him that night, that each of us who was there will long remember. It was their way of saying goodbye and of beginning the mourning process.

I came back one more time to sing with them. This time the father was in much worse condition, no longer able to sit up in a wheelchair. But the music went on just the same. The family stayed together, and the music said what they felt when they could no longer find any words of their own that were adequate.

I learned from being with this family that our lives are sequential timetables of relationships and of events, and that life requires change, separation, and loss. The reality of life has to do with accepting the dynamics of change. Our natures resist, and so we try to hold on to the precious moments of the past. The music in that room enabled the family to slowly make the move from the past to the present and then to the inevitable future.

Mama Zahava was ninety-seven. She had been born in Lisbon and her roots went back to pre-Inquisition Spain. A natural Ladino speaker, she knew the most beautiful Ladino melodies. She had experienced much in her life, including the Hebron massacre of 1929, when she and her family were saved by their Arab landlord. Mama Zahava was a great-great-grandmother. At the end, she was still lucid even though her body was wearing out. And she stood out in the weekly music group that I led in the home for the chronically ill.

What made Mama Zahava special was her ability to accept the changes in her life. She sang the Ladino songs with enormous energy and recalled and shared with us the stories behind the songs. Her extended family often came to visit and to sing with her, and the atmosphere was always upbeat. She was not afraid to talk about her impending end. She saw it as part of an unending process. By accepting her death she transcended it, becoming an agent of change and transformation, for herself and for her family.

Her humanity was instructive to me and to all those who sang her songs with her. She was able to use music in order to access a whole range of feelings that most of us do not begin to know how to articulate, certainly not in words.

There have been occasions when the patient or members of the family suddenly begin weeping hysterically in the midst of my quiet, meditative guitar-playing. And when they do, I am never sure how to proceed.

I was in the hospice on Mount Scopus, strumming a niggun for a woman and her daughter, when suddenly the daughter burst out crying. I stopped playing, not saying anything, just waiting. In the sudden silence, the daughter began to apologize for crying, but the mother just continued singing, softly and sweetly. After a few minutes, the daughter joined in.

In this case, the mother and daughter were not yet ready to discuss their coming separation. If they had been, I would have put down my guitar and let them talk. But it was too soon, and so I kept on playing, letting the music gradually melt down the blocks until they would be able to really talk. Eventually, they were ready.

I have come to appreciate the wisdom of the Hebrew word for funeral. It is *livayah,* which means "to accompany." Just as it is a mitzvah to accompany a person who leaves your home, so it is a mitzvah to accompany a person who is preparing to leave this world. Dying is the most solitary thing that we ever do in this life. In the end, the dead go alone. We can only accompany them to the edge of the grave, as the sages of the Talmud say; from there on, only their good name and their good deeds can go with them. But I keep thinking of this word "accompaniment" as a very accurate definition of what we do when we work with the dying. It is a great privilege to accompany someone who is leaving.

Let me end with a story, not about music but about accompanying. I was on my way to a wedding a couple of years ago when I saw a crowd bustling about a person lying on the ground. I stopped my car and got out to see what was going on. There was a woman lying on the ground, her fists clenched as if she were holding on for dear life. It turned out that she was one of the four women who had been stabbed by an Arab in the Kiryat Hayovel neighborhood of Jerusalem. The medic was at her side, trying to resuscitate her. It was the first time in my life that I actually saw someone struggling, literally holding on to life, and gradually slipping away into death. I forgot about the wedding and sat down beside her, holding her, being with her. There was nothing I could do for her but that. The medic was doing his best. But I felt as if I had been "summoned" to stay with her. As I held her, I became very aware of this woman, of a life slowly but surely leaving this world. The gleam in her eyes gradually dimmed and the clenched fists eventually relaxed. I felt that I had "accompanied" her and that somehow this perfect stranger, whose name I did not even know, whom I had never met before—this perfect stranger was no longer a stranger.

At that moment, I felt closer to her than to anyone I had ever known.

Should We Tell the Patient the Truth?

Samuel Klagsbrun

After fifty years of marriage, an elderly man faced a terrible dilemma. His wife was sick. She had metastic cancer and was dying. This couple had literally spent their entire lives together, both in work and in private life. Together they ran a little scientific publishing house. Being old German-born Jews, they didn't know how to connive or pull punches. They were very straight shooters.

They loved each other, cared for each other. They lived a very routinized life at home, and never had a word of untruth passed between them, so they claimed. And I'm sure it was true. The woman was dying and they went to a major institution of higher learning in medicine and found a major figure in the field of oncology. The physician accepted the woman as his patient with one condition: that he, the esteemed physician, would be in charge of every aspect of her care; otherwise he would not be her doctor. The condition included this statement to the husband: "I will not tell your wife the nature of her disease. She will think she has some kind of inflamed lymph nodes that will just go on and not respond to treatment very well. That's what I will tell her. And on pain of my not continuing the treatment with her, you will agree to this statement. I've done this for many, many years. I know exactly what I'm doing. It is cruel to tell a patient," and so on and so forth. "She doesn't have much of a chance. I don't think she'll make it. But the treatment will proceed on the condition that you participate in this statement." Those were his terms. The husband grabbed on to this magician and was so thankful and thrilled to be in his care that of course at that moment of stress he agreed to the terms.

Every time rounds were completed and the doctor left her room, there would be whispered consultations outside her door. The woman would of course ask her husband as soon as he stepped into the room: What did the doctor say? And the husband would hem and haw and say that the doctor discussed his medical insurance and the bill. He would say: You know you're doing fine, it's wonderful. And the woman, seeing her husband's face and knowing his face very well, knew fully that something else was being said. She knew her condition, she understood her own internal system. Not knowing a pact had been made, she felt something was being withheld from her for the first time in their marriage.

The woman lapsed into a delirious phase at this point. Whatever the reason or the source of the delirium, she became incoherent and confused. After a while she became paranoid; she began accusing her husband of all sorts of things. She accused him of being a traitor to her, of betraying her. Of course there was an element of truth in it. Then her paranoia escalated into all sorts of other fantasies.

Her husband was in agony. He was decimated by the accusations, but because he was always fearful of the doctor, he was afraid to tell his wife the truth and ended up maintaining the promise to the doctor. The woman died in a paranoid state, filled with vilification against her husband, with rage and hatred. She died screaming at her husband. The husband after her death could not go back to the publishing house that they had both created. It was too filled with her. And so he sold it for a pittance. The husband, in a massive depression, was referred to me for treatment.

The treatment consisted of my helping him vent his rage against the unfair edict of the doctor which forced him to be with his wife in her dying in a way that contradicted completely the way he had been with her in living. It was a lie, a monstrous lie. Her death was a lie, a lie forced upon this man by the doctor's awful condition.

Let Them Know What You Want

Marshall Meyer

There is a moment in medical treatment when you need to make a decision. I faced precisely that moment when my brother was dying of cancer. He died at the age of forty-nine. I had come up from Argentina to give him my kidney because the disease was metasticizing and we had a perfect match. But unfortunately I came too late, and the cancer had spread to the liver. So I stayed on for a month to nurse him. He was in chemotherapy and had radiation and God knows what else.

He finally came home to Norwich, Connecticut. Our family always used Yale University Hospital in New Haven. Sometimes we used Massachusetts General, but it was usually Yale. And the doctor he had there was his very best friend. They grew up together, they went into the Navy together, they were in the South Pacific together. They were very close. And finally one day I said to him, "Harvey, what on earth am I taking him to radiation for every day? He can hardly walk. Why are we doing this to him?"

This was his best buddy, from the time they were ten. He said to me, "I can't stand not to do anything."

I said, "Harvey, it's not what you can stand . . . you're the doctor. It's what John can stand that counts! He's my brother."

He countered with a terrible question. He said: "*Is* that what John wants?" So I asked him. I asked my brother the terrible question. It was an awesome moment. He knew that he was dying. He could hardly move. It took me over an hour each time to get him dressed and to put him into the car. And so I said, "John, this is so . . . Do you want to do it?"

"No, just leave me in my bed. You know what I want. I just want some music. I just want to rest."

So we stopped it and we never went back to the hospital again. And in three weeks he was dead. He was listening to all his favorite arias and all his favorite operas, and he went into a coma. And that's what he wanted.

Do I feel guilty? I would have felt overwhelmingly guilty if I had continued treatment against his will.

It was relatively easy. He was lucid enough to answer the question. But what do you do when you can't ask the question? That's why I am so concerned, so passionate, so determined that people have living wills. You owe it to the people you love to make your desires known and to *write* them down! Because you don't know if one day you will be plugged in to a machine. You owe it to the people you love to say it in writing—*with witnesses*. If you don't want heroic methods, or if you do want to fight for life until the last breath, if you are willing to stay paralyzed without speech or brain dead for six years, whether you want to keep the machine going or not—either way, you owe it to those you love to let them know. There are legally binding documents that attend to that.

I am not a lawyer but I am a rabbi and I deal with this all the time. Once the patient is hooked up to a machine, no document can unhook him. But when you get to deciding *whether* to put him on or not, you have to have a signed release. And if you do choose to sign a release for your mother or your father or your spouse or your child or your friend or your loved one not to be hooked up, then the doctors don't have to do it.

Understand that there is a difference between this and euthanasia. We are *not* talking about euthanasia. We are talking about the difference between prolonging life as opposed to prolonging dying. I don't want my life prolonged by a machine when I no longer have a mind. According to Judaism as we understand it in the liberal tradition, brain dead is dead.

One of the main problems we have in dealing with this topic is that we always assume—perhaps for psychological reasons—that these decisions apply only to old people. We always deny that they could involve younger people. Rationally, we know how ridiculous that is. We have all been to funerals of people younger than we are. So the possibilities we are talking about are very real.

So I beg you—beg you—for yourself and for your loved ones, to make the proper statements about how you want these things to be handled. It's an awful thing to have people try to guess what you would have wanted.

The Traditional Vidui

If one feels death approaching, he should recite the Vidui. And he should be reassured by those around him: "Many have said the Vidui and not died, and many have not said the Vidui and have died." And if he is unable to recite it aloud, he should confess in his heart. And if he is unable to recite it by himself, others may recite it with him or for him.

And these instructions should not be given to him in the presence of tender-minded people lest they cry and upset him too much.

—Shulhan Arukh, Yoreh Deah 338

O my God, the God of my ancestors, accept my prayer and do not reject my supplication. Forgive me for all the sins that I have committed in my lifetime. I am ashamed and abashed for all the wrong things that I have done. Please accept my pain and suffering as an atonement and forgive my sins, for against You alone have I sinned.

May it be Your will, Adonai, my God and God of my ancestors, that I sin no more. With Your great mercy, cleanse me of my sins, but not through suffering and pain. Send a complete healing to me and to all those who are stricken.

I acknowledge to You, Adonai, my God and the God of my ancestors, that my life is in Your hands. May it be Your will to heal me. But if You have decreed that I shall not recover from this illness, I accept the decree from Your hand. May my death atone completely for all the sins and all the transgressions that I have committed before You. Shelter me in the shadow of Your wings and grant me a portion in the world-to-come.

Father of all orphans and guardian of widows, be with and protect my dear family, for my soul is bound up with theirs.

Into Your hand do I commit my soul. You have redeemed me, Adonai, O God of truth.

Shema Yisrael, Adonai eloheinu, Adonai ehad.

Kayla's Prayer

Lawrence Troster

Traditional liturgical responses to critical occasions are often meaningless to people for whom the concepts in these responses seem foreign or unsuited to their personal approach to God or to the world. Sometimes, too, we as rabbis find the concepts in the prayers difficult to reconcile with our own beliefs.

One such prayer is the Vidui—the deathbed confession. On those few occasions when I used it, I usually read it for someone unable to read it for himself. There was one occasion recently, however, when a person who was dying asked me if there was a prayer for her. This person was Kayla.

Kayla was a woman who died of cancer at the age of fifty, after suffering from her disease for many years. The week before she died, knowing that she was going soon, she asked me if there was a prayer to say for a dying person. I read her the English translation of the Vidui in the *Rabbi's Manual* put out by the Rabbinical Assembly. As I was reading it, I realized that this was not her prayer.

That was basically the first thing that she said to me. "I don't like that prayer. It doesn't say what I want to say." Before I left her that day, I promised that I would write her another prayer. I don't know why I offered. It just seemed the right thing to say at the time. She accepted my offer and I wrote something down later that day. The next day I took the prayer to her and, despite her pain and despite her drifting because of the morphine, we rewrote that prayer together until it became her prayer, her death prayer. The next day I completed the prayer and gave it to her, and we read it together. It was also read as part of her eulogy at the funeral, at her request. This is an example of a personal yet traditional liturgy that can be developed for people at critical times in their life. This then is Kayla's Prayer:

KAYLA'S PRAYER

Listen to my voice,
O Lord our God
And God of my ancestors.

I lie here on the brink of life,
Seeking peace, seeking comfort, seeking You.
To You, O Lord, I call and to You, O Lord, I make my sup-
plication.
Do not ignore my plea.
Let Your mercy flow over me like the waters,
Let the record of my life be a bond between us,
Listen to my voice when I call,
Be gracious to me and answer me.

I have tried, O Lord, to help You complete creation,
I have carried Your yoke my whole life.
I have tried to do my best.
Count my effort for the good of my soul,
Forgive me for when I have stumbled on Your path.
I can do no more, let my family carry on after me,
Let others carry on after me.

Protector of the helpless, healer of the brokenhearted,
Protect my beloved family with whose soul my own soul is
bound.
Their hearts depended upon mine,
Heal their hearts when they come to depend on You.

Let my soul rest forever under the wings of Your presence,
Grant me a share in the world-to-come.
I have tried to love You with all my heart and with all my
soul,
And even though You come to take my soul,
Even though I don't know why You come,

Even though I'm angry at the way You take me,
For Your sake I will still proclaim:
Hear, O Israel, the Lord is our God, the Lord alone.
The Lord is with me, I shall not fear.

The following comments are notes to Kayla's Prayer to explain the process by which the prayer was written. Many of the phrases come from the liturgy or the Bible, as I attempted to weave both her feelings and ideas about herself and God into traditional language.

"Listen to my voice."

This, of course, is a beginning of a traditional liturgical phrase. I deemed it appropriate to start this way, since Kayla was crying out to God at this point and there was a real need for her to speak, but it had to be her voice.

"O Lord our God and God of my ancestors."

Kayla insisted that it should be "my ancestors" and not "our ancestors," for although she could say "our God" as the God of the Jewish people, she had a great deal of personal discomfort with aligning herself with the community. She had felt, both as a person suffering from cancer and as a divorced woman growing up in a community when divorced women were an anomaly, that her connection to a common ancestry was sometimes rather tenuous.

"Seeking peace, seeking comfort, seeking You."

Her final desire was to have the peace of death, to have the comfort of knowing that her children and her family could carry on without her, to have the comfort of knowing that she had led a worthwhile life, and, finally, to seek the God whom she could not always easily address in her life.

"To You, O Lord, I call . . . Do not ignore my plea."

The repetition of the supplication shows her urgency and her deep inner desire to be heard. Kayla often felt that, during her life, her voice was not heard by those around her.

"Let your mercy flow over me like the waters, let the record of my life be a bond between us."

This, again, using traditional phrases, asks for mercy as well as asking that her life be a bond that will tie her to God and that the deeds of her life will bring her close to God at this moment.

"Listen to my voice . . . and answer me."

These traditional phrases end the first section, which deals primarily with seeking contact with God.

"I have tried . . . complete creation."

This introduces some of the themes that motivated Kayla during her life: the completion of creation—*tikkun olam*—was something that was part of her life in the work that she did in attempting to save Syrian Jewry. She worked in this great mitzvah to bring about the completion of creation.

"I have carried Your yoke my whole life."

The yoke refers to the *ol malkhut shamayim* (the yoke of the kingdom of heaven) of being a Jew, but also to Kayla's particular yoke, the suffering that she had to bear because of her divorce and her illness.

"I have tried to do my best."

This is Kayla's own idea that one who does her best has done as much as God can expect and that this should be sufficient for God, if not for those around her. In her case, her best was a great deal.

"Count my effort for the good of my soul."

Unlike the traditional Vidui, where one's death is expiation for one's sins, Kayla's Prayer expresses her belief that one's sincere effort in life should be enough for God. She could not see her death itself as having any particular value.

If the traditional concept of death as expiation is to have any meaning at all, it must be reinterpreted. The following story perhaps can lead us to a new interpretation:

Rava said to Rav Nachman, "Show yourself to me [in a dream after you die]."

He showed himself to Rava.

Rava asked him, "Was death painful?"

Rav Nachman replied, "It was as painless as lifting a hair from a cup of milk. But were the Holy One, blessed be He, to say to me, 'You may return to that world where you were before,' I would not wish to do it. The fear of death is too great" (Moed Katan 28a).

The story tells us that while death itself is painless, the fear of death is the greatest fear that we have. Perhaps, then, we can say that the fear of one's own death brings expiation because it forces us to examine our life and leads us to repentence.

"Forgive me for when I have stumbled on Your path."

The forgiveness she seeks from God was for when she was not able to do what was normally expected in the tradition. This is not sin, but rather a stumbling on God's path.

"I can do no more, let my family carry on after me. . . ."

She saw herself as someone who worked for the good of everyone in addition to herself and her family. Now she could do no more and she needed the help that others could give her. It was her wish that her family would not only carry on without her, but would also carry on with her work. This is a direct reference again to her involvement in working for the salvation of Syrian Jewry.

This ends the second section, which deals with her summary of her life.

"Protector of the helpless . . . to depend on You."
This paragraph is a direct plea to God, as the healer of the brokenhearted and protector of the helpless, to help her family, who are so dear to her: her children, her mother, and her brothers. Since they depend so much upon her for strength, they should now be given strength by God to carry on without her.

"Let my soul . . . in the world-to-come."
Kayla did believe in a life after death. She did not know what to expect, but she did believe there was something beyond her life and therefore she wished to be a part of that.

"I have tried . . . my soul."
This expresses Kayla's idea that she tried to love God when she could, even while God is in some way responsible for her death.

"Even though . . . the way You take me."
This is an expression of Kayla's anger at God for her inability to understand why she was chosen to die of this disease. She is angry at God for doing this, when she had so much left to do and to live for.

"For your sake . . ."
Despite this anger, Kayla could still say the Shema. Despite her

doubts, despite her fears, she could still proclaim it and say: "The Lord is with me, I shall not fear."

(I would like to thank the family of the late Kayla Armel for their support and encouragement. I would also like to thank my good friend Cantor Paul Kowarsky for his suggestions and help. Danny Siegel pointed out to me the source of the story about Rav Nachman, and it is his translation that I have used.)

Saying Goodbye

Steven Saltzman

You are called to the deathbed of your father, and you don't know what to say. But you know that you have to say something.

Your father has arrived at the end of his life. He has only one more thing left to do . . . which is to die. It is something that he has to do alone. No one has any past experience in dying. There are no means, no guides, no resources to muster. Nevertheless it is something he has to do. He will do it either well or badly; he will do it either bravely or not; resolutely or cowering, but he will do it. Your father has known for some time that he will have to do this. He has often thought about it. He has often prayed and willed to do it well. He has prayed for courage, for to die well takes courage.

You are called upon to be there when your father is at the limit of his life. You are at the limit of your powers of language. You know that there is something to be said and you are not sure what it is.

The nurses say, "We are glad you have come." They have done their part, making him comfortable and calm. The nurses and the physicians know that you must now do something that they cannot do. You have to say something to the one who is dying.

What should you say? You have to say something that language cannot say, something that is not within the resources of common discourse to express. Anything that comes to mind sounds glib and insufficient, vacuous and absurd. You think to yourself: Perhaps I don't have the skills. Or: I can't think of the right thing to say because I have no experience in this kind of situation.

You have a friend who, when he was summoned to his mother's deathbed, didn't go. It was too frightening, involved too much responsibility. You have found the courage to answer the summons. Now you must say a word. You end up saying something like, "It'll be all right, Dad, it'll be all right." Then you feel stupid because you know it is not going to be all right, and so does your dad. He knows that he is dying, and in some ways he is braver than you are.

But he does not reproach you for what you said. Maybe in the end it doesn't matter what you say. What matters is that you were there, and that you said something—anything. Maybe it was important that your hand was in his as he died and that the warmth of your voice joined with his breath as he breathed his last. Maybe the light of your eyes met his as he turned to where there is nothing to see.

A tale found at the very end of the Torah tells of children who were summoned to the deathbed of their father and what they learned when they got there.

God spoke to Moses *b'etzem hayom hazeh,* which means "in the middle of the day" or "on that very day." On that very day God said to him: Moses, you shall die on the mountain that you are now about to ascend and you shall be gathered to your people.

Why did God insist that Moses die in the middle of the day, when everyone would be standing about watching, waiting, and wondering. Why not in the small hours of the night instead, in peace, in quiet, in private?

Rashi, the great biblical commentator, notices that this phrase *b'etzem hayom hazeh* is found three times in the Bible, in connection with three events.

B'etzem hayom hazeh—in the middle of the day, Noah and his family went into the ark, as God had commanded him. And the

Lord closed the ark and then the rains began to fall. Rashi explains that Noah entered the ark in full view of the people of his generation. Perhaps they wanted to stop him or stone him or prevent him from entering. But they couldn't.

The flood was inevitable, and so was Noah's entering in the ark. Nothing—no force on earth—could stop that flood that God had decreed.

B'etzem hayom hazeh, in the middle of the day, God took the Jews out of Egypt. There were Egyptians who, even after the ten plagues, still did not want to let the Israelites go or wanted to block their way. But there was no way that they could do so. Just as no human being could hold back the flood, no human being could hold back the Exodus.

And now, God has decreed that Moses will die—*b'etzem hayom hazeh,* on that very day. Israel will try to stop or put off the decree. They will pray for him, they will cry for him, they will protest for him, they will try to hold him back. He was their guide, their teacher, their protector, their sustainer, and their leader for forty years, through all the vicissitudes of the Exodus, so they could not bear to let him go. They will try to hold on to him in every way they can, but just as with the flood and just as with the Exodus, so no one could hold back the death of Moses. God has willed it to happen, and no force on earth can stop it.

All of Israel saw Moses ascend the mountain that fateful day. They were summoned by God to his deathbed like a son or a daughter being summoned to the deathbed of a parent. They had to be there, just as a child must be there when the parent's time arrives. And yet the Torah does not record a single word that the people said to Moses as he took his first steps away from them. They must have said something! They must have tried to clutch him, to hold him back, to persuade him to stay. Perhaps their hands were extended out to him; perhaps their eyes met his. But were there words? They probably said nothing, since nothing is recorded. If not to say something, then what is it that they were summoned to do, *b'etzem hayom hazeh,* on that very day?

I think I know what happened that day on Mount Nebo, on the

day Moses died, and what the people of Israel learned that day. I
think that they learned the same truth that Joy Gresham taught
C. S. Lewis, as they are portrayed in the film *Shadowlands*.

C. S. Lewis was a Catholic theologian, a don at Oxford University. He was a stodgy, typically English bachelor who spent his days
reading and teaching and writing theology. He lived with his brother, and together they had a secure, regulated, dull kind of life,
until he met Joy Davidman Gresham. This lovely, free-spirited
woman broke through Lewis's humdrum existence and brought a
whole new spirit into his life. Never before had he been so open
with anyone or so involved in someone else's life. They loved each
other deeply and planned to be married when Joy discovered that
she was terminally ill with cancer. They married—there was a
remission in her illness—but it was only temporary and then she
began to deteriorate. She knew she was dying; only their love for
each other sustained her and gave her the strength and will to keep
fighting the cancer.

Toward the end of the film, ravaged by the disease, Joy turns to
Lewis and says, "You have to let me go. You have to give me permission to die. I can't leave you—I don't want to leave you unless
you tell me that it is all right for me to go."

It was the hardest moment of his life. But in his love for her, he
found the courage to say the one thing that a person can say to
someone who is dying, to a person whose death is inevitable, who
has reached the limit of his life. He says to her, "I love you. If you
cannot hold on, if you are too tired, if you are too hurt and weary,
if you are in too much pain, you can let go. I will be all right. My
life will be immeasurably diminished, but I will go on until it is my
time to join you."

The people of Israel, according to one midrash, were summoned to watch Moses ascend the mountain, to begin a journey
from which there would be no return. They would do for Moses
what C. S. Lewis did for Joy Gresham: they would give Moses
their permission to leave them. It was his time. He was tired. They
would have to let him go *b'etzam hayom hazeh*—on that very day.

The people assembled at the base of the mountain that day, feel-

ing many different emotions. Their silence is the silence that all families share at a moment of imminent loss and pain. But the midrash
took that silence and translated it into words, sacred words, words
so important that it is God Himself who speaks them:

> God cried out and said:
> Who will stand up for me against evildoers?
> Who will stand up for Israel when I am angry?
> Who will stand up for them in battle?
> And who will ask for mercy on their behalf when Israel has
>   sinned?

Even God mourned Moses. Even He had to come to grips with the
world that He created—a world in which death comes to even the
most beloved and most precious of souls.

God did not want to let Moses go. But it was time. He had lived
long enough and he was tired. It was time.

> At that moment, God kissed Moses,
> And God drew out his soul with a kiss.

The people who stood at the foot of the mountain learned three
things that day. First, they learned that when you are summoned to
a deathbed, you must go. Otherwise, you live the rest of your life
with the knowledge that you were not there. Part of you will feel
guilt that you were not there and part of you will feel relief, but
you will live the rest of your life with the knowledge that you were
not there. So if you are summoned, you must go.

The second thing that they learned when they got there was that
sometimes the only thing you can do for a loved one at the limit of
a life is to extend a hand, to offer a kiss, to share a sigh, and to say
something—something that gives permission to your beloved to
let go.

And the third thing they learned that day is what Judaism would
have us learn ever since: they learned that in truth no one ever
really dies alone, for God is there.

This is why the one psalm that most people know by heart, and

which has come to mean so much to so many, is the one that
declares:

> Yea, though I walk through the valley of the shadow of
>   death,
> I shall fear no evil,
> For Thou art with me. . . .
> And I shall abide in the house of the Lord forever.

Letting Go

Janet Roth Krupnick

I began visiting patients at the Ritter-Scheuer Hospice of Beth
Abraham Hospital at the same time that I started to study in the
Cantors Institute of the Jewish Theological Seminary. The dean of
the Cantors Institute, Rabbi Leifman, has a program whereby he
sends his students to hospitals and nursing homes to visit patients
and residents. I never really thought of those visits as pastoral in
nature until recently, when I had been out of school for several
years. And it was only then that I began to understand the truly
powerful nature of these visits.

Although I grew up in the city of Chicago, I had spent three
years studying music in a small town in north Texas prior to coming to New York, and everything about New York City was a
shock to my senses. The hospice was in the far end of the Bronx.
To get there I had to walk to 116th Street, take a subway down to
96th Street, walk up and down stairs, and transfer to the train to
the Bronx—all this carrying a guitar in a heavy wooden case and a
backpack or some sort of book bag. The ride to the Bronx was
replete with strange subway characters, and by the time I reached
Allerton Avenue, there were generally only a few people in the
car. Then there was the walk to the hospital through a neighborhood with all sorts of interesting ethnic stores—Korean and
Puerto Rican groceries, and Middle Eastern corner stores.

Finally, at the end of several blocks was the hospital. The hospice occupied half of a small wing. My first time there I received a brief introduction to the hospice from the director of hospice volunteer services. She acquainted me with the administrative procedures, filling out forms, documenting each individual visit to every patient, and signing in and out. Then, guitar in hand, I went to visit the patients.

I was instructed to ask each resident if I could sing to them, because sometimes they didn't feel well enough to be entertained. And sometimes, for whatever reason, they just did not want me to come and sing to them. So there was always that element of possible rejection, standing at the foot of someone's bed, asking for permission to sing. The first time I went to the hospice, most of the beds were full and it seemed that I sang to almost everyone there. There were young AIDS patients, older cancer patients, and not-so-old cancer patients. There were Jews and Hispanics, black people and white people. I sat in a chair at the foot of the patient's bed and sang what I thought each person could relate to and would enjoy. There wasn't much conversation, sometimes a thank-you or an introduction to a family member in the room. Mostly I sat with my guitar and sang one, two, or even more songs; face-to-face with the patient, sitting at the foot of the bed.

That first time at the hospice, after about an hour with various patients, I went to make what I had decided was my last visitation of the day. David Cohen was in the day room, a lounge of sorts, and several members of his family were gathered around him.

My singing opened up the conversation. David had been in Israel just at the time the state gained independence. He spoke some Hebrew, and he was delighted to hear old pioneer songs and to reminisce about the time he had lived in Israel. I sang for quite a while, maybe twenty minutes, and he and his family joined in. Then, all of the sudden, exhaustion hit me. I needed to leave. I didn't say goodbye or "I'll see you next time." I just excused myself and left. I filled out the numerous forms at the office and headed back to Manhattan.

All week long I thought about how rude I had been to David. I hadn't even said goodbye to him! At the next week's visit I planned to be sure to say goodbye to David and to everyone else I visited.

The next week I schlepped out on the subways to the Bronx and went eagerly to the hospice with a new mission of politeness added to my singing. The head nurse stopped me at the nursing station. "Janet," she said, "you remember David Cohen from your last visit? He just loved your singing!" (Here I began to feel very good about myself.) "He talked about it all afternoon." (I am feeling even better about myself.) "His daughters came that evening and all he did was talk about your singing." (I am thinking how wonderful I am—isn't it great how good I am making everyone feel?) "And then he died." There is a silence. Guitar in hand, I run into the nearest bathroom to cry, banging the guitar on the door as I escape into the small space.

When I emerged, the head nurse explained to me why she was so happy. The singing and the music had allowed him to let go and to die. After all, as the rabbinical intern at the hospice explained to me, that's why people come to the hospice—to die. "Don't come here looking for a grandmother or grandfather," he said. "People are here to die." And we were there to help them.

So that is what I had done. I had helped David Cohen free his soul and he was able to die. There had been only a little conversation, and certainly no discussion of God, or death, or the world-to-come. Mostly there had been a small gathering of people, listening and singing, sharing a small amount of time together, connected by words and melody. The power of music. The intimacy of the situation. The death of a human being.

Eventually I would visit the hospice for most of the four years that I was at the seminary, at first going every week and then, in the last year, only on occasion. I visited Geraldine Smith, a black woman who was ornery with the nurses but who radiated warmth when I would sing for her. Geraldine once asked me if I believed in heaven, and at that moment I did. I believed that heaven existed and that Geraldine's soul would go to heaven when she died.

It may have been prejudice or merely an attempt to find music that people would find meaningful, but I tended to sing music that

I thought each patient could relate to. So to Geraldine and other elderly black patients I sang spirituals, and to the elderly Jewish patients I sang in Yiddish or in Hebrew. To the Hispanic patients I sang Spanish and South American folk songs. Once, by the time I got to a patient whom the nurses wanted me to visit, he had already died. So as they were putting the corpse into a body bag, at the request of one of the nurses, I sang an Irish folk song. I'm not sure whom I was singing to at that point, the nurses or the dead patient, but the nurses sang with me from behind the curtain as they dealt with the dead body.

I have a very strong memory of singing for an elderly Hispanic man. At least ten members of his family were in the room, and as I sang a simple Cuban folk song, they all sang with me. It was one of the most powerful moments I experienced at the hospice—a man dying in a room filled with his close family, and everyone singing together.

The hardest people to sing for were the young. It was the younger patients who were more likely to turn down an offer from me to sing. And it was for the younger patients that I had the hardest time finding music I thought they would enjoy. I felt inadequate because I didn't know contemporary rock music, and I thought that this was what the younger patients would want to listen to. There was Walter, a young black man, the son of a minister, who was dying of AIDS. He was in tremendous physical and mental agony. I went to visit him over a period of weeks. Each time, he had deteriorated more and was more distressed. Sometimes he would listen to a little singing, but for the most part he was in too much agony to enjoy the music. So I would read a psalm or pray with him.

There was a young boy of about seventeen years who was dying of brain cancer. Either his mother or his sisters were always there with him, and they were always happy to see me. But I was never able to make a connection with him, through either music or words. I felt very frustrated. At first I didn't understand that his deteriorated mental state was a result of his illness and that he had been at one time a normal, athletic teenager. Every year the hospice holds an interfaith memorial service; I would sing there, and I remember the year his mother and sisters came. I cried when I saw them.

I will tell you about two more patients. There was Hirsch, a man of about forty years old, dying of AIDS. Hirsch was Jewish, and although his was not a religious family, they spoke in Yiddish to each other. It was not very common to see a Jewish person with AIDS at the hospice. Even with a repertory of Yiddish songs, I could not find music to relate to Hirsch or his parents. I could not find a way to connect with them, but I felt an overwhelming need to reach out to them. I was very affected by this situation, this middle-aged, Jewish man dying of AIDS, speaking in Yiddish to his parents.

When I got home that evening, I called Rabbi Leifman. I asked him if he would visit Hirsch, because he would be able to speak to him in Yiddish. I am sometimes amazed that I was so moved by Hirsch and his family that I dared call the dean of my school. But knowing Rabbi Leifman, it is not surprising that he went out to visit Hirsch several times.

When I sang at the hospice, I always had a great desire to make the patient feel better. I wanted somehow, through music, for that person to be made more comfortable, or to experience a moment of pleasure or happiness or nostalgia, or to be moved in some way. I think I believed in some sort of cause and effect—that my effort could and would somehow change that person's experience of reality, if only for a minute or, as in the case of David Cohen, for an eternity.

The last person I will tell you about is Josef, a Jewish man in his late forties. He was a successful businessman, and then he was hit by a very aggressive form of cancer that had severely disfigured his neck and face and had left him virtually blind. He didn't want to be visited by his family or anyone. He did not want to speak to anyone. He was alone in his anguish and misery, just waiting to die. For some reason he agreed to have me sing to him. I don't know why, but it struck me to sing some old Beatles songs—"In My Life," "Blackbird." Then he started to talk to me. It turned out that a long time ago he and a friend had arranged some music for the Beatles. He was able to talk about this, about the Beatles and his dealings with the pop-music industry.

The nun in charge of pastoral visitations went to visit him later, and he was able to tell her about these experiences and to talk more with her. She and the nurses were amazed and thrilled that the music had reached him, enabling him to express himself and be in touch with his past.

I went to visit him once or twice more before he died, but he was deteriorating rapidly and the communication between us was never as strong as during that first visit. I was thankful to have been able to make that one connection; to be able to open that door for him, through music, through a simple song; maybe to ease his dying, maybe to help him let go, to free his soul.

It has been three years since I have been to the hospice. I still think about the people. I remember those very powerful moments, sitting at the foot of someone's bed singing, sometimes having them sing with me. I think about David Cohen and how he was able to let go. What a powerful act that is—that ultimate letting-go. I think about Geraldine Smith and wonder if she made it to heaven. Did Walter and Hirsch ever find peace, and how have their families moved on?

I cannot say that my work with hospice patients has resolved any major life issues or crucial religious problems. I think that it has been more a basic experience of being with other human beings on a primal and intimate level. I feel blessed that I have been able to use my music to share such moments. *Zichronam livrachah*

A Prayer for Health-Care Providers to Offer When a Patient Dies

Nancy Flam

The purpose of this prayer is to offer Jewish health-care providers a way to acknowledge the death of a patient within a religious context. Western medicine does not always encourage spiritual expression on the part of health-care providers. And yet they are involved in work that holds inherent power to move the spirit: caring for others, witnessing vulnerability, aiding the healing process, and, of course, being present at death. This prayer highlights one moment when modern health-care providers might deepen their sense of spirituality in care-giving.

I was motivated to write this prayer because a number of physicians had asked my help in sanctifying a patient's passing. When a patient dies, there are many things to do: make the pronouncement of death, fill out forms and certificates, contact and comfort family and friends. But the moment of a patient's death calls for more than the fulfillment of professional obligations; there are personal needs as well. We need a way to pray for the soul's eternal rest; we need a way to acknowledge our grief for having cared for this person—however briefly—and of having lost him or her; we need to summons strength to continue providing care for others; and we need to stand before the awesome mystery of being and nonbeing and affirm the eternal oneness we call God.

I imagine this prayer being offered at the bedside of one who has died and whose soul has begun to travel on. It might be said in private reflection or together with a colleague. The words of the prayer might be written on an index card and placed in a pocket or purse, ready to be drawn out when needed. There are surely myriad ways, yet undreamed of, by which we might integrate our spiritual sensibilities into our provision of health care.

May it be Your will, O God,
To grant eternal rest and peace
To the soul of _____ who has now surrendered life.

Help him/her pass gently into the world to come
And shelter him/her with Your love.

Help me bring Your comforting presence
    to family and friends
Who need strength in this hour of pain and loss.

O God,
Open my heart that I may grieve this loss.
I truly cared for _____;
I mourn his/her passing.

Give me strength
That I may continue my efforts
On behalf of others who are under my care.
And help me grow in wisdom and judgment.

As I dedicate myself to enhancing life,
Let me humbly accept
That there is a time
We must each let go of living.

Adonai natan v'Adonai lakakh,
Yehi Shem Adonai mevorach.

The Eternal has given, the Eternal has taken back;
Blessed be the Eternal.

Shema Yisrael
Adonai eloheinu
Adonai ehad

Chapter Three

Hevra Kadisha: The Holy Society

Jews have had many institutions and organizations; there is only one that was given the name Hevra Kadisha, or holy society. This was the group, once found in every Jewish community, of those who volunteered to take care of the preparation of the dead for burial. Those engaged in this sacred task were always volunteers because it was considered a great honor to carry out the last good deed that we can do for those who have died. Rabbi Shneur Zalman of Ladi, the founder of the Chabad dynasty in Hasidism, was a member of a Hevra Kadisha, and Sir Moses Montefiore in his diary expresses great pride in the fact that he was elected a member of the Society of Lavadores of the Spanish and Portugese Congregation of London and fulfilled his duties with meticulous care. In Jewish law no material benefit may accrue from the dead and so no private commercial firm was permitted to engage in the preparation of the body. The duty was upon the community as a whole.

Rabbi Arnold Wolf used to say jokingly that "the most innovative thing that you can do in suburbia is the tradition—because no one has ever heard of it." That quip surely applies to the new interest in the Hevra Kadisha in our time. Who would have ever predicted that the Hevra Kadisha, of all things, would make a comeback? Of all the traditions in Judaism, this idea—that a group of volunteers should take upon themselves the tasks of guarding, washing, and dressing the body for burial—seemed most unlikely. Who would have imagined that young people would be willing to volunteer for this difficult mitzvah? We are a highly professionalized society, one that usually prefers to pay money so that someone else can deal with a problem, and yet we now see people performing this mitzvah instead of turning it over to undertakers.

The revival of interest seems to have started in Minneapolis where Congregation Adath Jeshuran, under the leadership of

Rabbi Arnold Goodman, decided that the mitzvah of burial was too sacred a task to be left only to the undertakers. So they worked out a plan whereby their members could make their funeral arrangements in advance of need, through the synagogue, instead of at a time when their families would be emotionally distraught and vulnerable. As part of this plan, they offered simple pine coffins, which is what the tradition teaches we should have. These were fashioned by the young people in the congregation, with the help and guidance of some carpenters. They offered *shmirah,* members who would volunteer to stay on duty watching over the body of the dead until the funeral while reciting psalms or studying sacred literature. And they offered *taharah,* the ritual purification and washing and dressing of the *met* (the dead), done carefully and reverently as an act of lovingkindness and respect, and with no financial compensation of any kind.

This idea is catching on, and now we begin to find such groups springing up in liberal synagogues, not only in traditional ones, in small towns as well as in big cities. In this chapter, Daniel Troy, who is an attorney in Washington, D.C., Margaret Holub, a rabbi in Mendocino, California, and Debbie Friedman, a folksinger and composer, tell us how the Hevra Kadisha works in their communities and what they have learned from taking part in this act of lovingkindness.

A Sacred Duty

Once, when Rabbi Hamnuna [a fourth-century Babylonian sage] came to Daru-Mata, he heard the sound of the funerary bugle, and, seeing some people carrying on with their work, he said: "Let these people be under the *shametta* [ban]. Is there not a person dead in the town? How dare they go about their regular business affairs?" They told him that there was a Hevra Kadisha in the town. "If so," he replied, "you are permitted to work."

—The Talmud, Moed Katan 27b

The Burial Society

Daniel E. Troy

It is a truism that we moderns are uncomfortable dealing with death—and especially uncomfortable dealing with dead bodies. Troubled by the very idea of our own mortality, we try to avoid its reminders, among which an actual dead person is certainly the most powerful. So it is no wonder that among modern Jews, knowledge of, and interest in, the Hevra Kadisha (literally, holy society)—the group of lay volunteers who prepare a Jewish body for burial—has declined over time, or that membership in such a society, although considered by Jewish religious law to be among the most laudable of activities, is now often thought to be exclusively the province of the black-garbed ultra-Orthodox.

This is unfortunate, because Jewish law relating to the newly dead has much to teach us, as I myself have learned from experience. Ever since my best and oldest childhood friend died suddenly eight years ago, my interest had been piqued by the Hevra Kadisha. Until I married, however, my inclination to join such a group was dampened by my general squeamishness concerning medical matters, as well as by my uncertainty about the level of religious observance required for membership. (Although I attend an Orthodox synagogue, keep kosher, and observe the Sabbath, I do not adhere to every jot and tittle of Jewish law.)

My wife's family, however, holds membership in the Hevra in high regard. Her maternal grandfather participated in one in Germany, and her maternal grandmother was a member in Kansas City. (Men are allowed to attend only to dead men. Women technically are permitted to prepare both men and women for burial but, as a practical matter, women attend to women exclusively.) This heritage provided the impetus I needed, and thus one day I found myself volunteering on what I told myself was purely a trial basis. The rabbi assured me that one need not be a tzaddik—an especially righteous person—to join, only a committed Jew willing to do one's best.

This tolerant approach may reflect the relatively late development of the Hevra Kadisha as an organized institution. The earliest mention is in the Talmud, which reports that Rav Hamnuna (ca. 290–320 C.E.), arriving in a city where someone had recently died, observed the inhabitants going about their business. Irate, he threatened to excommunicate them for violating the injunction that burial of the dead takes precedence over all else. But then, upon hearing that burial societies existed in the town, Rav Hamnuna concluded that ordinary citizens were indeed permitted to continue work. Rav Hamnuna's ruling made the establishment of a Hevra Kadisha a top priority in most European communities. When Jews came to the United States, this was among the first institutions they established.

In Washington, where I live, many synagogues have their own Hevra, contacted when a member of the community dies. Thus, a few weeks after my conversation with the rabbi, I was called upon to assist in my first *taharah,* or purification. When I arrived at the funeral parlor, I was told that the sixtyish man we were to prepare for burial weighed over three hundred fifty pounds and had died of "chronic obesity." I guiltily squelched an adolescent urge to grin, and was doubly chastened as I watched Ben, our team leader, a physician in his early thirties, call around asking for a few more volunteers to help us deal with the difficulties created by the weight of the *met* (dead person). His tone in discussing the *met* was intensely respectful, and this set the stage for what I was to learn was the paramount directive in this experience: to show reverence for the person who has departed.

Judaism has always considered burying deceased loved ones to be a mitzvah, a religious duty and good deed, of supreme importance. Traditionally this view is based on Abraham's actions upon the death of his wife Sarah, when he turned to the neighboring sons of Heth and said, "A stranger and a sojourner am I with you; give me the possession of a burying place with you, that I may bury my dead from before me." This verse, the rabbis held, placed the responsibility for interment first on the family, and from there on the community as a whole. By the period of the Second Temple (ca. 465 B.C.E.–70 C.E.), according to the testimony of Josephus, to "let anyone lie unburied" was considered inhumane under Jewish law.

Jews try to bury their dead immediately, as befits a people whose origins were in the desert, where bodies decompose rapidly. The rabbinic teaching is that, unless necessary for the honor of the dead, "no corpse is to remain unburied overnight." Today, in most cases, a Jew is buried within a day after having died. This custom allows the family to begin coming to terms with the loss as soon as possible. Anyone who has experienced the death of a loved one knows that the time before burial is essentially a period of "limbo" (in Jewish tradition this condition is called *aninut*) and that only after the funeral can a family proceed with the difficult task of mourning.

As we walked to the room in the basement of the funeral parlor where we were to perform the *taharah,* we passed the *shomer,* or watcher, a man who stays with the recently deceased at all times. There are both practical and religious explanations for the constant presence of a *shomer*—as there are, incidentally, for most of the Hevra's ancient procedures. Practically, the *shomer* was originally needed to ward off mice and other animals that might inflict indignities on the corpse. He also may have helped guard against thieves who trafficked in dead bodies.

Today, when such considerations are less pressing, the *shomer* continues to serve a vital function. In the interval right after death and before burial, the deceased is especially vulnerable, having not yet reached a permanent "resting place" either in body or, so far as we know, in soul. (I well recall that when my friend died, his mother begged me to ensure that he was "not alone"; she did not want any further harm to befall his mortal remains.) The Hevra has thus traditionally served to reassure the family that their loved one is being protected and cared for, a function reinforced by the custom of having the *shomer* be a respected and, presumably, well-known member of the community.

But this concern about the "address" of the newly dead is not solely for the sake of the surviving family. (Nor is it exclusively Jewish, as we can see in the proliferation of lawsuits against funeral parlors that confuse or switch bodies.) Judaism's regard for the body itself lies behind the determination to ensure that it, in its wholeness, be accorded a place after death. This is but one of the many reasons why Jewish law prohibits cremation. Aside from manifesting a disregard for God's handiwork, incinerating a body leaves it without any definable, knowable location in the world.

Although I was aware of some of these Jewish laws and customs concerning the body, I had never seen a dead person before. I was therefore quite fearful as I followed Ben and the four other members of our team down to the purification room in the funeral parlor. The room in which the *taharah* took place was in the basement, immediately adjacent to the embalming room. It was stark and relatively small, with two sinks, a cabinet, a drain in the middle of the floor, and a steel table that tilted for drainage purposes. Ben noticed my trepidation and reassured me: nothing was expected of a beginner other than to watch. I was free to do only what I felt comfortable doing and to leave anytime I wanted. Ben warned us that smoking, eating, drinking, unnecessary talking, and praying near the body were all forbidden. Nothing was to distract us from the primary task at hand—preparing the *met* for eternal rest.

We entered the room, and there was the *met,* covered in a sheet, lying on a table. Ben explained the fundamental rules. As much of the body as possible is to be kept covered at all times, even while being washed. It is particularly important that the face and the genitals be shielded. At no time is it permitted to place the body face down. It is absolutely forbidden to pass anything over the body—a sign of profound disrespect, and a violation of the "personal space" of the *met;* if we had to give an item to someone on the other side of the table, we were to walk around and hand it to him.

The prohibition against passing objects over the *met* affirms the humanity of the person whose body is lying before us; it seeks to ensure that the members of the Hevra continue to accord a dead person the respect normally given to those still alive. This consideration is by no means peculiar to Jews: for essentially the same reasons, people visiting a cemetery are reluctant to step directly on the spot where someone is buried. But in Jewish tradition the space above a *met* is reserved for him not only in the immediate vicinity but all the way "up to the heavens," so that his path to the divine will not be impeded. This suggests that we should respect a dead person even more than we do a living one, precisely because, in death, the *met* is thought to come face-to-face with his maker and judge.

After Ben's explanation of the procedures, we began by reciting the *hamol* ("forgiveness") prayer, which asks God to take mercy on the *met,* pardon his transgressions, and allow him to rest with our fathers Abraham, Isaac, and Jacob, as well as the other righteous of Israel. Jewish prayers often characterize God as the reviver of the dead (in the time of the Messiah); unusually, the *hamol* prayer adds that it is God who causes the living to die.

Stealing glances during the prayer, I was surprised to observe that the *met* had a large tattoo. Since Jews are expressly forbidden by the Torah to tattoo their bodies, it seemed that this man had been far removed from Judaism in his life. And the distance became even more palpable when I heard his name—Yehudah ben (son of) Herman.* In other words, Yehudah's family did not even know his father's Hebrew name. Yet here he was, tattoo and all, being prepared for burial just as his ancestors had been for millennia. The stark contrast between Yehudah's apparently irreligious life and his choice to be buried in the ancient Jewish manner, in a shroud and in a closed, plain pine box, moved and confused me.

Ben assigned me the simple task of filling buckets with lukewarm water. The requirement that the water be set at the temperature at which most people feel comfortable taking a bath seemed yet

---

*I have changed the actual name but preserved its flavor.

another reminder that the *met* should be treated as sensitively as possible. Ben explained that the goal in a *taharah* is to replicate the immersion of the body in a mikvah (ritual bath). There are, again, at least two reasons for this ceremony. The first is ritual: to remove symbolically any impurity which the *met* might have brought upon himself during his lifetime. Humans can assist in eliminating this type of pollution, because it has arisen at the hand of man—i.e., the deceased. (The inherent impurity that comes from being a dead body, however, can be removed only by God.) The other reason is related to the vulnerability of the newly dead and the role of the *shomer*. Death completes the cycle of life. Practically the first experience of a baby is being washed and wrapped in swaddling clothes. It is fitting that this experience be mirrored in death.

Performing the *taharah* is uncomplicated. First, the entire body is fully washed, from head to toe, with water poured from a ladle backhanded, to indicate the sadness of the situation and that things are not "normal." Even the fingernails and toenails of the *met* are cleaned. Then, to ensure that as much as possible of the person be covered with water at one time, washed-down white wooden planks are placed under the body to lift it off the table. The *met* is next doused with at least three buckets of water simultaneously. This is the actual *taharah*.

Turning the *met* first on one side, then the other, we washed the body according to the specified protocol: first the head, then the right side of the body starting with the hand, up the arm; then the left side, also starting with the hand; then the right side of the back, followed by the left side of the back.

I was struck by the common sense of the order. We are, first and foremost, identified with and by our face and head. Inside our head resides our brain, seat of our conscious mind and therefore also of our "personality" (that which makes each of us unique), while our face is what we present to the world, often expressing outwardly our innermost being. By the time we reach our thirties, our face has started permanently to assume a shape that is determined by the expressions we have employed throughout our life. Often more than our eyes, our lines and wrinkles are windows to our soul.

After the head and face, the second most important part of ourself seen by the world is our hands. These, almost as much as our
face, embody who we are. The laborer's hands are calloused, the
scholar's soft. And moving from the face directly to the hands also
stresses the connection between the spiritual and the physical. The
hands make real the soul's wishes. With our hands, we make love,
hold our children, write, and mold the physical world in accordance with the dictates of our mind. It is therefore appropriate that
we wash the head and hands for the last time in tandem.

While the others washed, I was given the task of cutting off
every part of the covering sheet that contained any blood, so that
it could be put in the coffin and buried with the *met,* as required by
law. This rule is an extension of the strict prohibition against
autopsies. Every part of a person—even a few spots of his blood on
a sheet—is to be treated with equal respect and interred with him.
Although the rule making the dead body inviolable has the effect of
transforming every organ transplant into a difficult moral and legal
question, it also establishes a very clear line, permitting transplants
only under narrowly circumscribed conditions where there is an
identifiable beneficiary.

In this case, the *met* had undergone a tracheotomy before death,
and the endotracheal tube had to be removed before burial. (The
tube was also placed in the coffin.) This proved somewhat bloody,
and I quickly understood why my synagogue has a policy of having
a doctor present at each *taharah.*

Although shifting the *met* onto the reclining table had not been
difficult, placing the white boards under him and trying to establish
a sufficient distance between him and the table to enable water to
engulf him completely was somewhat trickier. Gently rolling the
boards once we had placed them under the *met,* we were able to
elevate him off the table.

We then performed the actual "immersion"—throwing the pails
of water on the *met* while reciting a prayer that recalls Rabbi Akiva,
one of the best-loved figures in rabbinic Judaism. It was Rabbi
Akiva who opined that the Lord in heaven will cleanse those in need
of purification. After the water was poured in a continuous stream

over the departed, we recited in unison: "*Tahor hu; tahor hu; tahor hu*" ("He is purified; he is purified; he is purified").

We next proceeded to dress the *met* in white linen garments, covered his head in a hood, and draped a tallit (fringed garment worn in prayer) around his shoulders. Judaism considers all people equal in death and requires that everyone be treated alike. Ornate clothing and fancy coffins are expressly prohibited. This custom originated with Rabban Simeon ben Gamaliel II (in the first half of the second century C.E.) who, alarmed at the extravagance and expense of funerals, ordered that his own funeral be extremely simple.

We slipped the *met* in his white linen shrouds into the *aron,* or ark (a much nicer word than coffin, especially since it recalls the place where the Torah scroll is kept in the synagogue). Spread on the bottom of the *aron* was dirt from the Mount of Olives outside of Jerusalem, where Jews have been laid to rest since the time of the Temple. This custom is based on the statement in Deuteronomy that "the earth shall atone for His people": the only earth believed capable of expiating the sins of the dead is that of the land of Israel.

Once the *met* was in the *aron,* we deposited pottery inside the head-covering, over his eyes. This is to address the mystics' concern that as long as the eyes of the *met* look upon this world, he cannot properly focus on the world-to-come. We also sprinkled dirt on his head, heart, and sex organ. The dirt, like the clay pottery, reaffirms the scriptural injunction "Dust thou art, and to dust thou shalt return."

We next placed the cover on the *aron,* bringing the *taharah* effectively to an end. The law strictly forbids reopening the *aron* for any reason. One of the many explanations for Judaism's insistence on a closed coffin is the lack of reciprocity inherent in the relationship between the *met* and those who remain alive. We may look at him, but he cannot see us. In this necessarily one-sided relation, we are voyeurs trafficking in the "disgrace" of his exposure. To prevent the dead person from being, as it were, embarrassed by his state, the coffin is closed.

The demand for a closed coffin is also another step in affirming the finality of death. It forces family members to begin thinking about the person as they will for the rest of their lives—as a memory; and it begins the separation process. It may also palliate the intensity of a family's grief. Finally, the prohibition on an open coffin avoids any temptation to cosmeticize the dead or to visit upon him indignities of the type prevalent in modern American funeral homes and practices.

After the coffin is closed, but before leaving, each person in the Hevra is instructed to beg silent forgiveness of the *met*. This apology is made in case anyone has inadvertently performed a part of the *taharah* in a manner not in accordance with the personal customs of the *met*. Jewish law also requires that each person speak aloud the name of the *met*.

At first this requirement seemed a little silly to me. Were we to pretend that Yehudah ben Herman had his own "customs" with respect to the Hevra Kadisha—or that he had ever given a moment's thought to ritual purification? The notion of us standing around a dead body uttering aloud his slightly ridiculous Jewish name made me uncomfortable, to say the least.

I was wrong. To accomplish any *taharah* requires a degree of distance from the *met*. That depersonalization ended the moment we spoke Yehudah ben Herman's name. We were reminded that a man, like us, lay before us in the *aron*: a man with a wife, children, coworkers, friends, and loved ones who were affected by his death. The little custom of speaking Yehudah's name drove home to me the genius of those who had formulated the rules. Just as the practices of the Hevra reinforce the Jewish prohibition against autopsies or any other purely utilitarian use of the body, they guard against what Leon Kass of the University of Chicago has called the "commodification of human flesh." The Jewish approach takes account of the powerful sense residing in every human being that the body should be respected, even after the person who inhabited it has left.

The rabbis describe participation in a Hevra Kadisha as a *hesed shel emet* (a true act of kindness), since no reward can be expected from the dead for whom the service is performed. Although the prospect of meriting such high praise may have been thought necessary in order to motivate people to join a Hevra (or to ensure that only sincere people join), in my view the rabbis were being deliberately hyperbolic. Clearly the Hevra experience does offer many rewards. For one thing, having esteemed members of the community care for a dead person makes an enormous difference to that person's family. For another, the Hevra sees to it that all people, high and low, are treated equally in death, and that their funerals and burial garments do not become a cause for ostentation. Finally, and perhaps most relevantly to our own day, the respect shown to a dead person by the Hevra can affect profoundly the way those of us who remain alive view our own humanity. In all these regards, the laws of the Hevra Kadisha serve the dead *and* the living.

How Tradition Brought One Community to Life

Margaret Holub

In the small and relatively youthful Jewish community that I serve as rabbi, there are not a lot of deaths. But each person who has died in our community has been a teacher to me and to all of us. We have changed because of the ways that people here have died and been mourned. I am going to describe several of these deaths and how we have evolved along the way. I have changed the names of the dead and their family members. But of course those who have died are not here to ask permission of. I hope that, were they to know how much they have helped their rabbi and their community to grow, for this at least they would be pleased and proud.

A few months after I moved to the north coast of California to be the rabbi, a man committed suicide. Steven was Jewish but had never involved himself with Jewish life. His wife, Jane, was not Jewish. In fact, Jane's first call after learning of her husband's death was to the Protestant minister of the church where their two young children went to preschool. A neighbor had found the man's body and had meanwhile called me. The minister was out of town, and I showed up at the house. So I became a kind of rabbi-by-default to Steven's family in the weeks and months that followed.

I remember well driving over to the house after I had received that first call from the neighbor. "What have I got to offer?" I kept asking myself. "Who do they think I am?" In fact I offered whatever I could. I held Jane's hand before and after she told her children of their father's death. I washed dishes, answered the phone, and deflected business calls from people who didn't know that Steven had just taken his life. I went to the mortuary with Jane and her six-year-old, who had clearly and courageously requested to see her father's body. I sat in the mortician's office with Jane as she numbly arranged for a cremation.

I didn't know how to advise Jane otherwise. Steven had long ago left behind whatever Judaism he had known. I knew well that Jane would look at the price list at the mortuary and see that for $850 his body would be cremated and delivered to her in a shoebox-sized carton in two days. Or she could pay the $650 basic fee to the mortuary, plus several hundred dollars more for a gravesite, plus another hundred to have it opened, plus $700 to $1500 for a kosher casket, which would have to be bused in from the nearest Jewish mortuary, four hours away, plus the cost of several days' refrigeration for Steven's body, since all this would take time to arrange. Not only that—our community didn't have a Jewish cemetery, the mortician had never been involved in the mechanics of a Jewish burial, and none of us, myself included, knew anything about what was involved.

I agonized over creating the memorial service for Steven. There was so little to turn to that would be meaningful to the people who would gather. I said that Steven's death was three times sad: it is a sorrowful thing when anyone leaves this life; more so if the person was young; and all the more so if he left in despair. I quoted Koheleth, avoiding the obvious *"ha-kol hevel"*—"all is vanity." Ours is a wonderfully supportive community, and neighbors and customers of Steven and Jane's business had been at the house all week helping out. Many people came to the memorial service, and they spoke kindly of Steven. It could have been much worse.

Afterward the family was left with the shoebox of ashes. We had some conversations about one day burying them under a tree on their land—but would Jane and the children stay in that home? Every time I talked with Jane over the next few weeks and months, we talked about the ashes. But I don't recall there ever being a resolution. Within the next few months, she sold the family business and moved away with her children to another small community, where I hear they are all doing well.

It seemed to me from the experience of Steven's death and funeral that it was monumentally more difficult to choose to bury a family member than to cremate one. Cremation was relatively inexpensive and took little planning. By contrast, burial—especially anything resembling a Jewish burial—cost a substantial amount and enmeshed a grieving family in a morass of details. In a community like ours, some people will always choose cremation. But it didn't seem right to me that one would have to be so much more knowledgeable, assertive, and wealthy to choose the option of Jewish burial. I thought that Jewish burial should be accessible in our community to all who wanted it.

It was around this same time that an elderly, very ill woman moved to this community to spend her last days near her son. Mrs. Steinberg was an Orthodox Jew from New York—our beautiful village in the wilds of northern California couldn't have been more foreign to her. She was moved into a small nursing home, and her son brought kosher meats up from San Francisco and instructed the cooks there about at least a few of the complexities of kosher cooking. They were constantly mixing it up. A few people from our Jewish community would visit, those who could speaking in Yiddish with Mrs. Steinberg. But the cultural gap was enormous, and, as she got weaker, it became more and more difficult for us to bridge it. The months in the nursing home were lonely and, I suspect, frightening.

One of Mrs. Steinberg's most insistent concerns was that she have a traditional Jewish burial. I spoke with her son about having her body driven down to San Francisco when she died, where she could be cared for in a Jewish mortuary and buried in a Jewish cemetery. But the advice didn't sit well with me. Mrs. Steinberg was, in however minimal a fashion, part of our community. She lived here; she was going to die here. Again it seemed that we were lacking something crucial if a Jew couldn't have a Jewish burial in the Jewish community where he or she had lived.

I put a notice in the *Mendocino Megillah,* our local newsletter, inviting anyone who wanted to study Jewish burial traditions to meet on a certain evening. I had no great expectations of anyone coming to this meeting. But in fact about ten people showed up, which, for our small community, was a significant number. It was a curious group. About half the people were actively involved in many aspects of Jewish life, and it was not surprising to see them here as well. But there were also a number of others who did not outwardly appear very connected to Judaism. It turned out that many in the group had lived through the death of someone close to them. Some had experienced the care of a Hevra Kadisha, a traditional Jewish burial group, and appreciated it. Others had been aggrieved by the mechanical way that death is so often handled in our society. When they were in mourning, they had wished for a more intentional approach to death, and these Jewish traditions offered that possibility—if not for them, then for others.

Nothing in my rabbinic training had prepared me to form a Hevra Kadisha. We all read and discussed some basic books that outlined the Halakhah of burial and mourning. We also began acquiring the buckets, sheets, and so on that are needed for the task of *taharah,* washing a body in the traditional fashion. Finally we began a process of research and negotiation with our county to designate a Jewish space in a local cemetery. We rehearsed what we would do when notified of a death, and set up "telephone trees" to schedule *shomrim,* attendants to sit with the body from death to burial. We went over and over the mechanics of *taharah,* worrying over details to which we had no answers. For example, the books we read said that, after a preliminary washing, the Hevra Kadisha holds the *met,* the body, upright and pours twenty-four quarts of water over it in a continuous stream. How exactly does one prop the *met* upright? We did not know then what we know now—that there is a certain amount of art as well as science in these practices.

In the middle of all of this—after we had met with the local mortician and apprised him of our plans, but before we had consecrated our cemetery—Mrs. Steinberg died. I was out of town when she passed away, and the Hevra Kadisha did beautifully. *Shomrim* attended her body from within moments of her death. The *taharah* went smoothly. What none of us could have known from reading books was that being present for her in this way would be such a powerful experience of *kedushah,* of the holy.

Over the next year or so there were several other deaths, and the Hevra Kadisha was involved in various ways each time. Our Hevra Kadisha is different from many more urban Hevrot in that we typically do much more than just orchestrate the *shemirut* (guard duty) and the *taharah*. Our Hevra Kadisha is the group that organizes every kind of support we can think to offer when there is a death. Within the next year there was a death in our community which touched us all very deeply and showed us just how essential, and extensive, our work can be.

We were getting ready for a big wedding during that time, when the news came that the twenty-four-year-old daughter of the prospective bride had gone out of remission from her leukemia, which was itself secondary to treatment she had taken for Hodgkin's disease four years earlier. With that one phone call we knew that there was little chance that she would get another break. Wedding plans continued, sobered by the new hope that Janet would live to see her mother remarry.

Janet's mother, Helen, had moved to our community two decades earlier, and Janet had grown up here, though she now lived in the town where she had gone to college. Both mother and daughter were extroverted, community-minded, and much loved. A few days before the wedding weekend, Janet had what became her final health crisis, which lasted three months. At the last minute the wedding was postponed, and Janet moved back to her mother's house, bringing her own fiancé with her. The entire local community, and the Jewish community within it, rallied around Janet and her family. This was possible in part because Helen and Janet were gifted at receiving help. They each had a remarkable ability to articulate what they needed and to receive what was offered graciously. This is often not so, as we all know. Our community was able to provide several meals each week, housing for relatives, and myriad other specific kinds of assistance, especially during those last three months.

While Janet's illness was progressing, our Hevra Kadisha began making plans for her burial. Of course we all hoped, or perhaps wished, that we would not have to use these arrangements. But we knew that we probably would, and Helen, Janet, and both their partners were open to making some of these plans in advance.

Our Hevra Kadisha had been talking for some time about whether we needed the mortuary at all. It was decided that we would try to care for Janet's body at home, bypassing the services of the funeral home altogether. We wanted to try this in part to avoid unnecessary expense. But more importantly, we are a rural, back-to-the-land Jewish community, and we like to do things ourselves when we can. Helen had built her own house and homesteaded successfully for two decades. The decision to care for her daughter's body at home was in keeping with her values and those of our Jewish community. In our rural area, there is somewhat less regulation of funeral procedures than I suspect there is in more urban communities. Nevertheless, an extraordinary amount of logistical planning had to be done. We ultimately learned what that "basic fee" at the mortuary really pays for.

We got hold of a blank burial permit and made arrangements to have it properly signed and filed within hours of Janet's eventual death, even if it was a night or weekend. A local craftsman built a simple wooden coffin, pegged together in the traditional fashion, which actually took more time and materials than we might have guessed. The coffin then had to be stored somewhere where it could be gotten to at any time. We procured a woman's shroud from San Francisco. We began to think about details such as how we were going to transport Janet's body to the cemetery and how we were going to lower the coffin into the grave. Some tasks, such as digging the grave and transporting the coffin, we did not want to do in advance. It just didn't feel right. So we had to have people lined up to do these tasks quickly when they were needed. Meanwhile, in the last weeks and days more and more relatives were arriving in town. We were able to provide housing for those who needed it and more and bigger meals for everyone gathered at Helen's home.

Janet died at home the morning of erev Hanukkah. Helen called me at about 7:30, and I went to their house. Someone else was already there to sit *shemirah,* to "guard" Janet's body. Within another hour or two, three other women from our Hevra Kadisha arrived. All three women happen to be mothers themselves, and I remember Helen weeping and saying, "The mothers are here." We did the *taharah* outside on a deck overlooking Helen's magnificent flower garden, which is itself overtaken by a white rosebush that Janet had planted years earlier.

There were complications, if that's what you would call them. Helen's closest friend, who was almost another mother to Janet, wanted to assist us with the washing. It felt odd to us to include her, as these ritual tasks are not usually done by people very close to the one who died. But it seemed less appropriate to refuse her request. She joined us on the deck and helped, but she was unfamiliar with the practices. At one point she objected to part of the *taharah.* It was a heart-stopping moment for all of us. We stopped and talked with the friend for a few minutes, telling her that we had come to appreciate the organic nature of the ritual, even if we didn't fully understand every part. We said that we hoped that she would trust the tradition and trust us. With her agreement, we moved on. The coffin hadn't been transported from the builder's garage to Janet's house by the time we did *taharah,* and so we didn't have it to put her body in and close up immediately after we had completed our task, as is customary. So we dressed her body in the shrouds and set her back in her bed. Visitors to the house kept making their way to the bedroom to view Janet's body, something that is not traditional and gave us some uneasy feelings. Our Jewish cemetery was still not a reality, and the burial was going to be in a site that had to be dug by hand. It took three adults eight backbreaking hours to open the grave, which caused some anxiety and delay.

The most serious mechanical problem was that it became unrealistic for several reasons to bury Janet the next day. This meant that her body would be at home for forty-eight hours or so, and we didn't know whether it would begin decomposing. Fortunately it was winter, and we opened the doors and windows of the room in which she lay. *Shomrim* sat in that cold room wrapped in sleeping bags and parkas around the clock for two days and nights. Our fears about decomposition did not come true.

On the day of Janet's burial, we placed the coffin in the back of a friend's station wagon, which had been laced with redwood boughs and flowers. At the cemetery, several hundred people stood in a circle offering stories, words of comfort, and prayers. We said the traditional prayers and lowered the casket into the grave, using three ropes with knots at each end. After the Kaddish, we all hand-filled the entire grave, which took another hour and a half, singing songs and prayers the entire time. We returned to Helen's home, lit the Hanukkah menorah, and had an evening service. It was no problem at all to get a minyan together for the rest of the week, as people gathered there continually.

These experiences have taught me some important lessons about ritual and community, as well as about death. I was not unlike many other rabbis when Steven died. I was caring and personally present, but I had little to offer beyond what any caring person could give. More importantly, our community could offer very little. We did not yet have our cemetery, our Hevra Kadisha, our knowledge of the obligation to comfort mourners, our arrangements for letting the community know about the death of a Jew, our customs of visiting and bringing food, our network of helpers. Because Steven and his family did not relate to Judaism—but equally because our community did not know what Judaism had to offer—his family did not receive either the ritual comfort or the human comfort that our tradition and our Jewish community should have offered.

These rituals provide comfort by structuring those agonizing hours and days immediately after a death, and far beyond as well. In one sense, it doesn't even altogether matter what the content of the ritual might be—just that one lights a candle, opens a window, tears a shirt, covers a mirror, provides comfort, does *something* to begin recovering from the rending of death. It is additionally comforting that these rites have been performed by our ancestors for generations, that they are observed in memory of others in the community, and that they will no doubt be conducted on our behalf one day as well. And behind the particular symbols and words of Jewish burial tradition there is a theology that is wise and coherent. Mourners may not be thinking about theology, but the water, the light, and the roundness are all comforting and healing at whatever level they are received.

Jewish traditions also provide an opportunity for the Jewish community to extend itself to a person in grief. Janet and her family were well known and loved. But many of the people who visited, cooked, dug, built, hauled, and mourned were not close friends. They were community, and they knew that a mitzvah needed to be done. I am quite certain that almost every person who helped out while Janet was ill and after she died counts it as a privilege to have been involved. Had we not known and practiced these Jewish traditions, there would have been no less goodwill. But it would have been much harder to figure out how to demonstrate it.

Since we have been organized, our Hevra Kadisha has offered its services to other households in which neither the person who died nor the survivors have identified themselves as particularly Jewish. The fact that our community is becoming knowledgeable about these customs—that we have dedicated a Jewish cemetery, that we store a kosher coffin and shrouds right there with our Torah-school supplies and prayer books, and that we as a community have found meaning in these mitzvot—has made them accessible to people who might not know to request them on their own. Family and friends in our Jewish community who have elected traditional burial for their loved ones have inevitably been moved and comforted by the traditions themselves and by the *kavvanah,* the intentionality, with which we offer them. And these experiences have drawn people toward other facets of Jewish life as well.

Over and over, both Jews and non-Jews have remarked to me how lucky the Jewish people is to have this remarkable body of tradition to offer for comfort and healing when there is a death. It has been true for us, and not just about death. I believe that these practices have made us more connected to each other and to the rest of Jewish tradition. Our *b'nei mitzvah* celebrations are more festive than they were. When my husband and I married last year, our Jewish community was present for us in ways that still overwhelm us when we recall them. I don't think that this would be true were it not for the experiences we have had struggling to be present when someone here has died. These traditions that surround death have brought us Jewishly to life.

Bubby's Last Gift

Debbie Friedman

She was so rigid. It was unlike her. There was a time when she was free and easy and open. When I touched her, she didn't respond to me at all. Her smile was gone, her touch was cold. She would not look at me. And no matter how loudly I called to her, she would not answer me.

It was hard to be angry with her. After all, this was all beyond her control. She would have been different if she could have been. I know that.

Once she was five feet two. She was only about four feet eight now. She was ninety-two. Soon she would be ninety-three.

She had put on some weight since she had stopped walking. She had forgotten her routine. Her body had more wrinkles than years. One knew by looking that this was a body that had endured years of challenge and hard times. One could see that perseverance and determination kept her alive. It filtered down to all of us as well.

Though our wrinkles were not yet showing, we were who we were because of her.

She was so cold. I guess they kept her in the refrigerator. It was hard to imagine that she didn't need a blanket or a sweater or something to keep her warm. I wondered if she was even there. I think that she had finally left to go be with all of the family and friends whom she so loyally and routinely blessed in Gan Eden every Shabbat as she blessed the candles.

I have often stood at the kitchen sink preparing dinner. I have scrubbed the vegetables clean to make certain there was no mud and have attempted to use a special solution from the health-food store that would neutralize and ingest any toxic chemicals present.

I have stood at the sink night after night in preparation for bed. First I flossed, then I put toothpaste on my toothbrush, and soap on my hands and face, and washed myself so that I would be fresh for bed.

I have often snuggled with my dog and found a flea or two, and in a frantic neurotic moment, I have run her into the shower with me and covered her with herbal antiflea shampoo to suffocate the fleas and attempt to make the eggs very unhappy.

It was December 1992. It was not time for bed, there were no insecticides present, there were no fleas. Bubby had died.

I had called the mortuary to make arrangements for Bubby's funeral. I explained that she was to go back to Utica, New York, that she was not to travel on Shabbat, and that she was to have *taharah.* They charged $175 for the *taharah,* but I did not care about the money. There was nothing too good for my bubby. I knew that this was a mitzvah and that it was inappropriate to charge for such a service.

I found out also that the Palm Springs "*Taharah* Queen" did the *taharah* herself and when she finished, she called the undertakers to help her with the body. This was not acceptable to me. Bubby was going to have a kosher *taharah* even if I had to do it myself.

I called my friend Devorah Jacobson, who was a rabbi. She had been part of a Hevra Kadisha in St. Louis. I asked her if she would help me. She said, "It would be an honor."

"Devorah," I said, "would it be okay if my mom and I helped you?" She told me that it would be fine. Mom said she would do it and arrived at the funeral home the next morning to help. Two other close friends joined us. We would need at least four people to do this.

When I was little, I walked upstairs every morning to help Bubby get dressed. She wore a bra that had about a hundred fifty hooks and eyes. For her it was an arthritic nightmare, but I helped her fasten her bra every morning. It was a big job, but I always got my reward. I got to stay upstairs and have oatmeal with Bubby and Zadie every morning. I can only imagine how she managed all those years that we were separated.

The *taharah* was to begin. "Put on rubber gloves," they said. I didn't want to do it. There was nothing of which I was afraid. My bubby was not diseased, she was dead. I put the gloves on at their insistence. They said that you never know what you might pick up in a hospital.

"Bubby," I said, "if I do anything to humiliate you or cause you embarrassment during your *taharah,* I ask your forgiveness in advance. I ask that you know that I would never do anything to cause you shame or humiliation or embarrassment."

Bubby said nothing to any of us. We all knew that she understood that we were there to help make her passage one of gentleness and comfort.

We had three very large pails filled with water. We read psalms, we read *Eishet Chayil* ("A Woman of Valor"), and poured the water from the head down to the feet as we held her and whispered, *"Taharah he,"* "She is pure." We did it again and again. I took off the rubber gloves, figuring that throughout the course of history they did not have such gloves. I wanted to touch her, and I knew that God would not only understand but would keep me from contracting any disease.

As the water washed down her body, it splashed on our aprons and clothes and the floor. I flashed on what it was that I was washing away. I continued to recite, *"Taharah he."* I knew full well that the need for purification had nothing to do with the way Bubby lived or behaved. I winced as we took the third bucket of water. It was getting close to being finished and I did not want it to be over. I did not want her to go away. I continued to recite, *"Taharah he."*

She bathed me when I was little. She dried me and put the towel over my head and rubbed my head and chanted, "Where did Debbie go?" And I said, "There she is!" I was struck by the awareness of what was to come. I would never find her again from beneath a towel, or putting on a bra, or making my oatmeal. I would never watch her meditate or stretch or walk in her Nikes. I would never hear her say to me, "Honey, I don't ever want to be a burden to you," or, "The old gray mare, she ain't what she used to be," or, "I'm having a hankering for something sweet," or, "Honey, when it comes my time to go, God will take me." Where did Bubby go? There she is. . . .

There she is. We took the towels and dried her. I wanted to put some powder and hand cream on her, but she did not need it where she was going.

Every part of her was dried now. We opened the package wrapped in cellophane. Out came three pieces: a shirt, and pants with "feeselach," little feet, attached. They were made of linen. They resembled Dr. Denton's pajamas. They were simple and not something that one would find at their local Bloomie's or Nordstrom's. They had a character all their own. The third piece was a bonnet to cover her head.

One arm at a time, one leg at a time. I thought: These were the arms that once cradled me, that kept me safe when I was terrified. These were the legs that walked with me and taught me to keep moving and trying even when it hurts. These were the legs that said, "You must always go forward." These were the little hands that always reached back to me when I reached to them—the same hands that "pached" my tushy when I stuck a napkin in the Shabbat candles and started a little fire in the house one Friday night.

Where did Bubby go?

I wanted to keep her false teeth. I loved them. I used to love them in my bathroom at night when she stayed with me. She told me that when she wanted to diet, she took them out so she wouldn't eat.

Unfortunately the Halakhah said that they had to be with her. I could not keep them. Eating with Bubby was like being in the percussion section of the symphony orchestra. Those teeth, though functional, were very noisy. For every bite she took, we could get up and dance the samba.

It was time. We were almost finished dressing her.

In 1978, the man she married after Zadie's death had died. A week later, I received a phone call from a woman. Out of the blue, she told me that she was the granddaughter of a friend of Bubby's and that the two grandmothers were to arrive in Houston that evening. I thought that it was a joke, but it wasn't. That evening, I picked her up at the airport.

I had a one-bedroom apartment. She slept with me in a queen-size bed. The first day she was there, I was awakened suddenly by a set of seventy-eight-year-old gums sunk into my biceps. "Are you awake?" she said. I said, "Bubby, what are you doing?" She said, "I used to bite you all the time when you were a little girl."

I said, "Bubby, what time is it?" She answered, "Four-thirty. I have to meditate. Meditate with me. All you have to do is say, 'One, one, one.' Your sister Barbara taught me how to do it. Come on, it's good for you."

My sister had taught her "omm." Bubby did her own variations on a theme. Her arrival at my home reestablished our relationship as it had been when she and Zadie lived upstairs on Baker Avenue.

In 1980 she had a heart attack. We sent her to Pritikin. She walked three miles every day. She did her stretching and her volunteer work. She went three days a week and on Shabbat to the Home for the Aged, where most of the residents were her age or older.

I would ask her to come visit me and her response was always, "Honey, if I am not at the home, the volunteers don't give the people the right Pokeno cards and the people are all confused. The volunteers don't help the residents with the Kiddush wine and cake. If they are not helped, they spill all over. They count on me. I'll come see you soon, but better you should come here."

When we were together, we walked every day. I ran from her and then back to her. And so continued our exercise routine. One day I lost her in the park. I told her where to turn around so that she could meet me, but she kept going. Everyone jogging in Balboa Park had their eyes out for her. My bubby, the Queen of Balboa Park.

We sent my aunt out to look for her. Given that they were from the same gene pool, it came as no surprise to any of us: my aunt got lost as well. Both were well exercised.

On our walks together we would talk about ideas and feelings. I said, "Bubby, you and I need to talk about what you want when you die. You have to tell me so that I make certain that you have exactly what you want."

"I want it kosher," she said.

"You want *taharah?*"

"Yes."

"Does it bother you to talk about it?"

"Honey, when it comes my time to go, it's my time to go. God will take me when He's ready."

We put her into the coffin. I kissed her forehead just as she had done to me all of my life. I did not want her to go. I was flooded with memories but I would not cry. She did not like it when I cried. I was intent upon honoring her ways. These were, after all, her last moments.

When I turned to walk out of the room, I turned back one more time to see her. I talked to her under my breath and said, "I stayed as long as I could, Bubby. I was with you until the last possible moment. You will be with me forever, in every song and every thought and every act of lovingkindness that I may muster up in my life. You taught me what I know about love. It felt funny to do *taharah* on you, Bubby, you were so pure. I'll miss you."

The undertaker waited for us to leave the room. In his funereal voice he asked, "How will you be paying for this?" Jokingly, I said, "Do you take Visa? I would love to get mileage." He said yes. I could hear Bubby laughing at my having gotten mileage for her funeral arrangements. She loved a bargain. She loved life.

Some think that dead bodies are frightening. Some people flinch at the thought of touching or being in the presence of a dead body. I believe that the fear arises from the confrontation with our own mortality. There are those who have the same response to live bodies. The thought of closeness, the thought of touching or being touched either physically or emotionally by another human being is frightening. This fear may be connected to the idea of loss. The fear of death and the fear of life may be one and the same: that a being suddenly disappears from the realm of our physical existence may be more than we care to acknowledge. This idea of potential loss may rule our lives and even keep us at a distance from the relationships we want most in our lives.

There was great comfort in knowing that for the first time in my life I could do something for someone who could not say, "Thank you." For me, this was a special gift. My life has not been the same since then. I am aware of the fact that caring for the dead is the highest mitzvah that one may perform, but it seems that another lesson has to do with the notion of *kal v'chomer* (how much the more so!). If one is capable of giving to one who is dead, how much more so to those still in life. This insight was Bubby's last gift to me.

Chapter Four

The Burial

Jews respect the image of God in the human body even when the soul has departed from it. This accounts for many of the unique practices concerning burial. This is why we bury our dead instead of destroying the body. This is why we hold no public wakes, and this is why we ourselves do the shoveling to provide a permanent resting place. All these rites are expressions of respect for the person and for the image of God in the human body.

These traditions are also helpful to the survivors. In this section, Marcie Hershman writes about what the experience of being a pallbearer at the funeral of her grandmother meant to her. Elie Spitz makes the case for why the tradition opposes cremation and insists on burial in the earth. Ron Wolfson explains why the tradition of participating in the shoveling of the earth into the grave by the mourners is excruciatingly painful and yet healthy and healing.

In Eli Wohlgelernter's piece, we see the lengths that one family went to in order to provide a proper grave to honor its dead. There is a wonderful pun in the title of this essay, *HaMakom Yenahem.* The traditional Jewish expression of comfort to mourners is "May *HaMakom* [which literally means 'place,' but here is another name of God] comfort you, together with all those who mourn for Zion and Jerusalem." Here the phrase is taken literally: it is the very fact that the dead have a grave, and that it is in the land of Israel, that brings a measure of comfort.

What Rabban Gamliel Did

Formerly, they used to bring food to the house of mourning, rich people in baskets of silver and gold, poor people in baskets of willow twigs; and the poor felt ashamed. Therefore, a law was passed that everybody should use baskets of willow twigs, in deference to the poor. . . .

Formerly, they used to serve drinks in a house of mourning, the rich serving in white glasses and the poor in colored glasses [which were less expensive]; and the poor felt ashamed. Therefore, a law was passed that everyone should serve drinks in colored glasses, in deference to the poor. . . .

Formerly, they used to bring out the deceased for burial, the rich on a tall bed ornamented with rich covers, the poor in a plain box; and the poor felt ashamed. Therefore, a law was passed that all should be brought out in a plain box, in deference to the poor. . . .

Formerly, the expense of burying the dead was harder for a family to bear than the death itself, so that sometimes family members fled to escape the expense. This was so until Rabban Gamliel ordered that he be buried in a plain linen shroud instead of in expensive garments. Since then, people have buried their dead in simple shrouds.

—The Talmud, Moed Katan 27a–b

The Funeral of Franz Josef

The funeral procession halted in the New Market before the monastery of the Capuchin monks, where the members of the Hapsburg dynasty were traditionally interred. The gate of the monastery was locked, as if no one had been expected there that day. The royal master of ceremonies stepped forward and loudly pounded on the gate with his ornate staff. From within a monk called out: "Who is that, demanding to be admitted?" The master of ceremonies, uniformed and standing at attention, answered loudly and distinctly, stressing each syllable, so that the monk should not misunderstand him: "*This is His Royal, Imperial, and Apostolic Majesty, Franz Josef the First, Emperor of Austria, King of Hungary, King of the Lombards and Venetians, King of Bohemia, King of Galicia, King of Croatia and Slovenia, King of Jerusalem, Prince of Silesia, Prince*

*of Bukovina, Prince of Styria, Salzburg, Carinthia, Carniola, and Wind-
shnark, Count of Tyrol, and Ruler over Trieste."*

The voice of the unseen monk answered briefly and curtly from within: "I know him not."

The master of ceremonies announced the more condensed and modest title of the deceased, instead of the fully detailed one. But again the monk flung it back with "I know him not." The third time the master of ceremonies said, "A poor, sinful man seeks admittance," and now the monk replied, "I know him," and opened the gate.

Hayim Greenberg, based on From Werfel

Suggestions to Those Who Plan My Funeral

David Vorspan

I became increasingly frustrated each time I met with families in order to help them grieve and prepare for the funeral of their loved ones, only to have our time together spent arguing and guessing as to how the deceased would have wanted to be buried. One family member would appeal for a closed casket; another would insist that the deceased would have wanted it open. All kinds of discord would erupt just at the very time when the family needed harmony and cohesion in order to get through the ordeal that faced them.

This is what led me to prepare a form so that the members of my congregation could make their wishes known and prevent the guessing and the bickering that so often accompany these difficult decisions. The results have been surprising, even to me. I thought people would be reluctant to fill out such a document, and truth to tell, the practice started slowly, but by now well over a hundred families have filled out the form. Some of these people have subsequently died, and in each case the family found the form very helpful. One young man, for example, was insisting that he wanted his mother's casket open during the service and that he wanted viewing to take place the night before. His siblings said no, and soon they were yelling and screaming at each other. When I showed him her instructions, in which she specifically asked that there be no viewing, he accepted the decision with no further argument. And the family was able to mourn together in peace.

SUGGESTIONS TO THOSE WHO PLAN MY FUNERAL

My Name _____

Hebrew Name _____

ben/bat (son/daughter of) _____

Residence _____

List your immediate living relatives:

Funeral Arrangements (please check when applicable)
*designates in accordance with Jewish law

_____ 1. *Please bury me in a modest wooden casket

_____ 2. *I do not want to be embalmed unless absolutely necessary

_____ 3. *I would like my privacy respected by not being viewed by any relative or guest at my funeral

_____ 4. *I do not want to be made up by a cosmetologist

_____ 5. I want to be dressed in (shroud or clothing. If clothing, please specify)

_____ 6. *I want the family to try to remain until the conclusion of the interment (lowering) service

_____ 7. *I do not want to be cremated

8. I would like the following rabbi(s) and cantor(s) to officiate if available:

9. If possible, I would like the following to serve as casket-bearers:

10. Please mention the following about me:
a. I have been a member of these clubs and organizations:

b. I have the following hobbies and interests:

c. These aspects of my personality I would like mentioned:

On the reverse side, please list additional information (including, if available, location of will, prearranged funeral programs, etc.)

Signed _____

Date _____

A Rabbi's Ethical Will

Stanley J. Garfein

The ethical will of Rabbi Stanley Garfein is unique in more than one respect: the first draft was addressed orally to his congregation, Temple Israel in Tallahassee, Florida, on Yom Kippur day in 1972. It was part of his sermon for the memorial service that day. In it, he urges the congregants "to revive the custom of the ethical will . . . and to include in it our funeral instructions . . . because the kind of funeral one has should reflect the values he admires in life."

Many rabbis of all streams in Judaism have waged an ongoing battle against the modification or abandonment of traditional Jewish funeral practices. This will, therefore, in addition to declaring the wishes of the writer about his own funeral arrangements, is instructional to all, like all true ethical wills.

Yom Kippur, 5751
September 29, 1990

Dear Friends,

In traditional Judaism, death was not a subject that people avoided.

Death was looked upon as part of the whole fabric of life. There was a time to live and a time to die.

Among most of our members, however, there *does* seem to be a reluctance to talk about the end of physical life. Of our entire congregation, only one or two have given me instructions about the conduct of their funeral.

This is unfortunate, because it leaves one's final business unfinished. It's like not taking out life insurance because of the fear of death. But once you face the necessity of protecting your family, an emotional load is lifted from your shoulders. Without your direction at the time of death, there is likely to be great confusion among your next of kin. Family and friends must play guessing games as to what you really wanted in terms of funeral arrangements. Petty power struggles sometimes break out over who is to decide what.

Traditionally, this wouldn't have happened. Mourning procedures among Jews were standardized. When death actually had occurred, *and not a moment before,* the Hevra Kaddisha, or burial society, came in and took over. Last rites were performed with dispatch and simplicity.

The members of the burial society were usually laymen, who offered their services without charge. Such participation in the burial of the dead fulfilled an important mitzvah. Perhaps it is due to the professionalization of undertaking and the disappearance of lay burial societies that death became distant and not talked about.

Another tradition that has fallen by the way is the ethical will. We're of course familiar with regular wills that dispose of material possessions. An ethical will, on the other hand, provided *spiritual* instruction for one's family. It is a sad commentary on our modern sense of values that people can't wait to open a regular will but don't even expect an ethical will.

I would urge each of us to revive the custom of the ethical will. Moreover, I would like to suggest that we include our funeral instructions in the ethical will; *for the kind of funeral one has should reflect the values he admired in life.* Finally, may I recommend that we not merely lock our ethical wills in safe-deposit boxes. A will is not likely to be found there till sometime after the funeral. Instead, one should distribute copies to his executor, to his next of kin, and to his rabbi.

In order to provide an example of what I mean, here is a draft of my ethical will.

TO MY DEAR ONES WHO SURVIVE ME,
SHALOM ALEICHEM!

You know how I've always tried to plan ahead and avoid last-minute confusion. Permit me now to offer this guidance in the making of my funeral arrangements.

Let two Jewish principles govern planning: (1) simplicity, and (2) expression of true feelings.

Following the Jewish tradition, the coffin should be the least expensive there is. I do not ask that it be all wood, as that might be costlier. Nor do I require a vault, unless that be a cemetery rule.

The funeral should be as soon after death as possible. If embalming is not required by civil law, you may dispense with it.

Leave any pulpit robes to my successor. Remove all jewelry, so that it may be used by the living.

Clothe my body in casual, informal garments. Cover my shoulders with my tallit and my head with the yarmulke I've worn at the pulpit.

Keep the casket closed. I have no desire to be viewed. I prefer to do without statements like: "He looks better now than he has in many a year." Remember me instead as I was in life.

Prior to the funeral, let there be no visitations at home or in the mortuary, except for consultations regarding arrangements.

Do not bring in anyone from outside the congregation to conduct the funeral. Our congregation is blessed to be able to count three rabbinical colleagues in our membership. They have been good friends and supportive resources to the congregation. Please call on them to aid in the services. Also, since I've always felt that lay people should be highly involved in the conduct of worship, I'd like the Worship Committee to read a service from one of my *Rabbi's Manuals.*

If the board of trustees consents, let the service be at the temple, and last not more than twenty minutes.

The tone of the psalms and prayers that are selected should match the nature of the death, be it sudden and tragic, or in the fullness of time, with the cup of fulfillment running over.

In place of a eulogy, I would feel honored if three or four excerpts from my sermons would be read. For I spent a large portion of my life in the preparation of my sermons. They reveal the concerns of my rabbinate.

In place of flowers, let contributions be made to Temple Israel, the Tallahassee Federation of Jewish Charities, or the United Fund of Leon County. I have no objection to flowers for the living, but I do object to banks of flowers at a funeral. Let there be no camouflage of the reality of death.

As a lover of music and singing, I would like our organist and soloist to render the Twenty-third Psalm and the *El Maleh Rach-amim*. These selections and any background music should fit the mood of the occasion, be it tragic or grateful.

Let the Worship Committee decide on whether or not to have pallbearers. Except for the hearse, do not rent special cars to go from home to the temple to the cemetery.

The service of committal at the Jewish cemetery should be short and traditional. I want no artificial grass concealing the earth. Lower the casket before Kaddish.

After Kaddish, I would consider it an honor if my friends would each shovel some of the good earth into my grave. I deem this a meaningful custom, because earth so beautifully symbolizes the ongoing cycle of life. Viewed from the perspective of the totality of God's creation, death is just a necessary phase of this ongoing cycle of life. Individual mortality is thus transcended by nature's immortality. I find *this* concept of immortality very appealing.

When the committal is over and my family returns home, light the shivah (seven-day) candle. I would appreciate it if the Sister-hood would provide a simple mourners' meal. Round rolls or bagels and hard-boiled eggs symbolize the ongoing cycle of life. They thus bear a message of comfort.

Avoid other gifts of food, heavy feasting, levity, or casual con-versation. I think it is undignified. It distracts the mourners from expressing their grief. Don't try to distract the mourners with ner-vous, idle chatter. Instead, make them feel comfortable about expressing their feelings.

For five nights following the funeral and not including Sabbath or Holy Day, I would appreciate having a minyan at home led by the Worship Committee. I would, of course, have you abide by the traditional diminution of mourning should a Holy Day occur.

Let calls on the bereaved family be distributed over several weeks. It is cruel for everyone to pile in at once the day of the funeral, only to abandon the mourners during the subsequent, try-ing weeks of bereavement.

I do hope that my family will say Kaddish with special fervor at

Sabbath services for eleven months following my funeral. I ask that they not attend purely social gatherings for at least thirty days, except if a Holy Day occurs in this period.

Most of these requests I make not just because they're traditional, nor because I would appreciate being offered respect in such ways. I make these requests because I'm convinced that it is psychologically good for the mourners to work through their grief, instead of denying it with false heroics. The practices of our tradition serve to make us face reality when we most want to deny it. This is good for the sake of subsequent mental health.

At the end of eleven months, dedicate a low, flat stone at my grave. Let my name be inscribed in English and Hebrew, with dates of birth and death according to the Hebrew and civil calendars. If my dear ones can find a verse from the Psalms that applies to me, I would feel privileged to have it inscribed on the stone.

On the yahrzeit, light a candle at home and say Kaddish with special fervor at synagogue services. These observances are important to me. I do not, however, require a perpetual memorial cast in bronze.

This will has been reviewed by Vivian. Should there be any questions about the execution of its details, the Worship Committee shall defer to her wishes. Should she be unable to render a decision for any reason, the authority shall pass to either one of her dear parents.

Here ends the list of my wishes. By carrying them out, your expression of grief will be intense at first and then gradually taper off, so that you can return to the routine of the living and function therein.

I am now prepared for the end of life, whenever that may be. Whatever awaits me beyond the grave is God's decision to make. "Into His hands do I commit my spirit."

I know that whenever I leave this world I shall be far from perfect. But I do feel a sense of satisfaction from the fact that my hands have not been idle, and I have achieved some good not only for myself but also for others.

To Vivian, Rebecca, and Susanna, let me say: I could never have functioned as well without your love, affection, encouragement, and help. How can I express in words the love and gratitude I feel?

God has granted me strength in sorrow, inspiration when I needed fresh ideas, good cheer during hours of celebration, and a wonderful family and friends, with whom I could share life's experiences.

May He bless you all and help you fulfill your highest hopes.

No Burden Too Heavy

Marcie Hershman

"Put your foot right on top of mine," she'd say. "That's good, *mamelah*. Now come stand on me with the other one."

"But doesn't it hurt you, Nanny?"

"Hurt me?" With a laugh, she smoothed the loose strands of blond hair back into my ponytail. "Why, you're so light, you weigh nothing. You're like a pinch of air. Other foot on top, come on—*up!* That's good: balance on me. And put an arm around my waist so no one falls." Playfully, my grandmother took hold of my free hand and wove her fingers with mine. Her fingers were thick and wrinkled; mine so thin and smooth and squirmy they seemed a different species entirely—kin to the freshly struck No. 2 pencils I was learning to write with in school.

"Don't be afraid; let what happens happen. But don't let me slip out from under," she warned.

"I won't."

"So?" Her square chin lifted even higher. She was smiling over the top of my head to whoever was watching. "Oh, how we are going to dance!" Taking a deep breath, she took a first simple step sideways, and my foot stepped, too, with hers. Then she took a bigger step; my whole leg was lifting.

"Oh!" I explained.

"See how easy?" Nanny said. "Easy as pie."

Clinging to her wide, warm, familiar body, giggling and gasping, I spun with my grandmother in giant circles across the dark parquet floor of the living room. Occasionally I slid off her feet (my anklet socks wouldn't hold), but I always scrambled right back. We danced on and on, unequal partners who in those moments absolutely loved all the inequalities about us, the jokiness, the seriousness. My grandmother was singing; her voice was loud and clear. She spun me for a long time. Our heads thrown back, legs stepping, arms pumping, our fingers intertwined.

"Now," said the funeral director, with a nod. And at that signal we lifted the casket. It was—she was—so light. She weighed nothing, like a pinch of air. I'd been afraid that I wouldn't be able to hold her up. I'd feared that I wouldn't be able to balance the casket and that it would tilt and my grandmother's body would fall out at my feet. But, really, she was so light, held by the six of us. I had no idea it would feel like this to be a pallbearer. Gentle. Cradling. Maternal.

We'd slid the plain wooden box out of the back of the hearse and started up a path of icy snow that wound among the standing gravestones to where the rabbi waited by a deeply dark grave. I wanted to carry her safely. Carrying now was a responsibility given over to me—it was completion and connection.

The Hebrew phrase associated with pallbearing is *hesed shel emet,* an act of truthful and pure lovingkindness. It is pure because the giver can have no expectation of reciprocity. Watching from the sidelines of the burial processions of others I'd loved in the past, I'd never known how the lovingkindness in the act overflowed, how it returned to fill the hearts of those who raised the casket and carried it to its measure of earth.

I'd thought of pallbearing as gloom, oppressiveness, darkness, a struggle to remain upright under both a physical and atmospheric—an impossible—weight. That narrow box of a world with all light extinguished, all weight given over, yielded only effort and loss. Pallbearing was connected to destruction. And like war in its soldiering, it traditionally has been shouldered by men. Men, who it seemed could bear up under the burden where women would not.

When my grandfather died, I'd just turned sixteen. I recall standing with my three younger brothers as his casket was carried past. What I wanted most to do for Papa then was to keep my chin high and not let any tears fall, because three years earlier I'd watched Jackie Kennedy grieving that way during JFK's televised funeral. The image of a woman who stood erectly, quietly, sadly, was rebroadcast countless times—and gradually it became embedded in the culture itself. The First Lady's stillness and bearing showed us a way we, too, might act to pay our last respects.

My mother doesn't like to think of herself as radical or unconventional, but on that sad morning her mother was to be buried it was she who broke first with tradition. I was writing a eulogy when she came quietly into the room. She waited a moment, then suddenly asked if I'd like to serve as one of the pallbearers.

"Mom?" I looked up at her, my eyes wide. The possibility had never entered my mind.

Months later, I asked if she'd ever seen a woman serve as a pallbearer before. Mom said, "Come to think of it, no."

"Then why did you think I could be one?"

"I guess I was upset and wasn't thinking clearly right then," she said distractedly. Then she caught herself. "No, not true. I really thought, well, this is the last honor someone can do for a person they love. And I knew you loved Nanny. You loved her as much as anyone did."

I stood up with my brothers and two of our cousins and went to an alcove off the main chapel of the funeral parlor. A man waiting there for us held out a basket filled with black cloth gloves. Along with the others, I selected a pair, the smallest they had. Gloves for pallbearing are made for a man's hands. I pulled them on; they fit. Two male assistants wheeled Nanny's bier into the room. The six of us positioned ourselves around it. The funeral director went over to the double doors that led to the parking lot. Family and friends would gather out there; I knew the aisle they'd make by standing on the sidelines would guide Anna Weiss's casket to the back of the hearse. The director opened the doors. The December wind blew right in.

"Ready?" he asked. We each grasped a side handle.

"Okay," he said, waving us forward. "Lift."

Lift.

"Now," said one of my brothers. "Together."

We lifted—and my arm was pulled downward, but that was all. As we slowly moved into the wind, I didn't buckle. For how absolutely steady Nanny's last weight was; how perfectly still. How little it asked of me. Only that I carry her gently. As so many times she had on her own carried me.

Keri'ah: The Tearing of the Garment

Joseph Ozarowski

The practice of tearing a garment as a tangible show of grief goes back to the Bible. There are numerous instances in the Torah where people tear their clothes to show sorrow. *Keri'ah* is the graphic act manifesting the anguish one feels at the loss of life.

While many situations in earlier times warranted tearing, *keri'ah* today is done for the closest relatives for whom one mourns: parents, children, siblings, and spouse. One may also tear for other relatives.

Rabbinic sources offer half a dozen possible reasons for the practice of *keri'ah*:

1. It deepens the sense of pain and sorrow.

2. It confronts the individual with the recognition of the sanctity and importance of life at a time of loss.

3. The loss of an article of clothing graphically symbolizes the personal sense of loss.

4. The cathartic process rids the heart of cruelty and anger by sensitizing it to loss, thereby fostering return, reconciliation, and repentance.

5. Tearing the clothing is symbolic of the rending of the relationship between the deceased and those still alive.

6. It serves as a substitute for or sublimation of ancient pagan self-mutilation rituals not permitted in Jewish law.

Keri'ah is done on an article of clothing worn on or near the heart, such as a jacket, sweater, vest, shirt, blouse, bodice, or, minimally, a necktie or neck scarf. Rabbinic sources describe this as *m'galeh et libo,* revealing the heart. The tearing of a garment near the heart symbolizes the emotions felt in the heart at this time. The tear is made on the left side for parents and the right side for other relatives.

When mourning a parent, as opposed to other relatives, the obligation to tear always remains, even long after the initial mourning period has concluded. The Talmud explains this as a function of the duty to honor one's parents, which continues after the death of the parent. But this raises questions in cases—more and more frequent—where the child feels no emotional bond with the parent. We might well ask if an abused child or one with large emotional distance from the parent still must tear. Halakhically, the answer is yes, because, at the very least, the biological bond has been severed. One acknowledges the fact that the deceased parent brought the survivor into the world, even if he or she did not fulfill the obligations of parenting.

The torn garment may be basted or repaired after the mourning period, yet it will never look as it did before. This symbolizes that while life goes on, it can never be completely the same after the loss has occurred. In the case of the death of parents, it also connotes the fact that the mourner is no longer fully able to fulfill the mitzvah of honoring them.

The Talmud states that the tear has to be done *b'shaat himum,* literally at a time of great emotional turmoil or pain. It can be argued that anytime one feels this way can be considered *b'shaat himum.* Our custom today is to tear at the time of greatest emotional feeling. Usually, this is just before the funeral service, though it is occasionally just afterward, or sometimes at the gravesite. After the initial shivah week of mourning is over, the garment need not be worn.

Unlike most of the other mitzvot that come from the Torah or rabbinic tradition, *keri'ah* has no specific blessing recited over its performance. The rabbis were reluctant to attach a blessing to a seeming act of destruction, even one warranted by the Torah. However, there is a very important blessing associated with the grief period and, since medieval times, said before performing *keri'ah*. The blessing is *Dayan Ha-emet*: "Blessed are You, Lord our God, sovereign of the universe, the true judge." While this blessing is traditionally said anytime one receives very bad news, it takes on special meaning here. It has been classically explained as the attempt to justify God's actions, be they good or bad. This flows from the traditional belief, expressed in the Talmud, that "whatever God does is for the good." Jewish life certainly affirms this as a general tenet, and some mourners are able to accept the idea. Yet it is not always satisfying. When deep grief and loss strike, one is not always ready to accept standard theological wisdom or dogma. However, the basic idea behind this blessing acknowledges God's ultimate power over life and death. During *aninut,* the period between the death and the burial, the mourner attempts to come to grips with the tragedy that has occurred. By referring to God as "the true judge," the survivor is helped to recognize that death as well as life is part of God's ultimate plan. Much of the funeral service moves the mourner to face the stark reality of what has occurred, and *keri'ah* is the first step.

Another explanation sees this blessing not as an affirmation of faith in the face of tragedy but rather as a goal toward which to work. The ultimate hope of consolation and healing involves the reaffirmation of faith, but this does not happen immediately. Rather, the mourner can view the blessing as an agenda, something for which to strive within the mourning and healing process.

There is no question that historically and halakhically, the tearing of clothing has been a significant part of the Jewish process of grieving. Unfortunately, too many modern Jews have shied away from this psychodrama of sorrow. Some reject *keri'ah* because they simply reject halakhic practice.

Others, more well-meaning, desire to spare grieving family members a perceived "barbaric ritual." Thus, the black ribbon was developed as a symbolic substitute for *keri'ah*. However, the black ribbon seems more an imitation of the non-Jewish custom of wearing a black armband as a sign of mourning. Most people I speak with believe for some reason that the ribbon must be worn for a full month, though there is no source in Halakhah to indicate that a *keri'ah* garment is to be worn that long.

Most importantly, the actual tearing done by the mourner addresses the emotions that all mourners endure. The pain and loss felt in the heart, the confrontation with the finality of death, and the cathartic ripping of the material—symbolizing the ripping of the relationship, never to be fully restored—are all deep emotional issues which simply cannot be addressed by a ribbon. Indeed, the use of the ribbon may be part of the larger phenomenon in American culture of denying the finality of death and covering up its reality. Along with cosmetic tampering of the body and abandonment of the open grave before burial, these all avoid facing tragedy. But the healing process cannot begin until one has confronted the fact that loss has occurred. By acknowledging what has befallen through the ripping of clothing and God's ultimate power over life and death through the *brakhah* of *Dayan Ha-emet,* we begin this process as we address our deepest psychological needs as a mourner.

Why Bury?

Elie Spitz

A new trend has developed in recent years among non-Jews, and then, because Jews live in the midst of a non-Jewish culture, among Jews too. It is the tendency to cremate instead of to bury.

What is behind this trend? Perhaps the main motivation is that cremation is much cheaper; there is no casket to purchase, no grave to choose. But people are reluctant to give such a crass reason and so they offer nobler-sounding explanations. They tell you that there will eventually be a shortage of space in the world and so it is better not to have cemeteries. They tell you that cremation is quick and simple and less painful than burial in the earth.

Whatever the reasons for this new trend, Jewish teachers continue to resist it. There are at least three reasons why the Jewish tradition opposes cremation: our theology, our memory, and our concern for the welfare of the mourner.

First: theology. In the Jewish tradition, that which was once holy remains holy, and so the body is to be treated with respect, even after the soul departs. The tradition opposes self-inflicted wounds, intentional scarring, and tattoos, because the body is ours only on loan. Ultimately it belongs to God.

Even after death, the body is to be treated with reverence. *Kavod ha-met,* reverence for the dignity of the dead person, is the key to the manner in which the body is to be washed and dressed, purified and guarded until the burial. Burning the body is seen in our tradition as a desecration of what was once holy.

Second: memory. It is hard to comprehend how in this generation, which is just one removed from the time of the Holocaust, we can think of burning a body. Millions of our people were cremated in the death camps, and so cremation conjures up for us the horror of that time when Jewish bodies were treated as worthless.

Third: concern for the welfare of the mourner. Burial helps the mourner by providing a sense of closure. When the mourner sees the coffin being lowered into the earth and when he hears the sound of pebbles and soil hitting the coffin, it hurts terribly, but from that moment on he knows that death is real.

We may know intellectually that our loved one has died, but at some level it is very hard to really comprehend it. It is not unusual for a person to come back from the funeral and half-expect, half-hope, that the loved one will be there to meet him. Until and unless we perform the physical acts that mean goodbye, we are blocked from being able to come to terms with reality and begin to heal. Cremation always takes place out of sight of the family, for it is a violent act. And so, for the mourner there is no act that marks closure.

A grave is an address to which a family can come ever afterward in order to commune with its memories. Some people have told me that they want to be cremated because they know that "no one will ever come to visit or to take care of the grave anyway." We can sympathize with the pain that is reflected in such a statement, but it expresses a lack of trust in the family and in the community. Each person deserves a place and each family needs an address to which it can come in order to remember, in order to take strength, in order to give and to receive forgiveness, and in order to learn lessons in how to live.

For all these reasons, we continue to resist the trend toward cremation.

How We Bury

Ron Wolfson

Burial is the final act of love, the ultimate gesture of *kavod ha-met,* honoring the dead. The rabbi explains that it is not for strangers to bury our dead, but for each and every one of us to provide the blanket of earth for the final rest. You are taken to the grave and handed a shovel. As difficult as it is, you fill the shovel with earth and empty it into the grave. The dirt hits the top of the coffin with a thud, and that thud sends a shudder through your whole body, which you will long remember. You stand aside as your family and close friends take turns carrying out this last mitzvah—this mitzvah for which there will be no repayment, no reward except the knowledge that you have done a good deed, that you have brought the deceased to a final resting place. Friends approach you with hugs and words of condolence. They form two lines with an aisle between them. And as you walk by, they offer you the ancient words of hope and consolation: "May the place comfort you, together with all those who mourn for Zion and Jerusalem." You reach the car and collapse in tears in the back seat, numbed and exhausted. As you leave the cemetery you take one last, long look back, knowing that with this ending comes a beginning. The funeral is over; the mourning can now begin.

Why No Viewing

Harold M. Schulweis

One of the questions that I get most often at funerals is about the permissibility of a public viewing of the deceased. I try to explain that the Jewish tradition says no, because it is sensitive to the dignity of the deceased. The deceased is now a *nireh v'eyno roeh,* one who can be seen but who cannot see. To allow people to look at the deceased is to turn the comforters into spectators and to turn the person into an object. Better to remember those whom we loved as they were when they were free and active human beings, capable of relating, rather than as objects. Rarely, after they understand the concept behind the tradition, do the mourners object to the rule.

Why in Tachrichim?

Philip Roth

Later in the day, at the bottom of a bureau drawer in my father's bedroom, my brother came upon a shallow box containing two neatly folded prayer shawls. The older tallis I took home with me, and we buried him in the other. When the mortician, at the house, asked us to pick out a suit for him, I said to my brother: "A suit? He's not going to the office! No, no suit—it's senseless." He should be buried in a shroud, I said, thinking that was how Jews were buried traditionally. But as I said it, I wondered if a shroud was any less senseless—he wasn't Orthodox and his sons weren't religious at all—and if it wasn't pretentiously literary and a little hysterically sanctimonious as well. I thought how bizarrely out of character an urban earthling like my insurance-man father, a sturdy man rooted all his life in everydayness, would look in a shroud even while I understood that that was the idea. But as nobody opposed me and I hadn't the audacity to say, "Bury him naked," we used the shroud of our ancestors to clothe his corpse.

Why Stones Instead of Flowers?

David J. Wolpe

The final scene in the movie *Schindler's List* is puzzling. Survivors and their cinematic offspring file by the grave of Oskar Schindler. With solemn ceremony, they place stones on the grave. Why should they leave stones rather than flowers? From where does this strange custom come?

The practice of burying the dead with flowers is almost as old as humanity. Even in prehistoric caves some burial sites have been found with evidence that flowers were used in interment. But Jewish authorities have often objected to bringing flowers to the grave. There are scattered talmudic mentions of spices and twigs used in burial (Berakhot 43a, Betzah 6a). Yet the prevailing view was that bringing flowers smacks of a pagan custom.

That is why today one rarely sees flowers on the graves in traditional Jewish cemeteries. Instead there are stones, small and large, piled without pattern on the grave, as though a community were being haphazardly built. Walking in the military cemetery of Jerusalem, for example, one can see heaps of stones on the graves of fallen soldiers, like small fortresses.

For most of us, stones conjure a harsh image. It does not seem the appropriate memorial for one who has died. But stones have a special character in Judaism. In the Bible, an altar is no more than a pile of stones, but it is on an altar that one offers to God. The stone upon which Abraham takes his son to be sacrificed is called Even Hashityah, the foundation stone of the world. The most sacred shrine in Judaism, after all, is a pile of stones—the wall of the Second Temple.

In the words of the popular Israeli song, "There are men with hearts of stone, and stones with the hearts of men."

So why place stones on the grave? The explanations vary, from the superstitious to the poignant.

The superstitious rationale for stones is that they keep the soul down. There is a belief, with roots in the Talmud, that souls continue to dwell for a while in the graves in which they are placed. The grave, called a *beit olam* (a permanent home), was thought to retain some aspect of the departed soul.

Stones are more than a marker of one's visit; they are the means by which the living help the dead to "stay put." Even souls that were benign in life can, in the folk imagination, take on a certain terror in death. The "barrier" on the grave prevents the kind of haunting that formed such an important part of East European Jewish lore. The stories of I. B. Singer and the plays of the Yiddish theater are rich in the mythology of East European Jewry: souls that return, for whatever reason, to the world of the living. One explanation for placing stones on the grave is to insure that souls remain where they belong.

All the explanations have one thing in common—the sense of solidity that stones give. Flowers are a good metaphor for life. Life withers; it fades like a flower. As Isaiah says, "All flesh is grass, and all its beauty like the flower of the field; grass withers and flowers fade" (Isaiah 40:6–7). For that reason, flowers are an apt symbol of passing.

But the memory is supposed to be lasting. While flowers may be a good metaphor for the brevity of life, stones seem better suited to the permanence of memory. Stones do not die.

A beautiful answer takes it cue from the inscription on many gravestones. The Hebrew abbreviation *taf, nun, tsadi, bet, hey* stands for *"teheye nishmato tsrurah b'tsror ha-Chayyim,"* a phrase usually translated "May his soul be bound up in the bonds of eternal life."

Yet *tsror* in Hebrew means a pebble. In ancient times, shepherds needed a system to keep track of their flocks. On some days, they would go out to pasture with a flock of thirty; on others, a flock of ten. Memory was an unreliable way of keeping tabs on the number of the flock. As a result, the shepherd would carry a sling over his shoulder, and in it he would keep the number of pebbles that corresponded to the number in his flock. That way he could at all times have an accurate daily count.

When we place stones on the grave and inscribe the motto above on the stone, we are asking God to keep the departed's soul in His sling. Among all the souls whom God has to watch over, we wish to add the name—the "pebble"—of the soul of our departed.

There is something suiting the antiquity and solidity of Judaism in the symbol of a stone. In moments when we are faced with the fragility of life, Judaism reminds us that there is permanence amidst the pain. While other things fade, stones and souls endure.

Ha-Makom Yenahem:
The Place Gives Comfort

Elli Wohlgelernter

All Naftoli Wolgelernter knew about his grandfather while grow-ing up were the stories his father and grandmother told him, his great-uncle's eyewitness accounts, and sixty pages of a journal his grandfather kept during the Holocaust.

But that was all the twenty-three-year-old needed to fulfill his dream of finding his grandfather's remains.

Naftoli's grandfather was Rav Haim Yitzhak Wolgelernter, a descendant of the Seer of Lublin. A child prodigy, Haim Yitzhak left his hometown of Kazimierza, Poland, at thirteen to study with the Ostrowiecer rebbe, Rav Yehezkel Holztock. At seventeen, the rebbe honored his prize pupil with ordination.

Every Saturday night Haim Yitzhak wrote down the words his rebbe had said that day, which he published before the war under the title *Beis Meir*.

When the Ostrowiecer rebbe was killed by the Nazis in 1943, Haim Yitzhak, by then thirty-one and hiding in Dzialoszyce, com-posed a famous poem using the first letter of every line to spell out his name. Haim Yitzhak and his extended family had already been in hid-ing since the first Nazi action in Dzialoszyce on September 3, 1942.

The family split up to make it easier to hide but somehow main-tained contact and tried to keep each other alive. The attempt was

not always successful. Haim Yitzhak's sister Yuta was killed in Kazimierza, and his sister-in-law and daughter—living under Aryan
papers—were caught early on and sent to Belsen.

His wife, Chaya, and their two-year-old son, Feivel, Naftoli's
father, went north to live near Radom under assumed names, with
forged Aryan papers saying she was a war widow. Meanwhile,
Haim Yitzhak's brothers, Duvid and Meir, had gone into hiding
with their parents. They were in Dzialoszyce for two months
before hiding in and around Kazimierza, sixteen kilometers away.

"For two weeks we were in the hayloft of a barn," says Duvid,
who now lives in Toronto. "But the owner kicked us out, he got
afraid. So we went to the village mikvah, next door to a slaughter-
house, where we stayed for two weeks."

They were lucky. "Two days after they got there, the Germans
came and rounded up two hundred and fifty Jews and put them in
a school in Kazimierza," says Naftoli, quoting from his grandfather's journal. "The Nazis kept them there for two weeks and then
took them out to the forest and killed them. Duvid and Meir saw
the roundup from the mikvah."

Before the war, the seven thousand Jews of Dzialoszyce made
up eighty percent of the town's population. Yachet Platkiewicz,
Haim Yitzhak's mother-in-law, owned a clothing store there. It all
came to an end on November 9, 1942, when the Nazis conducted
the second and final liquidation.

After two weeks, one of the slaughterers told them that people
knew they were there. The four went to hide in the cowshed.
There they found another Jew hiding. It was a snowy day. The
other Jew went out to look for food. Heading back to his own
apartment, he found a Pole living there. The Pole went to the
police, and they found his footprints in the snow. On Sunday, the
SS came.

"When the Nazis came into the barn," says Duvid, "my brother and
I were in the hayloft. We jumped out the back window. My parents,
of course, couldn't jump with us. That's the last time I saw them."

Naftoli (a third cousin of this writer) has the letter that Meir
wrote to Haim Yitzhak, telling him of the last days of their parents,

Naftoli's great-grandparents. "The Nazis found a few other Jews hiding around there," Naftoli says, "and took them all to a school for a couple of days and then took them to the forest—probably the same place where the two hundred and fifty were killed—and killed them."

After a couple of days, Duvid and Meir found another place to hide, with a gentile woman. There they stayed for eighteen months. At first it was just the brothers, but soon eight other family members joined them.

"At the beginning the gentile woman was very friendly, my grandfather writes," says Naftoli. "She was doing it for the right reason, believing it was the Christian thing to do. But after that relations went down, and at the end they hated her. Eventually she threw them out because the Germans came, and she was afraid."

Again they were faced with the problem of where to hide. They found a small hamlet of some twenty people called Dembowiec, five kilometers from Dzialoszyce, and hid in a small barn owned by a man named Biskup.

The group swelled to eleven with the addition of another family member and two Jewish partisans. In times of danger, they would move underground through a secret trap door. Otherwise, they lived in the hayloft, behind an artificial wall.

Though he took a risk by hiding Jews, Biskup was hardly a Righteous Gentile. "My grandfather writes that Biskup was a bad guy," says Naftoli.

Biskup was paid five thousand zlotys a month to hide the group, money spent mostly on booze. The group made sure the money was not kept with them so Biskup would never have the temptation to kill them and take it. Once a month they'd send a courier—a blond, blue-eyed fourteen-year-old with Aryan papers—to pick up the money.

After five months, the group was forced to leave. "We used to go out at night to get food, and one night a friend in the village told us there was a rumor that there were Jews staying by Biskup's place," says Duvid.

Haim Yitzhak and one of the partisans knew of another hiding place about an hour's walk away, and they arranged to move immediately. "We couldn't all go together, it was too dangerous," Duvid says. "So we drew lots as to who would go that night—two from the group, and one partisan. Three that night, and the other eight would come the next night."

It was June 22, 1944, the first night of a new moon, Sivan 30.

As the others would have to help carry Haim Yitzhak's sixty-five-year-old mother-in-law, these first three carried suitcases and bags . . . and the journal kept by Haim Yitzhak. At 2:00 A.M., Duvid, his brother's nephew Feivel Erlich, and Avraham Schoenfeld, the partisan, headed out. "We walked to the place an hour away," says Duvid. "They made a place for us in the barn."

There they stayed, waiting for the rest to join them. By dawn on the second day, the first of Tammuz, nobody had arrived. The owner of the new place, named Zito, came out to the barn that morning with news.

"He told me that in another village nearby they found eight Jews and killed them. He didn't know that I knew these people, but I knew right away who it was.

"He also heard that there were a few who ran away, but I was afraid to say it was us, because I was afraid that this guy would tell us to leave."

Who killed them? Zito heard it was Biskup, and that it happened one hour after the three had left.

To this day, no one is sure. One Jewish underground fighter, Avraham Furman, says Biskup didn't do it. Furman used to travel between Jewish hiding places, bringing news, money, and articles that the Jews needed. He had heard a rumor in the village that it was members of the Polish underground army, led by General Wladyslaw Anders who was based in England.

"All the money they gave to Biskup went for drinking," says Naftoli. "So when he was drunk, he probably started talking. If the village knew, the whole area knew, and it was easy for the Polish underground to find out. Maybe Biskup helped."

Another theory has it that Biskup thought they had gold and diamonds sewn into their clothing. When he realized the group was getting ready to leave, he killed them to get at the hidden treasure.

The three survivors stayed with Zito until liberation about three months later. "Even after liberation, we stayed there another two weeks, and when we left Zito we didn't tell him we were leaving," Duvid says. "We were still scared that he might kill us."

A year later, Duvid went with Haim Yitzhak's widow to Dembowiec. They saw the place where the earth had been turned and prayed there.

But Poles were still carrying out pogroms against Jews. Indeed, Schoenfeld was later killed by Polish partisans. So the surviving family members departed without the bodies, hoping to return later.

It is now forty-five years later, and the teenage Naftoli Wolgelernter, who moved to Jerusalem from Zurich to study in a yeshivah, is working on the Yiddish journal of his grandfather, Haim Yitzhak.

As a child, Naftoli heard the story about how his grandfather and great-grandmother were killed. He was also told about the journal and how his great-uncle Duvid had saved it.

Naftoli remembers how his father, Feivel, didn't like to speak about those times. "He'd always answer me when I asked a question," Naftoli says. "He just wouldn't start talking about it by himself."

But Naftoli had the sixty-page journal, which Duvid had given Feivel on his wedding day, and that was all he needed to begin work on deciphering the almost microscopic writing. As he scrutinized the pages and got to know his grandfather better, he went looking for others who knew Haim Yitzhak.

One day early last year, Feivel Erlich, one of the three who survived that fateful night, gave Naftoli the Ashdod phone number of Furman, the underground fighter.

"Furman asked if I ever went to Poland," says Naftoli. "I told him no, why should I go? If I knew where the grave is, I would go.

"He told me he knows where it is. So I said: 'If you know where the grave is, why didn't you ever bring it over?' No answer."

Furman had a cousin in Dzialoszyce who was adopted by the Szczubial family. They had hidden Jews, including Wolgelernters. (The Szczubials were later named Righteous Gentiles.) A quick inquiry to Furman's cousin and it was confirmed: nothing had changed in the village, the ground was undisturbed.

So last March, Naftoli contacted Moshe Spiegel from Bnei Brak, an expert at locating graves in Eastern Europe. Spiegel said he could arrange with the Polish government to obtain documents needed for the journey, and could also get digging permits, diggers, drivers, and whatever else was necessary.

But would they find the graves?

Naftoli, who was in Zurich for Pesah, asked for his father's permission.

"He thought I was crazy," Naftoli says. "I told him, 'Listen, probably you're right, we won't find it. But you—it's your father. Did you ever try to do anything to take your father out of Poland? At the end of your life, you have to be able to say, "I tried." So let's try.'"

Feivel Wolgelernter is a fifty-three-year-old electronics engineer who runs a small computer company in Zurich. His is an exact world; this mission sounded too fantastic.

"When Naftoli came to me," Feivel says, "he said, 'Look, we'll go there, we'll find the place, and if everything works out—how much are you willing to pay?' I said if it costs fifty or a hundred thousand dollars, I don't care. So he said, 'Okay, I've agreed with Spiegel that if we don't succeed, we'll just pay the expenses.'

"And then the day grew closer, and I said, 'I can't let him go by himself, I've got to go with him.' My older son Haim also came.

"I didn't believe he'd pull it off. I didn't believe anyone knew the place anymore. I just thought, He'll get it out of his system."

Did Naftoli really believe it?

"I didn't think about it. Spiegel told me: 'Listen, there's a big chance we are going to find it.' That was enough for me.

"And Furman's cousin said it's still the same village of twenty people. Furman said to himself: 'There are old people there, we'll just ask them where Biskup's place was.' "

On Sunday, April 18, the three board a plane to Warsaw. It is Holocaust Remembrance Day. They meet with Spiegel and make plans. Early in the morning, they drive south to Crakow in a light rain. They arrive in Dembowiec and go to the home of the Szczubials.

There they pick up sixty-eight-year-old Bronek Gala, who at nineteen supposedly witnessed everything. He leads them to the end of the village, then turns right, past a strawberry field to the top of a U-shaped depression, full of trees and shrubs, used to dump rubbish. It is about two hundred meters from the barn in which they were hidden.

"Here they lie," says Gala. "This is the place where Biskup buried the eight people." Another elderly man points to a spot one hundred meters away and says, "Another body was thrown there."

Spiegel and his assistant, Baruch Goldberg, arrive with the digging permits, and a van comes with some strong diggers.

Gala insists his spot is right, but Spiegel and Feivel feel it is too steep a slope. They start digging a trench two meters long and one and a half meters deep a little farther down.

News travels fast, and for the simple village folk it is the event of the decade. From all around they come to watch. Some even help. All day they labor, but to no avail. Two elderly women insist the grave is on the other side of the "U." They sound convincing, so everyone moves.

Ten people ultimately dig three trenches, two meters long by one and a half meters deep. They find a cow's leg and the skull of a small animal.

"It became clear to me that we had little chance of finding anything this way," says Feivel. "Biskup surely didn't make individual graves."

The area was twenty meters by twenty meters, and at least one and a half meters deep—an impossible task by hand. Someone suggests getting a bulldozer.

Spiegel meanwhile gives out vodka to the diggers. He offers a

$100 reward to whoever finds the right spot first. They claw at the dirt. At 6:00 P.M., they stop.

"After the first day, I didn't feel sad, just disappointed," says Feivel. "At that point I said, 'So what, okay, so we won't find it.'

"I just wanted to be at ease with my conscience. I was always upset that I couldn't go to my father's grave, like everybody else in Zurich. Now that I'm over fifty, most of my friends' parents have died, and they can go to a *Beis olam* [cemetery] and pray at their graves—I can't."

That night Feivel and his sons went to Crakow to visit the Rema Synagogue. Next to it is buried Reb Moses Isserles, the Rema, and next to him is the grave of Natan ben Solomon Spira, a seventeenth-century rabbi known as the Megalleh Amukkot, after his famous book, which means "reveal the depths."

"I noticed Naftoli praying very hard," Feivel says. "Probably he thought, 'If this tzaddik wrote such a book, You, Master of the universe, should reveal to us what's in the depths.' To tell you the truth, I felt that nothing would come of it."

The next day Spiegel arranges for a bulldozer. It does in two minutes what eight men do in half a day. The two old women admit that Gala may have been right. Many trees are uprooted, and earth is piled all around. At 12:15, they stop for a break. Feivel has almost given up.

A half-hour later, they resume. Spiegel and Goldberg peer at the bulldozer's shovel. They spot one bone, then another. Spiegel sends the bulldozer on its way, so as not to disturb any more earth and break any bones. More than two and a half meters deep, and at exactly the spot where Gala indicated in the beginning, there is a grave.

"My emotions overcame me," says Feivel. "I started to think what a great thing it was."

As Goldberg worked with his hands, Feivel went back to the top of the ditch. "One shouldn't see the remains of your father," Feivel says.

As Feivel stands on top, his sons keep coming up to tell him what is happening. There are two pairs of long thigh and leg bones—it is Haim Yitzhak Wolgelernter and his brother Meir. The skull of Feivel's grandmother, Yachet Platkiewicz, is found, with its toothless jaw.

Goldberg thinks she was shot in the head. Another skull looks like it was smashed in. It raises the question: Why would Biskup kill them differently?

"If Biskup had a gun, he wouldn't have to kill them with a club," says Naftoli. "Since we found one of each, probably at least two people killed them."

After confirming the presence of three bodies, Goldberg sends up a message: Tell Feivel that it is his family.

Feivel tears *keri'ah,* but there is no sadness. "I was thinking, What a miracle. No crying—I wasn't even sad, more a happy feeling.

"I opened my Psalms, and just like that it opens on chapter 94: *Kol nekomos hashem*—To God belongs vengeance. And that's what I'm thinking, that all the Jews will have a proper vengeance."

The afternoon operation takes four hours. There are many small bones, fingers and toes. But there is no doubt—they find the expected eight skeletons, no more, no less. The bones are intertwined, indicating that the bodies were thrown in at random. They are sorted out as well as possible and laid on eight sheets.

"I felt pain that they had killed them," says Naftoli. "Especially at first, when I came and knew it was the place."

A coffin is brought, and the bones are put in. Feivel passes out $5 and $10 bills. These are good Poles, he thinks, not like their predecessors. He decides to reward the village with a $1,000 donation.

That night, they go back to Warsaw, and Feivel calls his mother. "I told her: 'You tear *keri'ah,* now and sit shivah until evening.' It did her good, because she had never sat shivah for her mother, her brother, and her former husband."

Before leaving Dembowiec, Naftoli goes to take more pictures, while Feivel and Haim say goodbye to the Szczubials. The van to pick them up never arrives. Walking back to Dembowiec, they see a barricade of trees and a tractor blocking the van.

The discussion is loud: the village people want to be compensated, at least $20 per tree, $200 altogether. It turns from nasty to ugly. Says one woman: "Twenty minutes from here, they used to burn you."

Naftoli is not surprised. "I was telling him all the time that they're still Polaks. He says no, the Poles had changed. I wasn't surprised. I was wondering why they weren't ashamed that they killed these Jews. But no shame. That's how they are."

For Feivel, it is beyond belief.

"I felt confused and amused," he says. "Had I been able to talk Polish, I would have said: 'Isn't it enough you had a part in murdering them?' I would have told them: 'Look, I had in mind to make a donation to your village of a thousand dollars. Do you think it's worth it, to lose that donation? You've been so nice all day, yesterday and today you helped us.' But it was like talking to beasts.

"I wasn't afraid, because I knew it was a problem that could be solved by money, either two hundred dollars or a hundred and fifty."

They settle on $90, and everyone leaves. Three days later, the reburial takes place on Har Hamenuhot in Jerusalem. Feivel Erlich and Feivel Wolgelernter say Kaddish, Naftoli gives a eulogy. A few old Dzialoszycers attend. There isn't a dry eye among them.

"For a few months after that, I kept thinking it was truly a miracle," says Naftoli. "Spiegel, the man who does these things, told me it's *mamash a nes* that they found it.

"I felt very much I was doing a favor for my grandfather and father. I never saw him so happy," says Naftoli. "And for my whole family, that they now have a burial spot to go to, in a Jewish cemetery. My grandmother gives me blessings for what I did."

For Feivel Wolgelernter, knowing where his father is buried makes him feel whole again.

"I too can now go to the grave of my father," he says. "I have done my mother a big favor. She too can come, she finally has what she wanted, but much more. Instead of just taking her there to *daven,* I've given her back her mother, her sister, her former husband, two brothers-in-law, a nephew, and a niece. There's a lot I feel. Gratitude toward Naftoli, because he really did it. He could have done it without me. I just was there.

"A chapter in my life has closed, something has come to an end. It doesn't bring back my father and how I grew up without him. All these books that keep appearing about children of the Holocaust—that's me, that's me. So it's a very, very deep satisfaction I get thinking about it.

"What I've done—no one ever did such a thing. Most of them went up in smoke. Some were able to take out bones from one cemetery to another, where there were known graves, or from one that was destroyed. But not where Jews were murdered and dumped in a grave by a goy."

And for Duvid, who felt the sadness of having lost his brothers just three months before liberation, the joy at eighty is not only in finding them, but in finding them a spot to rest.

"There's a phrase we use when someone dies, *Ha-makom yenahem et ha,* meaning 'God should comfort you.' But *ha-makom* also means 'place.' Now finally we are comforted, by knowing the place where they rest."

Chapter Five

Shivah

Why do we sit shivah for a week? Because the world was made in a week, and each person is a world, a world that never was before and never will be again.

People no longer know how to sit shivah or how to make a shivah call. The mourners think it is their task to act as hosts, entertaining and feeding those who come. But as Rabbi Bernard Lipnick explains in this chapter, the mourner is supposed to be a guest, a guest in his own home, and not a host. And people no longer know what they are supposed to do when they make a shivah call. As Ron Wolfson observes, they fill the house with noise and talk about everything except the real reason they have come.

I remember once, many years ago, when a man in my congregation died suddenly. He left two bewildered teenage daughters. The house was full all week with people who came and spoke about sports, about business, about everything except what had happened. They spoke to each other but stayed away from the daughters—out of embarrassment, out of fear that they might say the wrong thing, or for whatever reason.

When the week was over, the two girls asked me, "Are you not allowed to talk to the mourners, according to Jewish law?"

In this chapter some of the rituals that take place during shivah, such as the minyan in the home, the covering of the mirrors, and the special psalm that is recited in the house of mourning are discussed, and a new ritual created to mark the end of shivah is proposed.

The First Meal

The first meal eaten by the mourner after the burial is called the *seudat havra'ah,* literally, "the meal of recuperation." At this meal he is forbidden to eat of his own food. It is a mitzvah for the friends and neighbors to bring him food.

The custom is to include round cakes or eggs in the meal of recuperation. The mourner should not peel the eggs himself, so as not to appear ravenous.

—Shulhan Arukh, Yoreh Deah 378:1

The Therapeutic Function of Shivah

Joyce Slochower

In memory of my father, Harry Slochower, with gratitude to Dr. Sharon P. Kaplan and Minyan M'at.

Most of us know only too well that the death of close loved ones, whether dreaded or wished for, is a profound and wrenching experience. This is especially so when we lose a central and irreplaceable relationship—a parent, sibling, spouse, or child. Deaths like these affect our life in profound, not necessarily temporary ways. Our immediate experience of loss reduces our capacity to be involved in the world of real relationships or activities and may permanently alter our sense of our place in the world.

Loss of this magnitude requires that we allow ourself to mourn. Mourning is a process whereby death is directly addressed—the mourner expresses grief about the loss, sorts out memories and mixed feelings about the death, and lives through a temporary depression. Ultimately, the work of mourning allows us to give up the lost relationship as a real, alive one, while forming and preserving an internal relationship to the deceased person in all its complexity.

Jewish tradition has provided us with a remarkably detailed,

and, I believe, a brilliant structure within which to address death—
the customs of shivah. Yet few Jews outside of traditional communities fully observe these customs, and many are completely unfamiliar with shivah rituals. This should not be particularly surprising:
death continues to be a subject that is treated gingerly by contemporary culture, very much reinforcing our own natural discomfort
with such pain. It often seems easier simply to get on with life and
to relegate traditional mourning observance to the antiquated customs of our grandparents' generation. We may view as excessively
restrictive and time-consuming the requirement to set aside a full
seven days (shivah means "seven"), during which we withdraw from
the world and face our loss. In fact, for many, "sitting shivah" has
come to describe a brief social afternoon following a funeral, during
which the mourners provide a spread for the guests. Such a setting
is actually antithetical to the intent of shivah observance and, I am
convinced, is most unlikely to facilitate mourning. Yet the traditional laws of shivah have become inaccessible and even alien to
many of us.

The very complex Jewish laws of mourning outline aspects of
observance from the moment of death and for a full eleven months
thereafter. (Norman Lamm's 1988 book, *The Jewish Way in Death
and Mourning,* describes mourning ritual in detail and is an excellent reference.) One sits shivah only for a parent, sibling, spouse,
or child—those with whom we have the most irreplaceable of
relationships. The mourner first concretizes his loss in the custom
of *keri'ah:* at the moment of death or at the funeral, a tear is made
in the mourner's outer garment. This will be worn throughout the
week of shivah, which formally begins when the mourner returns
home from the burial. The mourner washes his hands before entering the home (this symbolizes a cleansing following contact with
death). All mirrors (traditionally associated with vanity) are covered. Those who gather at the mourner's home join the mourner
in a symbolic meal of condolence. The community, not the
mourner, provides this meal, which includes foods associated with
life, such as bread and hard-boiled eggs. The mourner lights a
memorial (yahrzeit) candle that will burn for the seven-day shivah

period. Traditionally, shivah lasts for seven days, throughout which time the mourner remains at home unless the shivah house is elsewhere and the mourner cannot reside there for the week.

The laws of shivah alter virtually every aspect of ordinary social behavior for both mourner and visitor. The mourner's grief is concretized in a variety of ways: he does not wear leather shoes (traditionally associated with comfort and vanity). The mourner neither bathes nor changes clothing, especially the rent garment. The mourner does not use cosmetics, cut his hair, or engage in sexual contact. The study of Torah is also forbidden, since such study is believed to bring joy. The mourner is free to walk, stand, lie, or sit but only on a low stool or chair. Contrary to popular belief, the chair need not be hard or uncomfortable. Instead, the low seat symbolizes the mourner's lowered emotional state. The mourner does not rise in order to greet the visitor; in fact, the front door is left ajar to free the mourner from this obligation. The mourner is excused from all household tasks (cleaning, et cetera) and does not prepare or serve food for others or himself. The mourner is thus freed from all social obligations and distractions and is expected to be involved solely with the mourning itself.

A shivah caller operates under similarly unusual rules. A shivah call is considered its own good deed and obligation (mitzvah). In traditional communities, such calls are paid by most of the mourner's community, whether or not they were personally involved with the mourner. Callers generally come unannounced at any time during the day or evening. The purpose of the shivah call is explicit: to support the mourner in his grief by offering an opportunity to speak about the loss and by sharing with the mourner memories of the deceased. Shivah callers are not permitted to greet the mourner; instead, they wait until the mourner notices and greets them. Conversation must be initiated by the mourner, who may choose to speak of the deceased, of other things, or to remain silent. The caller does not, however, attempt to distract the mourner unless the mourner indicates such a need. Thus, at times, the caller may simply sit silently with the mourner; at other moments, the caller may be engaged in conversation of more or less emotional depth. The caller, who is not expected to stay long, does not say goodbye and instead utters a traditional phrase, "May God comfort you among the mourners of Zion and Jerusalem." The mourner does not respond to this farewell and remains seated when the caller leaves.

At the end of the seven days, the mourner "gets up"—resumes daily activities in most respects. However, during the subsequent thirty days (shloshim), certain activities (such as attending parties) designed to bring joy are curtailed. Many male mourners refrain from shaving throughout shloshim. This represents a most powerful and visible expression of bereavement. In fact, for a full eleven months following a death, the mourner is expected to acknowledge this loss concretely by saying Kaddish daily, and, in the case of a parent's death, also limiting social activities and festivities.

When my own father died last year, I sat shivah for the first time and found it to be an extraordinarily reparative experience. As a psychoanalyst, I was struck by the degree to which the shivah situation evoked many of the most healing aspects of psychoanalytic treatment. Although psychoanalysis is popularly viewed as a situation in which the analyst offers interpretations to the patient, I believe that noninterpretive aspects of the therapeutic situation play a critical role in the treatment process. D. W. Winnicott, who was both a pediatrician and a psychoanalyst, described this dimension of psychoanalytic experience as a "holding environment." The psychoanalytic situation holds the patient figuratively, by protecting him in ways that allow a full experience of the self to develop. The analyst who provides a holding environment functions not as an interpreter of the patient's experience, but as a reliable, available, potentially empathic presence who communicates confidence in their mutual survival. When the analyst maintains a holding stance, subjective responses to the patient are contained by the analyst to establish an emotionally protective setting within which the patient can expose private experience, often for the first time.

In thinking about what it took for me to assimilate my father's death, it became increasingly clear that the structure of shivah created a therapeutic holding environment that tremendously facilitated this task. From the moment he died, I derived comfort from the knowledge that my own community rather than strangers were caring for his body. At the cemetery, I experienced something simultaneously raw and essentially real as my family, according to custom, shoveled earth upon the unprettified pine casket. The denial of death was impossible, and the shock was intense.

I returned home to the comfort provided by my community; I was both protected from and deprived of the external distractions that might be viewed as relieving the pain of loss. I did not work, or shop, or cook for myself or my family. Yet I was far from alone; a stream of shivah callers appeared who set aside their own concerns and allowed me to talk about my father when I needed to and about other things when I did not. They came and left unrequested, and so freed me from the burden of having to ask for the company that I did not always know I needed; at the same time, they made it possible for me to retreat in privacy when I wished to do so. They made sure that there was a minyan so that I could say Kaddish and provided a meal for Shabbat. Many shivah callers brought food; few ate mine. Some were close friends or relatives; many were more casual acquaintances, yet most made it possible for me to talk, to stay with the feelings of loss as long as I needed to. Their traditional farewell offered the comfort of community, reminding me that I was not alone in this experience. I emerged from this very intense week of remembering exhausted but relieved. My recovery did not end there, but was steady, and at the end of the year I found myself largely at peace with this loss.

How did shivah help? I was forced to express my grief in multiple concrete ways. My shoes, clothing, lowered chair, et cetera, underlined my state of mourning and interfered with the possibility of "putting on a face" (false self) to the world. Yet the community's visits, even people's parting words, required no acknowledgment from me. The shivah custom requiring that I speak first, for example, facilitated a direct response to me and to death by the community by making it harder for us to escape into social convention. The prohibition against ordinary greetings and farewells was awkward for many of us, yet it served as a compelling reminder of the visit's nonsocial nature.

Taken together, what at first appears to be a rigid set of rules creates an environment designed to facilitate mourning by creating an emotionally protective setting that is reminiscent of the analytic holding environment. The community of shivah callers collectively provides this hold, which is symbolized by both concrete care and emotional space. The shivah setting makes a demand on the community: to permit the mourner to use people within the community without regard for the community's needs. In this sense, the mourner is permitted to express and experience the self in a way that mimics many aspects of the psychoanalytic holding situation.

It was not until I experienced shivah as a healing process that I became aware of the ways in which shivah is often distorted. When the mourner's community is unaware of or uncomfortable with shivah ritual, observance becomes a burden rather than a support for the mourner. The mourner in this sort of environment often feels obligated to entertain visitors and to distract them both from the uncomfortable knowledge that the mourner is in acute pain. I vividly remember a previous shivah, when those present (who were unaware of shivah tradition) sat in strained silence interspersed with self-conscious political comments as they ate a meal provided by the family. The mourner's grief had no place in this context, and "shivah" provided no relief at all.

Yet even those who are familiar with shivah rules may struggle with the obligation to visit the mourner, which requires us to tolerate our own anxiety and social awkwardness about facing death and encountering what may be an unfamiliar set of people and traditions. To enter a shivah house and not to greet anyone, to sit in silence (often among a group of strangers) waiting to be acknowledged, is an intensely uncomfortable experience. It can leave us wanting to fade away, to leave as quickly as possible, even to wish not to have come at all. To further complicate matters, the mourner will not necessarily express gratitude for our visit.

I have never paid a shivah call without some degree of discomfort; further, I have rarely found the visit to be what I expected.

The "house of mourning" will be most variable; I have entered homes to discover mourners sobbing in grief, chatting about their own lives in an attempt to gain some emotional relief, or laughing in an apparently disconnected emotional state.

It shouldn't be surprising that different mourners respond to death differently, of course, depending on their own tolerance for grief, and also depending on the nature of their relationship with the deceased. For some, death represents a shock too great to assimilate with overt grief. To the degree that a mourner is defended against the experience of loss, grief may emerge in a diverted form or may be apparently absent. When the mourner is someone with little tolerance for emotional experience, a powerful need not to experience grief may be communicated. The mourner may behave as if nothing is wrong, as if the shivah call were, in fact, a social visit. In paying a shivah call, then, we may feel puzzled, bored, shut out, even judgmental of the mourner's apparent lack of grief. What do we do? How do we behave in such a context? Do we join in the social atmosphere, or sit silent, as if it is we who are grieving? Shivah custom would imply that we neither introduce nor distract from the subject of death. That is, we need to do our best to remain with the mourner as he is and not demand that the mourner express real feelings. From my perspective, such a stance gives the mourner both space and potential contact. Eventually, this space may permit the mourner to feel safe enough to confront the loss and to connect to it in a fuller way.

To the extent that the mourner's own feelings about the death are complex and involve guilt about past actions or inactions, feelings of hatred toward the dead person, et cetera, the mourner is likely to experience expressions of concern ambivalently. When we pay a shivah call to a mourner in this state, our very care may intensify the mourner's guilt about felt failures vis-à-vis the deceased. At other moments, the caller's concern may frustrate the mourner by its inadequacy in the face of loss. The mourner may react to the caller with irritation or respond with anger or guilt to expressions of sympathy that inadvertently evoke guilt. To say the "wrong thing" during a shivah call can be chillingly uncomfortable; an irritable mourner is hardly likely to relieve such feel-ings. It is far from easy to tolerate being unappreciated, unhelpful, or even hurtful to the mourner. Yet by remaining emotionally pre-sent but not intrusive, we communicate confidence about the mourner's ability to survive the difficult feelings generated by the grieving process.

Despite my familiarity with shivah tradition, I have often found the shivah call to be painful or uncomfortable, especially when I was not personally involved with the mourner and/or the deceased. It was not until I sat shivah myself that I became aware of the powerful impact of people's visits during shivah. I felt "held" by these visits, by the fact that I could count on my family and best friend to turn up each day and by the calls of people I had never been personally involved with (including someone I had never met before). I had often hesitated to pay shivah calls to people I knew only superficially. Most paradoxically, I found these "superficial" visits to be extraordinarily moving; they made me aware in an immediate sense that I was part of something larger than myself or my grief. Some of these shivah callers followed Jewish tradition to the letter while others did not. What mattered was not the specifics of form but rather my sense that the caller had come to be with me during a period of intense grief.

For those readers who feel outside of traditional Jewish obser-vance, then, I would like to urge you to consider the shivah process to be a gift that you can provide yourself when you face a death, and one that you can offer others in the same circumstance. The details of ritual observance are far less important than is the setting aside of a week within which to do little other than remem-ber. As a mourner, allow others to do what they can for you and do your best not to entertain. Set out photographs of the deceased, or mementos that will make it easier for you and for others to enter the process of remembering. Try not to feed or serve others. Most important, make use of people's visits in the way that is best for you—no one cries all the time, and laughter is not prohibited. Simply living through a week of suspended life is therapeutic.

When contemplating paying a shivah call, consider visiting in the early evening if you prefer to be with a large social group, or during the day if you would rather talk alone with the mourner. Some people prefer to phone ahead and ask whether a particular time would be a good one. Take your cues from the mourner and remind yourself that your presence itself is of value, even if you don't know the mourner well. Many people feel uncomfortable about the formal farewell and simply say, "May we meet again on a happier occasion." Finally, remember that you don't have to stay long; a half-hour visit is fine.

It is clear that the laws of shivah are largely designed for the protection of the mourner and make powerful demands on us as a source of support during shivah. To require that we enter a situation perhaps unique in its social discomfort only to tolerate the difficult range of feelings evoked by a mourner is a considerable demand. Shivah laws do, however, take into account the vulnerability of the community. Interestingly, as shivah callers, we are protected in ways similar to the protection provided the analyst. Shivah calls are short, ordinarily paid not more than once by any individual. The mourner's larger community is expected to assume the ongoing obligation. The holding function of shivah is thus shared by the community, falling lightly on its individual members.

On the seventh day of shivah, the mourner must "get up," whether emotionally "ready" or not. The community is thereby automatically freed from further obligation at the end of the shivah week. Further, shivah is interrupted by Shabbat and is actually cancelled by major holidays. These laws may in part reflect the community's need to remain involved in life, in joyous or religious events that supersede even the needs of the individual mourner. Like the therapist who ends sessions or takes vacations despite the patient's need for treatment, shivah laws place the mourner's needs within the larger context of community need. It is evident that the mourner may be quite unable to suspend grief just because Shabbat or a holiday interferes. To the extent that this failure in adaptation to the mourner's needs was preceded by a period of holding, however, it may be strengthening rather than traumatic. A break in the shivah experience may actually begin to draw the mourner back into life, much as a disruption in holding may facilitate an integrative process in a patient. There are times, however, when community needs do interfere and even prevent the grief process from fully unfolding. When a major holiday falls during shivah, the shivah period is actually cancelled. In such an instance, the mourner's need for a holding is overridden by the community's need to be involved in ritual observance.

Thus, while Jewish tradition views the mourner's needs as great, they are not paramount—they do not consistently override the needs of the shivah caller. It may be that the limits placed on the mourner's needs are actually what permit the community to tolerate the very great demand that is made of it during the period of shivah observance. It is, of course, not uncommon that the practice of shivah fails to hold the mourner, because either the mourner or the community cannot tolerate the discomfort generated by such an experience. Shivah cannot provide a holding in the absence of some degree of cohesive community, which is absent for many contemporary Jews.

Yet in the context of community, shivah laws meet an individual's temporarily intense need in its varied aspects while protecting the larger group. These laws are, in many ways, a brilliant prepsychoanalytic adaptation to a universal human need, reflecting the capacity of society to provide a temporary holding for its members while also insuring that the community remains a going concern.

Who's the Host? Who's the Guest?

Bernard Lipnick

Contrary to what many people think, the entire tone of the shivah is set by the mourner. The mourner should think of himself as a guest in his own home, not as a host. Those who come to visit should act as hosts, not the other way around. A case in point is food and drink. If mourners think of people coming to their home as guests, they think that it is their place to offer them food and drink. Once that happens, the tone is set: "I am your host, you are my guests." The drinks flow, the food is eaten, there is boisterous conversation (what do you talk about with a drink in your hand?), the evening passes, and the guests leave. And the mourner feels as though he's been clobbered, run over by a Mack truck. Why? Because all the emotions he has had and wants to give vent to and wants to sort out have been denied. He has been the host when he should have been the guest.

In the traditional shivah house, you, the mourners, are to be served, waited on hand and foot, so that you can deal with your grief. All your physical needs are to be taken care of by family and friends.

That's why I always recommend that absolutely no food be offered to visitors in a shivah home. Not even a cold drink. Not even coffee. Nothing. Zero. When it comes to mealtime, a friend can say, "Excuse us, the mourners have to eat their dinner." And the mourners can get up and go to the kitchen or dining room to eat the meal. Most consolers will get the message and say, "Excuse me, I didn't realize it was dinnertime," and leave. The consolers will always follow the lead of the mourner.

The Art of Making a Shivah Call

Ron Wolfson

We are not alone. This is the fundamental message of Judaism about death and bereavement. Every law and every custom of Jewish mourning and comforting has, at its core, the overwhelming motivation to surround those who are dying and those who will grieve with a supportive community. While some may argue that facing death and coping with grief heighten one's feeling of aloneness, the Jewish approach places loss and grief in the communal context of family and friends.

Comforters are obligated to tend to the needs of mourners. For instance, since a family sitting shivah should not prepare meals, it becomes the responsibility of the community to feed them. Some people send prepared foods from local caterers, and many Jewish newspapers carry ads for "shivah trays." With our busy, frenetic lives, it is certainly convenient to turn to these sources. Yet personally prepared and/or delivered food is a more traditional act of comfort. Liquor, candy, or flowers are not usually sent. A donation to a charity designated by the mourners would be another appropriate way to honor the deceased, while comforting those who mourn.

As a comforter, making a shivah call is one of the most important acts of condolence. But all too often those visiting a mourner's home are not sure of the appropriate behavior. David Techner, funeral director at the Ira Kaufman Chapel in Detroit and a leading expert in the field, suggests that many people do not have the slightest idea as to why they even make the shivah call. "People need to ask themselves: 'What am I trying to do?' When people say things like, 'At least he's not suffering,' who are they trying to make comfortable? Certainly not the mourner. People say things like that so that they do not have to deal with the mourner's grief. The comment is for themselves, not the mourner."

In my interviews with rabbis, funeral directors, psychologists, and lay people for my book, *A Time to Mourn—A Time to Comfort,* I discovered that the act of comforting the mourner is quickly becoming a lost art. We do not know what to do, so many people avoid making a shivah call altogether. We do not know what to say, so many people say things that are more hurtful than helpful. We do not know how to act, so often the atmosphere is more festive than reflective.

The problem is exacerbated by mourners and their families who do not know how to set an appropriate tone. Many observances have become like parties, with plenty of food, drink, and chitchat. Of course, there are alternatives. In some shivah homes, the minyan becomes the focus. During the service, the life of the deceased is remembered through stories and anecdotes.

Whichever type of shivah home you encounter, there are some basic guidelines for making a shivah call.

Decide when to visit. Listen for an announcement at the funeral service for the times that the mourners will be receiving guests. Usually the options are immediately after the funeral, around the minyanim in the evenings and mornings, or during the day. Should you wish to visit during another time, you may want to call ahead. Some experienced shivah visitors choose to visit toward the end of the week, when it is frequently more difficult to gather a minyan.

Dress appropriately. Most people dress as if attending a synagogue service. Depending on the area of the country, more informal dress might be just as appropriate.

Wash your hands. If you are visiting immediately after the funeral, you will likely see a pitcher of water, basin, and towels near the door. It is traditional to ritually wash your hands upon returning from the cemetery. This reflects the belief that contact with the dead renders a person "impure." There is no blessing to say for this act.

Just walk in. Do not ring the doorbell. The front door of most shivah homes will be left open or unlocked, since all are invited to comfort the mourners. This eliminates the need for the mourners to answer the door. On a practical level, it avoids the constant disruptive ringing of the bell.

Take food to the kitchen. If you are bringing food, take it to the kitchen. Usually there will be someone there to receive it. Identify the food as meat, dairy, or *parve*. Be sure to put your name on a card or on the container so that the mourners will know you made the gift. It also helps to mark any pots or pans with your name if you want to retrieve them later.

Find the mourners. Go to the mourners as soon as possible. What do you say? The tradition suggests being silent, allowing the mourner to open the conversation. Simply offering a hug, a kiss, a handshake, an arm around the shoulder speaks volumes. If you do want to open a conversation, start with a simple "I'm so sorry" or "I don't know what to say. This must be really difficult for you" or "I was so sorry to hear about ————." Be sure to name the deceased. Why? Because one of the most powerful ways to comfort mourners is to encourage them to remember the deceased.

Recall something personal: "I loved ————. Remember the times we went on vacation together? She adored you so much." Do not tell people not to cry or that they will get over it. Crying is a normal part of the grieving process. And, as most people who have been bereaved will tell you, you never "get over" a loss, you only get used to it.

Spend anywhere from a few moments to ten minutes with the mourners. There will be others who also want to speak with them, and you can always come back. If you are the only visitor, then, of course, spend as much time as you wish.

Participate in the service. If a prayer service is conducted during your call, participate to the extent you can. If you do not know the service, sit or stand respectfully while it is in progress. If the rabbi or leader asks for stories about the deceased, do not hesitate to share one, even if it is somewhat humorous. The entire purpose of shivah is to focus on the life of the person who has died and his or her relationship to the family and friends in that room.

If invited, eat. Take your cue from the mourners. In some homes, no food will be offered, nor should you expect to eat anything. In others, especially after the funeral, food may be offered. Be sure that the mourners have already eaten the meal of condolence before you approach the table. When attending a morning minyan, you will likely be invited to partake of a small breakfast. After evening minyan, coffee and cake may or may not be served. In any case, should you be invited to eat, be moderate in your consumption. Normally, guests are not expected to eat meals with the family during the shivah.

Talk to your friends. Inevitably, you will encounter other friends and acquaintances at a house of mourning. Your natural instinct will be to ask about them, to share the latest joke, to shmooze about sports or politics. You may be standing with a plate of food and a drink, and if you did not know better, it would feel like a party. But, the purpose of the shivah is to comfort the mourners.

You are in the home to be a member of the communal minyan. The appropriate topic of conversation is the deceased. Reminisce about his or her relationship to the mourners and to you. Of course, human nature being what it is, we tend to fall into our normal modes of social communication. This is not necessarily bad; however, you should be careful to avoid raucous humor, tasteless jokes, loud talk, and gossip.

Do not stay too long. A shivah visit should be no more than an hour. If a service is held, come a few minutes before and stay a few after. Mourners uniformly report how exhausted they are by the shivah experience; do not overstay your welcome.

Say goodbye. When you are ready to leave, you may want to wish the bereaved good health and strength, long life, and other blessings. The formal farewell to a mourner is the same Hebrew phrase offered at the gravesite and in the synagogue on Friday evening:

May God comfort	*Ha-makom yenakhem*
you	*etkhem* [many mourners]
	otakh [one female]
	ot'kha [one male]
	etkhen [more than one female]
among the other	*b'tokh sh'ar*
mourners	*a'vaylay*
of Zion and Jerusalem.	*Tzion v'Y'rushalayim*

Ha-Makom is a name of God that literally means "the place," referring to God's omnipresent nature, including at the life-cycle events from birth to death. It is only God who can grant the mourner lasting comfort. The comforter comes to remind the mourners that the divine powers of the universe will enable them to heal and go on with a meaningful life. Ultimate consolation comes only from the omnipresent God.

"*B'tokh sh'ar avaylay Tzion v'Y'rshalyim*" means "among the other mourners of Zion and Jerusalem." Once again, the message is "we are not alone." In fact, traditional Jewish practice requires a *minyan* (quorum) of ten in order to recite the *Kaddish* prayer. Personal bereavement is thus seen in the total context of the community.

The great genius of Jewish bereavement is to empower the community to be God's partner in comforting those who mourn. In making a shivah call in an appropriate and traditional way, we are the medium through which God's comfort can be invoked. In learning the art of coping with dying, we are, in fact, learning an important aspect of the art of Jewish living.

The Shivah Minyan

Bradley Shavit Artson

A few weeks ago, my community experienced an unusually high number of funerals within a short period of time. As a result, we endured the challenge and the trauma of providing several shivah minyanim simultaneously. Fortunately, the congregation takes the mitzvah of *nichum aveilim* (comforting mourners) seriously, so I didn't have to worry about whether or not enough people would attend the *Ma'ariv* services going on simultaneously in so many homes.

What I did have to ponder was my own embarrassment while forced to lead a prayer service praising God in a place where God's love and power were so hidden, so missing. After all, each one of these homes sheltered families that had suffered the death of a beloved spouse, parent, or sibling. How could I expect these people to be willing to praise God's greatness, to extol God's power, or to express gratitude for God's goodness. Still aching from the pain of death and separation, these mourners could no longer view God as either benefactor or friend.

Perhaps it was just such a moment of rage and sorrow that originally generated the Yiddish expression "If God lived on earth, all God's windows would get broken."

Yet it was precisely into those homes—homes filled with rage

at God's impotence, homes tormented by an overwhelming abandonment and isolation—that Judaism compelled me to stand and
to sing of God's enduring love and incomparable power.

In a home that reeled from the loss of a wife and mother, one of
its pillars of purpose, meaning, and identity—into that home I had
to proclaim the continuing habitability of the universe, the benefi-
cent purpose underlying God's creation.

And in homes ripped from communal moorings, uncertain of
the continuing relevance of friends, community, or Jewish fellowship—into precisely those homes poured friends and congregants,
awkwardly reciting the phrases and melodies of our timeless tradition. Did this strange practice make any more sense to them than
it did to me?

I, leading the prayers at the front of the minyan, represented the
anomaly of God's love in a place bereft of love, of God's purpose in
a home torn by the random cruelty of finitude and mortality, of
God's covenanted community in a place isolated by loneliness.

Small wonder, then, at my embarrassment and discomfort.
Leading the minyan of mourners in what could only feel like a
"prayer of the absurd," forcing mourners to mouth words they
could hardly mean, I, and they, needed to confront our puzzle-
ment and frustration at a tradition that imposed this farce on me,
this outrage on them. Despite the gap between the mourner's
embittered frustration and the rooted piety of Jewish tradition, I
and my congregants were obligated to bring our minyan, our
prayers, and our presence to these hurting people. Why?

Why does Judaism mandate seven days of minyanim in the
home of a mourning family?

Let's start with the reality of loss and rage following the death
of a lifelong spouse or a beloved sibling. For the person left
behind, a jagged hole looms in the center of the heart, an empty
space in the depths of the soul. Having built a life around the presence and cheer of one who was deeply cherished, we can only rage
against a universe in which such horrors as this death too frequently occur. The Mishnah's admission that "we cannot understand either the tranquility of the wicked or the suffering of the

righteous" provides no comfort, only the recognition of an often bleak and unfair reality. Not without logic, amorphous fury at what has transpired is often directed against God. After all, how can there be a God or how can God claim to be good if this outrage could happen to one so needed, so loved?

It's difficult enough to endure the death of a loved one, but to simultaneously lose the comfort of God's love, to exclude the strength and endurance that can emerge from opening one's heart to God, from sharing one's pain with the source of all comfort, can only make a painful situation excruciating. As Psalm 42 observes, "Day and night, tears are my nourishment, taunted all day with 'Where is your God?'" Isn't that precisely the crisis that every mourner faces? Just when God is most needed, the tragedy that produces such pressing need also renders the divine presence least accessible.

One central function of the shivah minyan, then, is to restore access to God's love. Words often remain superficial, and sermons regularly fail to penetrate the recesses of the human heart. But the silent presence of fellow Jews, the simple gesture of sitting together or offering an outstretched hand speaks more eloquently than the most lofty speech. God's presence cannot be articulated or alluded to. But it can be demonstrated. Just by being there, we embody God's love, and we make that love tangible. "To You, God, silence is praise."

Think again of the mourner's devastation in the wake of death. Not only is receptivity to God's love diminished, but a healthy sense of purpose and a willingness to trust is shattered as well. It is relatively easy to rely on the habitability of the universe while loved ones thrive. It may feel effortless to maintain a buoyant spirit and a cheerful countenance when blessed with health, companionship, and prosperity. But with the death of a loved one, our facade of control dissolves into fantasy. Suddenly, the world we inhabit appears random at best, cruel or deceitful at worst.

Life no longer makes sense. Without conviction, without an affirmation of purpose or meaning, human life becomes impossible. When the psalmist says, "Were it not for the Lord, I would have perished," he is using biblical language to maintain that we cannot flourish in a random world. Chaos is the enemy of our ability to thrive.

Into a family assaulted by chaos, battered by unjustifiable loss, the shivah minyan asserts continuing purpose, affirms a world view that stands in the face of death and proclaims the imperative of life, acting on the biblical charge for "one generation to laud God's works to another." Precisely by reciting prayers that acclaim God's goodness, we assert our determination to endure, to comfort, and to blossom. The shivah minyan restores a lost vision of how to live, how to retain order, goal, and direction in a shattered world.

Finally, a significant component of a mourner's devastation is the severed sense of belonging. Having lost one of the closest ties to the outside world, one of the most intimate of relationships, the mourner flounders in lonely isolation. Abandonment sets the somber tone of the mourner's mood.

It's impossible to be a Jew alone. While sociologists confirm that all human identity is formed in community, and object-relations psychology teaches that even an infant's sense of self derives from its interactions with others, nowhere is that need more pressing than in the isolation of a mourner. And nowhere is the assumption of community more pervasive than in the world of traditional Judaism.

The mourner, then, reels from the universal and human loss of context and belonging—a loss made more acute by the particular way Jews generally can presume the support of their community. The shivah minyan—because it occurs in the home, because it is composed of friends and fellow congregants—does more than remind the mourner of membership in a larger community. It creates that community—precisely where it is most needed. By physically entering the isolation of the mourner, the shivah minyan dispels it.

For all these reasons, the shivah minyan is needed most where it is desired least. In a place of anger, the practice of shivah offers acceptance and love. To a heart adrift, the shivah minyan restores direction. And to the agony of individual pain, the shivah minyan creates a portable and persistent community.

The Kabbalists spoke well when they pointed out that the only way to gather the shattered sparks of divine light—now held by the forces of chaos and despair—was to enter the *sitra ahra,* the side of darkness. The only place to provide healing, comfort, and an abiding sense of God's love and communal support is in the home of the mourner.

"Out of the depths, I called to You, Lord." And it is out of the depths that healing, community, and solace can hope to emerge.

Covering Mirrors

Lawrence Kushner

Mirrors at the time of death.

Culture's greatest creation for pondering the mysteries of self-reference, is, of course, the mirror. And it is just this invention, found everywhere in the world, that—according to Jewish folk tradition—must be covered up on the occasion of death. Is it not perhaps a way of saying that the ultimate outcome of self-reflection is death? Or perhaps even a way of saying that when the final gauze separating this world of life and the other world of death has been momentarily torn, we must be especially careful to keep the portal of the mirror closed, lest there be additional passages going this way and that, between life and death?

Let us instead cover the mirrors, doing the best we can to endure the mystery and pain.

Why Psalm 49?

Herbert J. Levine

Psalm 49 is said only in the house of mourning. It has no other liturgical use in the Jewish calendar. What is its special claim on the mourner's attention and on the attention of those who have gathered for a minyan in the house of the mourner? Why, of all the one hundred and fifty psalms in the psalter, was this one chosen for the house of mourning?

The psalmist begins, "My mouth utters wisdom / my thought is full of insight." That kind of introduction is characteristic of the wisdom psalms. It is a way of saying to the listener: Pay attention to what I am about to say. It is a lesson that you need to hear.

The lesson is very simple: death awaits every person, rich and poor, wise and foolish alike. Therefore, be not proud, you naive people who think that you "abide in honor." In reality, human beings are "like the beasts that perish."

Who is it that needs to hear this lesson? "Those who are self-confident," those who "are pleased with their own speech," those who boast of being responsible for their good fortune in life, and those who thrive on the envy of others. His targets are those who survey their achievements and look over their possessions and say to themselves: All who look upon you must admit that you did well by yourself.

What does all this self-regard amount to in the end? The arrogant may be rich now, but when they die they will take nothing of their possessions along; their wealth will not follow them down to the grave. Human beings, the psalmist repeats, are "like the beasts that perish."

There is only one line in this psalm that seems to make a different claim: "But God will redeem me from the clutches of Sheol, for God will take me." What can that line mean? It surely does not mean that the psalmist imagines that he is exempt from the laws of mortality that apply to all human beings. The medieval commentator Ibn Ezra said that it means that the poet is aware of an eternal soul that will survive the death of the physical body. Rashi, however, claimed that this verse means that God "takes" him to walk in God's ways *during his lifetime.* God's teachings will protect him from the arrogance and the naiveté of thinking that his possessions are his forever.

If Rashi is right, then the psalmist's focus is not on life after death but on life itself. What he is saying is: Do not focus on piling up possessions because you can't take it with you. Focus instead on how to live while you are on earth, for that, and only that, will bring you lasting honor.

This, then, is the claim that Psalm 49 makes in the house of a mourner: Your loved one is now gone. The time remaining to you may be short as well, so make the most of the time you have. Pay God what you owe God for the space you occupy on this earth by doing good deeds. Live while you are still alive, instead of spending your strength accumulating possessions that you will inevitably have to leave behind.

Knitting Up the Tear

Alisa Rubin Kurshan

From the moment that I learned of my father's death, I experienced immediate, utter, shattering chaos. My world, as I had understood and defined it, was no longer the same. The shivah was the beginning of a long, painstaking journey from emptiness and confusion toward a rediscovery of meaning.

Keri'ah—tearing one's garment—is the first act that the mourner is obligated to perform after learning of the death of an immediate family member. Whether done immediately upon death, as was traditional, or just before the burial, *keri'ah* is an act of acknowledgment of the newfound chaos.

Keri'ah is the mourner's first admission that life will never be ordered the same way again—the fabric of the mourner's life will never be whole anymore. That act is the admission that one's world has been torn asunder, and what follows is the liminal state of shivah.

The halakhic rituals of mourning guide the mourner through the dark, unknown paths of reentry to life. Hazal understood that, before reentry, one must deal with grief and pain. Therefore, shivah removes the Jew from the worries of everyday life and gives the mourner time to grieve. The mourner does not need to make any decisions during this period—all behavior is legislated by Halakhah.

One of the most puzzling aspects of the ritual of *aveilut,* mourning, is *keri'ah.* The act of *keri'ah* is an undeniably powerful moment. Yet, with all the attention that Halakhah devotes to the details of proper *keri'ah,* there is no mention of how to bring closure to the *keri'ah* experience. Precisely when, how, and with whom should the *avelim* remove the *keri'ah* garment? Should someone remove it for them or should they do it themselves? What should they recite while removing the garment? What should they do with the garment? In a system of Halakhah and Jewish custom which is so rich in detail, it is striking that there is no mention of what a mourner should do with the *keri'ah* garment.

Expounded upon in great detail are the halakhot of when and how to mend the garment. The general agreement among the poskim (rabbinic authorities) is that the tear can be only crookedly mended for a parent; for other immediate relatives, it can be mended straight. However, there is no mention of the removal of the garment.

The Halakhah probably focuses on how to mend because Jews did not throw away what was probably one of their few garments. In our day and age it is rare that a Jew mends a *keri'ah* garment and then treats it as any other article of clothing.

To the extent that *keri'ah* marks the first admission on the part of the mourner that chaos has intruded into his or her life, there must be a complementary experience of healing at the other end. In the transition between shivah and resumption of life's awesome responsibilities, some people need tangible reminders of the healing they must yet undergo.

When I sat shivah for my father, the *keri'ah* garment came to symbolize my grief and pain. When it was time to get up from shivah, something seemed amiss. The walk around the block with my family strengthened us as a family. We understood that this walk was not only to help our reentry into everyday life but an acknowledgment that the shared experience of the past seven days would always be part of our collective memory. Yet I felt the need for a ritual to help symbolize the private healing and mending that I needed to continue to experience in the future.

The guidance and strength that Halakhah had provided for me throughout shivah eluded me when I stood in my bedroom poised to remove the *keri'ah* garment. Throughout the shivah, I would look down at my scarf and recall the sound of the tear. I repeatedly asked myself during shivah: Will I ever recover from this rupture? Will I ever feel whole again?

When it was time to remove my *keri'ah* garment, I was confronted by questions that I could not answer. What do I do with my scarf? Do I throw it away? In a literal sense, it is only a piece of ripped cloth. But symbolically it had become emotionally associated with the experience of mourning and recollecting my father. Do I save it? If so, for what purpose?

After talking with many people, I have learned that many other people have wondered what to do and why Halakhah provides no guidelines. I became convinced that a ritual for personal healing involving the *keri'ah* garment was necessary to complement the family ritual of walking around the block.

This ceremony will not speak to everyone. Some cannot wait to remove the garment and to never look at it again. Yet for others the very act of throwing clothing away (simply for lack of direction from the Halakhah) seems improper and hollow—not to mention ecologically irresponsible.

Each mourner is still at a very early point in healing. The ritual of "*keri'ah* mending" described below fits this early stage. Although there is a shared grief among all the mourners, each mourner's memory is unique, as was each mourner's relationship with the deceased. Each will heal at a different pace and in a different way. Therefore, each mourner's healing process must be uniquely acknowledged. Each mourner must mend his own tear.

This ceremony would also coax mourners away from the prevalent practice of the black ribbon which is so common in Jewish communities today. The black ribbon does not sufficiently express the emotional intensity of a mourner's grief.

Also included in the ceremony is the recitation of Psalm 23. It has been chosen for several reasons. It should resonate for the mourners as part of the funeral service. In addition, its message of hope in the face of death is clearly appropriate. Also, there is a beautiful, soothing melody to the text that would be consistent with the mood in the room. Finally, its recitation might serve as an appropriate act of closure for the mourner. It will enable each mourner to express the hope of providing comfort and strength to the other members of the family.

A *KERI'AH* MENDING CEREMONY

As the mourners complete shivah on the last day, the immediate family leaves to take the traditional walk around the block together as the final act of the shivah. After they return and before they disperse to their own homes, they should each remove their own *keri'ah* garments and hold them in their hands as they sit together in a circle one last time in the room where they sat shivah. As they are seated on the shivah boxes for the last time, they prepare to mend their garments together. Each mends his or her own garment; however, all should begin at the same time. Everyone takes a needle and thread and sews broad, rough stitches over the tear. The mourner should not try to sew the tear so as to make the rip unnoticeable; just the opposite! By sewing large stitches, the tear will still be apparent to anyone who might look at the garment. There should be silence in the room, thereby allowing the mourners to reflect on the deceased and on the wounds each is bearing inside. When the last person has completed the basting, all the mourners should rise.

The family might choose to have each mourner reflect aloud on the fears he feels in having mended the outward sign of the gaping wound. Perhaps the family might choose to read the following paragraph or some version of it together in unison:

As we mend our garments together, we realize that our wounds are not yet healed. We are in pain and we remain vulnerable. As we have removed our *keri'ah* garments and repaired the tear, we know that we must work hard to mend our torn hearts. Give us the strength and the courage, Adonai, to face our pain and our grief. Help us to renew our lives even as we will always feel the absence of _____.

May we find a measure of comfort in Your presence and in each other.

The family then recites or sings Psalm 23. While the psalm will conjure up the memory of the funeral, it is also most appropriate at this time. After having walked in the valley of the shadow of death, the mourners must seek new sources of comfort and strength.

Each member of the family then recites the following adaptation of the traditional statement of comfort, addressing one another:

> Ha-makom yenahem otanu
> b'tokh sh'ar aveilei Zion V'yerushalayim.

The keri'ah garments should not be thrown away. Some might choose to donate the clothing to an appropriate tzedakah (charity), while others might choose to hold on to the garment as a reminder of the need to mend their inner wounds. Some might choose to put it away forever. Some might choose to wear it each day as they recite Kaddish. Still others might choose to wear the basted garment each year on the yahrzeit.

Chapter Six

Kaddish

It is a prayer that is said in Aramaic, not in Hebrew. It is a prayer that makes no mention of the dead. And yet the Kaddish is one of the prayers that has the strongest hold on Jews. People who do not bother to say any other prayer arrange their schedules and order their lives around the synagogue's schedule so that they can say this one, morning and evening, for eleven months. People who start out as strangers in the synagogue come in order to say the prayer, are welcomed and shown the ropes by the old-timers, and soon become regulars who greet and take in the newcomers who arrive after them.

What is this prayer and how has it come to have so much power in the lives of so many? In this chapter several people report on what the experience of saying Kaddish in many places, at many kinds of services, in many moods, has meant to them.

When Death Comes

Ruth Brin

When death comes to the person you love,
you will go down to darkness and despair
and in the depths of loneliness will find
your naked soul, craven and cold.

You whose mind has considered and doubted,
whose heart has faltered and whose courage has failed,
will wring out the final personal word
from your stricken soul.

And death has no truth but this: I believe.
Death has no victory but this:

to rise from doubt and cold darkness
to magnify and hallow the name of God.

A Commentary on the Kaddish

Bernard Lipnick

Why is it that the mourner recites the Kaddish at the end of the service? After all, there isn't a word about death in the prayer. It is a kind of benediction, a last "good word" before ending the service so people will go home feeling uplifted. The words remind us of what we came together to do—namely, praise God—and they encourage us to look forward to the establishment of God's kingdom, when there will be completion, peace. But why should the mourner be given this honor?

My theory is that there are three problems that mourners face that the Kaddish speaks to in a most direct manner. The first problem is loss of faith. If there is a God in this world, how could my loved one die? Maybe there is no God in this world; maybe the world is rudderless. The blow to faith is never more pronounced than it is at the moment when you bury a loved one. Yet here comes the Kaddish and proclaims faith in God. It isn't that the mourner is talked back into faith by reciting the Kaddish. But the fact that a mourner says the Kaddish in a minyan of Jews three times a day for a period of eleven months keeps the mourner in the community of faith. By standing up and proclaiming publicly, *"Yitgadal v'yitkadash sh'mei rabbah"*—"Magnified and sanctified is the great name of God"—the body and soul of the mourner have a chance to recuperate, to go through a healing process. The perspective changes from that first day, that first week, that first month. The mourner begins to see that there are magnificent mountains and blue skies and gorgeous flowers and lovely birds. You don't know that the day you bury your mother. But a month later, you do; two months later, you certainly do. The denial of the existence of God which wallops the mourner like a sledgehammer during that first week is blunted by the recitation of the Kaddish as the mourner gradually regains perspective.

Okay, so you say there's a God in the world? But what kind of God can it be? A good God would not have taken my child. A congregant called me last night to tell me that his nineteen-month-old grandson has a tumor on his brain the size of a baseball. It's malignant. The chances of a nineteen-month-old baby surviving this are very, very slim. Maybe one in five. This same man's wife died two years ago at the age of fifty-six. He says to me, "Eleanor I can understand. Fifty-six years old, with children and grandchildren. But a nineteen-month-old baby? Come on, what kind of God are we dealing with?"

The Kaddish speaks to this problem, too. It says, *"B'almah divrah khi'rutei"*—"Throughout the world which He created according to His will." There is a certain pattern to life and death in this world which seems to be inherent in creation. If God is the author of creation, then God created it as a place where people live and then die. I once talked to a doctor and asked him about the mortality rate. He said, "It's still one hundred percent!" The point is that the world was created according to God's will. Now, if you had created it according to your will, people, especially babies, wouldn't die. But you didn't create the world. God did. It's not that God is a bad God. Death happens when microbes get the better of us, or when accidents happen, when immune systems aren't what they ought to be. In this world, which operates according to the rules of physics and motion, which seem to have inherent time clocks, people die. God didn't choose that your father should die rather than somebody else; "somebody else" will die too. Your father died because his liver stopped working, or because he had bacteria that infected it—not because of a bad God. God really had nothing to do with it. God created the world, which operates according to certain rules. People, even nineteen-month-old babies, die because they get sick, because the cells go haywire. Now that it's happened, what we have to do is find a way to cure it. Let's call upon the divine powers within us and the universe to help us find a solution. The Kaddish says first that there is a God in the world, and second that God created a world according to divine will, in which death is the inevitable conclusion of life.

The third problem is: What's it all for? If this is the way it all ends, why beat your head against a wall? Whether it's eighty-nine years, or fifty-six years, or nineteen months, it's all over too rapidly. Now, people have different reactions to this awareness. Some say, "Eat, drink, and be merry, for tomorrow we die." Others say, "Withdraw from life. It will all be over soon anyway." The issue is: If it's all over so soon, why break our necks?

The Kaddish speaks to this. *"V'yamlikh malkhutei b'hayeikhon u-v'yomeikhon u-vhayei d'khol beit Yisrael"*—"May God establish His kingdom during our lifetime and during the lifetime of the house of Israel." When the prayer says "establish His kingdom," this is theological language for a perfect world, the messianic era. God's rule is to be perfect and complete. So, the mourner—at this moment when he or she is most sensitive to the issues of life and death and to his or her own inevitable demise—stands up and says, "There is a God who declares that it is our obligation as Jews to establish God's rule on this earth in our lifetime."

Jews are very sensitive to words. Words are very precious in Jewish tradition. This is saying that we undertake to solve all the problems in the world in our lifetime. Now, I'm sixty-six years old. If I live a normal lifespan, I've got another eleven years or so, maybe twelve. But, I've had a heart bypass, so who knows? Even if I make it to one hundred and twenty, is it realistic to expect that all the social problems of the world, all the political problems of the world, all the medical problems of the world, all the psychological problems of the world will be solved—all in the next twenty to thirty years? It would take that long just to list the problems! Yet, the tradition asks the mourner to stand up and make the statement "I'm expected to work toward the establishment of God's complete and perfect world in my lifetime." What does that say? It says: "Mourner, you have never been in a better position to appreciate the brevity of life and the fact that you have a mission in this life—to establish God's kingdom—and you don't have very long to do it! You must therefore redouble your efforts to bring God's kingdom into existence."

Who is more in touch with the realities of the human condition than the mourner? That's why Judaism decided that it should be the mourner who proclaims in the benediction to the service the ultimate meaning of human existence.

Going to Shul

Milton Himmelfarb

In the past months, since my father died, I have been in the synagogue twice a day to say the Kaddish. Other congregations would regard mine as observing bankers' hours, but even so its morning schedule requires arising in the dark and cold, especially in the winter. For afternoon-and-evening prayer the hour varies, depending—at least in principle and in Orthodox synagogues—on the time of sunset, but going every evening is not easy either.

Which is why not even the devout necessarily frequent the synagogue every day, contenting themselves with private prayer, particularly on weekdays. It is the man who is saying the Kaddish who must have a minyan, public worship. In most American synagogues, nearly everyone you see at prayer during the week is a mourner, together with most of those who are there from the beginning on Saturday morning. Inconvenience also helps to explain the tenth-man problem, quite apart from the big explanations we like better: the difficulty of belief, the difficulty of prayer. In few synagogues where the speech is English is it unnecessary to have a list of volunteers who can be telephoned in an emergency to round out the required number of ten.

In the Middle Ages it was thought that saying the Kaddish for a year was especially helpful to the dead if they had been wicked. Since no one wanted to imply that his father or mother had been wicked, today we say the Kaddish for eleven months. I do not know what proportion of Jewish men observe the full eleven months, but I suspect it is fairly high, especially when put beside our known propensity for staying away from the synagogue.

If this is so, why? Well, feelings about death, especially the death of a parent; guilt and anxiety, and the need to relieve them; ritual—all these can be interpreted along conventional Freudian lines and have been, often. For Freud, religion was a kind of public, collective neurosis. I take this idea seriously. It tells me better than anything else why the very inconvenience of saying the Kaddish morning and afternoon or evening every day for eleven months, and thereafter on anniversaries—normally at least two in a man's life—becomes a virtue, perhaps an attraction. It is expiatory, it is almost punitive, and we have been taught that guilt seeks punishment.

It is more, of course. Much has been said in dispraise of Jews who obey the rules of the Kaddish though otherwise they hardly ever pray at all. The contempt is unwarranted: the Kaddish must meet their needs better than anything else in the synagogue. And these are not only needs of the kind we have learned about from Freud, but also needs for style and tradition. Freud said that the collective neurosis of religion spares us the trouble of developing individual, personal neuroses. With the Kaddish, Judaism spares each person the trouble of developing for himself a style—etiquette, ritual, mode of expression, symbolic action—at a time when he wants it and when he knows he cannot devise something personal that will be as good.

If each of us were accountable for his own ritual of mourning, who would escape censure? Who would escape his own censure? The Jewish rites—the burial, the seven days at home, the Kaddish—have the advantage of being a tradition, a style. We need assume no responsibility for them, as we would for any personal or private symbolic action, nor can there be any question of their appropriateness. They are appropriate almost by definition, because of their antiquity, their near-universality, their publicness—*quod semper, quod ubique, quod ad omnibus.* Yet their publicness, so far from making them exterior and impersonal, makes them all the more appropriate to the particular relationship between mourner and mourned: the Kaddish I now say for my father, he said for his; and so back through a recession of the generations that exceeds what my imagination can grasp. Acting as my father acted, I become conscious that I am a link in the chain of being. Nor am I hindered from expressing particular, local, present emotion.

One of the things a person is supposed to say about someone who has died is the prayer that Abigail said for David (though in his lifetime and in his presence), that his soul may be bound up in the bundle of life. Saying this is of a piece with the rest of our ritual. Whatever its efficacy may be for the dead, it binds *me* up in the bundle of life, situates *me* in the procession of the generations, frees *me* from the prison of now and here.

Although we have been born when it is hard to believe in immortality, the Kaddish helps us to believe, a little. I know that it makes me think of my father often, more than twice a day; and it will keep reminding me of him after I have stopped saying the Kaddish daily, when I hear someone else say it and I make the appropriate response. To think of my father, to recall him, is to hold off his mortality—and because ritual is eloquent, to hold it off still one generation further. Where has Daddy gone? To shul, to say Kaddish for Grandpa. By doing what allows my children to ask this question and receive this answer, I also allow myself to hope that my own mortality will similarly be delayed.

A Year of Grieving, A Year of Growing

Shamai Kanter

In March 1989, after we buried my father, I began my Jewish obligation to offer prayers in his memory at daily congregational services, morning and evening, through the next eleven months.

The specific prayer led by mourners is known as the Kaddish. It is a praise of God, asking for the coming of His kingdom. Even Jews who are barely literate in their tradition are familiar with the chanting of its awe-filled Aramaic rhythms. (Christians, too, find it familiar in translation: many of its phrases are incorporated into the prayer they know as "Our Father" or "The Lord's Prayer.")

Over decades, as a rabbi, I'd always encouraged people to be regular in joining the daily worship and in reciting the Kaddish during their year of grieving for a parent. I assured them it would bring them comfort on many levels: the religious plane of closeness to God and the human plane of mutual support from other mourners. And of course this was true.

What I didn't expect was the form my own progress would take from the darkness of mourning to the dawning of consolation. Everyone is unique, of course, so I don't know whether it has been quite like this for others.

There's a phenomenon that often happens when you have something on your mind that greatly concerns you and you're reading. Words about that subject seem to leap out at you from the page. I know that when someone is in love, the words "love" and "marriage" seem to be printed in bold type in news stories. And it's certainly true for Jewish people, who are concerned about the safety of our ever-threatened people, that the words "Jewish" or "Israel" seem to jump off the newspaper pages as if they were bigger than the rest of the line.

So it was for me during the reading of each service. In the pages of the Psalms, there were certain phrases that would jump up to catch my eye in the same way the word "cancer" will jump at a reader waiting for a radiologist's diagnosis.

For example, in the Morning Psalms there is the line "God heals those whose hearts are broken and binds up their wounds. He counts the stars and calls each one by name." At first, encountering those words each morning was like a shock to my own heart; a reminder of my loss. Yet, at the same time, it was a promise of eventual healing that provided a kind of hope.

At a time when it was easy to feel alone, it reminded me that the One who names every star also knows each of us as an individual. We may feel anonymous, but we are not. Every morning that verse would wait for me, to catch my eye with its message and sometimes evoke a tear.

Later, during the month of June, I experienced a kind of transitional feeling. It was like a chord change in music, when the melody notes are the same but the harmony behind them changes. The same words would jump out, but they were softer somehow. Not that the sense of loss had gone, but it was muted and gentler. The healing had begun.

Grieving is not a straight-line progression. It's up and down as well as forward and back. Yet, as that line from the Psalms began to recede to "normal size," others would take its prominence.

"Your love and truth continually sustain me." The Hebrew there can also be read as "Your love and truth continually create me." It told me that our existence always depends upon God, who is continually creating us, and that creation is an act of love.

During the month before the High Holy Days, the special addition of Psalm 27 gave me the words "For though my father and mother might abandon me, the Lord will gather me up."

Those words spoke to the child inside the adult, the child who felt left behind and abandoned and who would have liked to be gathered up in someone's arms, partly because he realized that a parent's death had transformed him now into the "older generation."

As the fall holiday season progressed with its joyous special psalms, I was reminded: "Grievous in the sight of the Lord is the death of those who love Him." It told me that we do not mourn alone: God is with us even in our grief. As mourners, the sense of isolation we sometimes feel is illusory. God is even closer to us than the people who sit beside us, able to share our feelings.

One afternoon while driving, something occurred to me that surprised me. As a rabbi, the substance of my religious life doesn't normally include the Christian gospels. But something on the radio reminded me of the line from the Beatitudes, "Blessed are those who mourn, for they shall be comforted."

I had never given the words serious thought before. If anything, my reaction to them would have been: "What kind of blessing is that? It would be a greater blessing not to have to mourn at all!" But that afternoon I understood things a little differently. No one gets a free ride in life; all of us suffer the death of a dear one at some time. What then?

Many people find themselves incapable of mourning. They cannot weep. Their feelings remain bottled up as they rush to "get back to normal." Often I've seen their unexpressed mourning turn up months or years later in the form of depression or physical illness.

It is, indeed, no blessing to suffer personal tragedy. But when that happens, it is a blessing to be able to mourn. Because only when we do so can we pass through the dark tunnel of grief and emerge into consolation. Christian scholars can tell me whether or not that is the intended meaning of the gospel verse, but that's the wisdom it expressed for me.

It is a wisdom similar to the expression in the psalm "Lord, I am indeed Your servant, son of Your handmaid: You have freed me from the things that have tied me up." Being God's servant does open us to express grieving and to eventual healing.

I say "eventual," not immediate. As I approach the anniversary of Dad's death, I know the healing is not complete. The measure of that incompleteness for me is the number of cards and letters I received during that first week of mourning.

Those people who took the time and effort to write to me were a great help and support. Their kindness and concern helped make it possible for me to begin to return from the valley of the shadow. They will never be able to overestimate their importance to me.

And yet I have not been able to write them in response to tell them this. As far as I've come, that final step is the most difficult of all. It is almost as if writing those notes will indicate my full acceptance of something that a part of me just does not want to accept at all.

Of course I will get to it soon, most likely by the anniversary of Dad's death. When I do, another step along the way of grieving will have been completed.

Saying Kaddish: The Making of a "Regular"

Marian Henriquez Neudel

A little less than a year ago, my father died. When I had dealt with all the immediate logistics, I began working on the more long-term logistics of saying Kaddish.

My expectations were shaped by innumerable articles, biographies, and novels I had read about bereaved Jewish women who went through all sorts of unpleasantness to be able to say Kaddish in all-male minyanim which most emphatically did not want them around and disapproved of their taking on the obligation in the first place. Henrietta Szold's marvelously moving statement about saying Kaddish for her mother was perhaps the basic text I was operating on. I was braced to spend the better part of a year gritting my teeth. I'm not quite sure why, under the circumstances, I still wanted to assume the obligation. My father, while he undoubtedly would have understood why I chose to do so, would also have understood if I had not. Most of my other relatives would have trouble making sense of the ritual.

Additionally, I had the purely biological problem of not being a morning person. Until this year, I have had the luxury of being able to get up at 7:30, take an 8:25 train, and get to work slightly early for a 9:30 court call most mornings. Daily minyanim start at 7:30 A.M., or (downtown) 8:00 A.M. at the latest.

The egalitarian minyan I *daven* with on Shabbas doesn't meet during the week. It's twenty-five years old now and is unlikely to change its ways on this issue. Most of us have trouble enough getting to shul on time for a 9:30 A.M. service once a week.

AGAIN, A WANDERING JEW

There's a Conservative synagogue downtown, a stone's throw from court and not too far from the train. It serves a good breakfast after services in the morning. Breakfast is also (it turns out) a good place to meet fellow attorneys and talk shop. Seating is mixed, but women are not counted in a minyan. On the other hand, they almost always *have* a minyan. People are friendly. On the other hand, the Middle East politics of the rabbi and many of the regulars are only a hair to the left of Jabotinsky himself, and they *love* to talk politics at breakfast. That was one possibility.

There's another Conservative synagogue in my neighborhood, about eight blocks from home, which is a difficult walk on icy winter days, though rather nice in good weather. Getting there involves a walk through a park, among other things. They're also usually reasonable about letting me park my car in their lot on bad days. They're half a block from a train station. Breakfast is intermittent.

They count women in the minyan. On the other hand, some weeks, they can't *get* a minyan, even by counting women. (Most of the regulars are retired men who get sick or go to Florida to visit their kids or have doctor's appointments on a fairly regular basis.) Some mornings, they ask me to lead services, even though the Ritual Committee has not quite gotten around to ruling on this issue, even for Shabbas services. (This is the only daily minyan I know of that is ahead of the Ritual Committee on *anything*.) I get *aliyot* pretty regularly. *They need me.* To make a minyan, I mean. They need everybody they can get, male and female. When I don't show up for a couple of days (because the weather was bad and it was easier to go downtown), people ask if I'm okay and say they would have called me at home if I'd missed another day.

Architecturally, the shul is unprepossessing. And it leaks. Getting from the parking-lot entrance to the chapel on wet days is an obstacle course of pots, pans, and puddles. On *really* wet, windy days, the rain blows into the chapel through cracks in the leading of the stained-glass windows. Breakfast is also a disappointment. My most ardent revolutionary struggle of the year was the effort to get bran muffins for breakfast. Instead, breakfast dwindled away altogether when there were only two or three of us who stayed around to eat it.

AND WHAT IF YOU CARE ABOUT SPIRIT?

The *davening* is less musical than I am used to, and somewhat faster. (By Orthodox standards, on the other hand, it's pretty slow.) The men who lead it most of the time are serious about it. Their *kavannah* (devotion) shows. Their religiosity reminds me of my father's.

A minyan full of (mostly) older men becomes a very vivid reminder of the narrowness of the gap between those who say Kaddish, and those for whom we say it. Over the year, two of the regulars themselves have died. A couple of the others are looking a lot frailer, and I worry about them. At the same time, the rest of us move in and then move on—my last week of saying Kaddish turned out to be the first week for a friend of mine, who had lost *her* father.

I have become very fond of the regulars. I see my father in them. Temperamentally they have a lot in common with him. A couple of them are very frail men who have trouble seeing and walking, and go to a lot of trouble to get to shul. As my donation to the shul I have given a check earmarked for the construction of a railing on the *bimah* so they won't have so much trouble getting up and down for *aliyot*.

I sometimes joke about writing a "Mourner's Guide to Chicago Synagogues," rating them all (fifty-odd, I think) on liturgical quality (rating indicated by between one and five tiny *sefer torahs*), speed of *davening* (indicated by clock faces), odds of having a minyan at any given service (stated in percentage), nonsexism (indicated by the number of = signs), friendliness (one to five smiley faces), and quality and quantity of breakfast (forks?). But, obviously, I have made my choice.

Now that my eleven months are up, I find I do not want to get out of the habit. I find (much to my surprise) I even have trouble sleeping past 6:15. I have committed myself to showing up Wednesdays and Thursdays, to make the counting easier and more predictable.

In the process of becoming a regular, I have learned a lot about what the ritual is *for*. I know something of the history, but that doesn't have a whole lot to do with how it works *now*. For most of us, the eleven months of mourning is the first acquaintance we will ever have with daily *davening,* individually *or* in a congregation. It draws us into a community (typically a rather small one) at a time when grief might otherwise isolate us. It imposes a routine on us when we might be tempted to let chaos take over. It gives us something to do early in the morning when depression wakes us up earlier than usual.

UNDERSTANDING HESCHEL'S LEAP OF ACTION

And it gives us (many of us, anyway) our first sample of real, genuine Jewish petitionary prayer. Those of us who *daven* only on Shabbat and the holidays are, obviously, a lot more Jewishly literate than those who only go to High Holy Day services. But we still miss out on a lot. The Shabbas Amidah, the central prayer of the service, goes out of its way *not* to deal with the needs and concerns of the rest of the week. God, we figure, is *also* entitled to take the day off. So what we mostly do on Shabbas is praise Him. Which leads many of us to think of Judaism as more abstract and less nitty-gritty than the many other religions that surround us, with their endless and often very public and petty prayers for health, wealth, and peace of mind. That's okay in our younger days, when we don't usually feel any serious lack of those necessities. It's fine to have a religion that's above such mundane things. But our first major bereavement is likely to coincide with, or even mark, the passage into middle age, when health and wealth (or anyway, sustenance) and other basic necessities become harder to come by. And it also introduces us to the daily Amidah and plugs it into the nittiest and grittiest part of our daily life.

The alternatives and adjuncts to Kaddish also do a lot for us in the situation of bereavement. The tradition tells us that if you can't say Kaddish with a minyan, the next best thing is to study. Preferably Torah, for instance the *parashah,* the portion of the Torah that is read each week, or something very closely related to it. So (given the difficulties of our local shul in raising a minyan some days) I've done a lot more Torah and *Haftarah* reading than I ever did before. I've done a lot more reading on Jewish topics in general, for the same reason.

We are also supposed to give a *lot* of *tzedakah* (charity) during the year of mourning. I have become acutely conscious of the innumerable beggars on my regular path to and from work, between my office and court, and around my neighborhood. Some of *them* have become "regulars" in my life too. What the tradition had in mind, I don't know; but the admonition to give extra *tzedakah* makes me aware of other people's troubles when I might otherwise become absorbed in my own. One of the last things I was able to do for my father while he was alive but not able to write or calculate was to take care of his regular charitable donations for the year. Here again, the tradition has given me a very constructive, very personal way to feel close to him.

I used to be bothered that Jews, or at least the ones I come in contact with, see daily prayer as something to be done only in the context of bereavement. Now I realize how many of the regulars in our daily minyan were drawn into it during their various bereavements, and I suspect that they—and I, now—don't exactly see daily prayer as a mourning ritual. After all, we stay on past our year. Rather, we see bereavement as a kind of initiation into the *meaning* of the ritual. Now we know what it's for.

Chapter Seven

The Year and After

When does death really occur? In a sense, it is not when the heart stops beating but when the person is no longer remembered by anyone.

And so, for the mourner, life becomes a struggle of memory versus forgetting.

> Soon,
> of the two of us, neither will be left
> to forget the other.
> —Yehuda Amichai, *Love Poems*

The war against oblivion goes on, starting from the day of the loss of a loved one. That is why it is so difficult to let go of the clothing and of each and every memento. That is why the empty seat at the seder is so painful to look at, and why every birthday, every anniversary, every visit to a place that you shared with the one who is gone, every family *simhah* (celebration) is ambivalent. We all want to believe that everything we are and do is recorded up above and does not get lost, because here on earth whatever we do to preserve the memory eventually fades. Even words carved on stone wear out.

The tradition has constructed a whole network of ways by which we can fight off oblivion. The Yizkor prayer, which is said on the last day of each of the pilgrimage festivals and on the Day of Atonement, is a way to integrate remembering into the cycle of the year. And perhaps Arlene Rossen Cardozo is right in what she suggests in her essay here—that it is a way of coping with "the holiday blues" that mourners feel. The naming of a child after a dead loved one is only custom, not law, and only known among Ashkenazic, not Sephardic Jews, but it is a custom so widely observed and so emotionally resonant that it clearly strikes a powerful chord. And so with the other devices that the tradition provides to help get us through the year of grief and beyond.

In this chapter a number of people reflect on how the mourning rituals have helped them move from stage to stage.

The Law Sets the Limits

One must not grieve excessively for the dead. Whoever weeps more than the law requires must be weeping for something else. Rather, let one accept the schedule set down by the sages: three days for weeping, seven for lamenting, thirty for mourning.

—Shulhan Arukh, Yoreh Deah 394

The Five Stages of Grief

Linda Pastan

The night I lost you
someone pointed me toward
the Five Stages of Grief.
Go that way, they said,
it's easy, like learning to climb
stairs after amputation.
And so I climbed.
Denial was first.
I sat down at breakfast,
carefully setting the table
for two. I passed you the toast—
you sat there. I passed
you the paper—you hid
behind it.
Anger seemed more familiar.
I burned the toast, snatched
the paper, and read the headlines myself.

But they mentioned your departure
and so I moved on to
Bargaining. What could I exchange
for you? The silence
after storms? My typing fingers?
Before I could decide, Depression
came puffing up, a poor relation,
its suitcase tied together
with string. In the suitcase
were bandages for the eyes
and bottles of sleep. I slid
all the way down the stairs
feeling nothing.
And all the time Hope
flashed on and off
in defective neon.
Hope was a signpost pointing
straight in the air.
Hope was my uncle's middle name,
he died of it.
After a year I am still climbing,
though my feet slip
on your stone face.
The treeline
has long since disappeared;
green is a color
I have forgotten.
But now I see what I am climbing
toward: Acceptance
written in capital letters,
a special headline:
Acceptance.
Its name is in lights.
I struggle on,
waving and shouting.
Below, my whole life spreads its surf,

all the landscape I've ever known
or dreamed of. Below
a fish jumps: the pulse
in your neck.
Acceptance. I finally
reach it.
But something is wrong.
Grief is a circular staircase.
I have lost you.

Shloshim: The First Thirty Days After Burial

Alan Kay

The thirty days following burial, which includes shivah, is the period of *shloshim*. It embodies the full mourning period for all relatives except for parents, for whom mourning ends after twelve Hebrew months.

"The mourner is encouraged to leave the house after shivah," Rabbi Maurice Lamm writes in *The Jewish Way in Death and Mourning*, "and to slowly rejoin society, always recognizing that enough time has not yet elapsed to assume full, normal social relations. The rent clothing may customarily still be worn for deceased parents, and haircutting for male mourners is still generally prohibited."

Although mourners may greet another and respond to greetings of others, *"shalom"* is not generally used. But the mourner returns to a normal work schedule, surrounded with people outside the immediate community of family and close friends. The mourner has begun to return order to his or her life. The monument may be purchased during this period.

I "got up" from sitting shivah for my father on the morning of the seventh day of shivah. I returned to my school later that day, dressed in the black suit and tie I had worn at my father's funeral, the torn black ribbon, symbol of *keri'ah,* still pinned to the left lapel of my suit jacket near to my heart. I drifted mournfully through the day, lost between two worlds.

The thirty-day period of *shloshim* begins after interment. Rabbi Tzvi Rabinowicz reminds us that "in mishnaic times, Rabbi Judah Hanasi, before he died, gave instructions that the 'assembly for study should be reconstituted after the lapse of thirty days from the day of his death' [Ketubbot 103b]" *(A Guide to Life).* During *shloshim,* Rabbi Rabinowicz continues, "a mourner must not take part in any festivity or attend a place of entertainment whether on the Sabbath, festival, or a weekday. If he mourns a parent, this period of abstinence should continue for the full twelve months [Shulhan Arukh, Yoreh Deah 391:2]. He should not listen to instrumental music or play any musical instruments himself during the whole period of mourning."

Rabbi Rabinowicz informs us that it was custom at one time for mourners to wear black throughout *shloshim,* "since black was the symbol of death." Today, however, "Orthodox Jews do not wear black for mourning."

"The mourning period," Rabbi Simeon J. Maslin writes in *Gates of Mitzvah,* "is one of great personal vulnerability." On the day I "got up" from sitting shivah and returned to my school, I was particularly vulnerable and self-consciously wore my black suit and rent ribbon as much to draw people to me as to keep them at a distance: these were the two worlds in which I found myself on that day, the world in which I sought sympathetic, even empathic comforters, to ease my pain, and the world in which I desired to be alone because no amount of comfort could ever lighten my painful burden.

"Some pains are too deep to salve," writes Rabbi David J. Wolpe in *The Healer of Shattered Hearts,* "and too inexplicably awful to pretend they have explanation." With my wife, Jo's, quiet empathic strength borne out of having lived without her father for more than half of her life, I left my home that morning assured that resuming my own life would not mean forgetting my father. Jo, too, returned to her school that day. Even though it was not her father who had died, my father was the only father she had known for twenty-five years, and she had been observing her own personal shivah. Our daughters, Corinne, Lisa, and Adina, returned to school, and with my mother visiting in my sister's home, our home was empty that day but for the echoes of weeping.

What might others have said to me that day I returned to my school? What might I have said to those who approached me? After shivah, Rabbi Lamm instructs, the mourners "may initiate the greeting and respond to it. Customarily, however, the mourner is not greeted with *shalom* for the full year of mourning in the case of a parent's death, and for the thirty days after the death of other relatives."

In school, some colleagues and students came close to me with whispers of "I'm sorry"; others approached, touched my arm, and retreated silently; still others, at a distance, nodded their heads in acknowledgment of my loss and turned away. I was still cloaked in the mourner's shadow that day and believed that if others did not see the beat of my heart, they heard it. I whispered thank-yous to the whispers I heard, and I bowed my head in recognition of the silent messages of condolence. In the very acts of "getting up" from sitting shivah, returning to work, and surrounding myself with people outside my immediate community of family and close friends, I was beginning to return order to my life and learning how to live without my father.

We received many cards and letters during that first month in which family and friends found they were able to share what they could not share face-to-face. "I know your loss is a loss in the profoundest sense," one colleague wrote to me. "[I have been] told of the depth of your relationship with your father and its importance in your life. I can only offer a little something from my own experience. There is hardly a day when something doesn't happen to bring my dad to mind with such sweetness and such clarity that his presence is always with me. I am very far removed from a spiritual life, but this never fails to move me. For those of us who have been lucky enough to make our peace with our parents and felt their positive influence in our lives, the gifts are enduring."

Every word and whisper, every card, whether printed or original, every touch, every visit helps to build the bridge between the mourner's world and the world of normal relations that the mourner must reenter in order to resume a healthy life.

"I don't want his grave to be unmarked," my mother had said to me during shivah, after having read in Rabbi Lamm's book the chapter on erecting the *matzevah,* the monument. My mother wanted to select a stone for my father's grave immediately after shivah and I had agreed.

During the week following shivah, my mother and I visited the office and showroom of the monument maker from whom my mother and father had purchased the monuments for my paternal and maternal grandparents. I don't recall having talked with my mother in advance about the style of the monument or the inscription she desired. It was not until we entered the showroom—and with the expert, compassionate assistance of the owner—that she made her selection.

"Good taste, quiet dignity, and the avoidance of ostentation are the only guidelines for selecting the monument," Rabbi Lamm advises. "What is recommended is a short Hebrew descriptive phrase, in addition to the Hebrew name of the deceased and his father's Hebrew name, the full English name, and the Hebrew and English dates of birth and death. It may contain all of these or only the names. It is most appropriate, however, to include the Hebrew dates whenever Christian dates are inscribed."

Rabbi Lamm cautions against having the face of the deceased or figures of animals cut into the stone. Equally, photographs are inappropriate. "It does seem that a person should be remembered without having his portrait to stare at. If already erected, however, these tombstones should cause no disputes and are better left to stand as they are."

My mother and I walked among the monuments in the showroom and, as we touched the cold stone and read the sample inscriptions, as we stepped back and imagined first one stone and then another at the head of my father's grave, we shared ideas about how my father's monument should look and what it should read. My mother chose a monument with two tablets and, as she touched my arm, assured me that setting a tablet aside for her was in no way a sign as to her own state of mind. "There's no question where I will be buried," she said, "and there is no reason I cannot make a choice of a monument for both of us."

In addition to my father's Hebrew name and the name of his father, and that he was a Levite, we wanted him to be remembered as

Beloved Husband
Devoted Father
Loving Grandfather
Dear Brother

And so those remembrances were to be carved on the tablet after his name. Not that my father would not be remembered without those inscriptions, but when the grave is visited, the inscriptions will be read aloud and, in part, will be a prayer to my father.

We decided on a carving of the eternal flame to separate the two tablets. I was comforted by that symbol that so often had drawn my attention in the sanctuary. In the upper right-hand corner, a menorah would be carved, and in the upper left-hand corner, a pitcher, to represent my father's status as a Levite—and mine, as well.

My maternal grandfather, Samuel Ovshia Lubliner, was a *cohain*. According to Orthodox and Conservative Jews, a *cohain* is a descendant of Aaron, Moses' brother and the first high priest of the Temple in Jerusalem. During the Torah reading on the Sabbath and on festivals and whenever the Torah is read, a *cohain* is the first of the worshipers called upon to repeat the blessings and, later, to offer the priestly benediction.

The Levites are Jews who trace their ancestry to the Levites of biblical days. Then, in the time of the ancient Temple, the Levites were responsible for the physical care of the sanctuary. But they had another job as well.

Before my maternal grandfather would enter the sanctuary during the High Holy Days to offer the priestly benediction, my father and I would pour water from a pitcher over his hands. Perhaps more than any other ritual I performed in the presence of my father, this one linked me religiously to my father (and grandfather) and historically to my heritage. Here was the literal "passing down" from generation to generation of Jewish ritual: my father would pour water first, then hand the pitcher to me, and then together we would follow my grandfather into the sanctuary. Although I did not stand with my grandfather on the *bimah*, I was as much a part of him then as I was a part of my father, next to whom I proudly stood. In the sanctuary, when I was a boy I held my father's tallit; later I held his hand; and still later I draped my arm around his shoulders. A pitcher of water, like the tallit each of us later wore, had made us inextricably linked to each other and to our heritage.

As my mother and I left the monument showroom, I told her the day would come when I would visit my father's grave with my grandchildren and they would ask about the pitcher of water. I would tell them not only of their great-grandfather as Beloved Husband, Devoted Father, Loving Grandfather, and Dear Brother, but also of their great-grandfather as Affectionate Teacher.

A Way to Mark Shloshim

Arthur Gross Schaefer

An old man [in ancient Israel] was planting a fig tree when a Roman general happened to pass by. The general said to the man, "Don't you realize it will take twenty years before that tree will grow enough to give fruit, and you will be long dead by then?" The old man responded, "When I was a small child, I could eat fruit because those who came before me had planted trees. Am I not obliged to do the same for the next generation?"

The family and I stand around a freshly dug hole in their backyard. I remind them that a short while ago, we also stood at the side of another dirt hole. At that time, they, and not strangers, took spadefuls of dirt and placed earth on top of a coffin to pay honor to someone who was very special in their lives. I then tell them the above midrashic tale of the old man planting a fig tree. I again request that they take up spadefuls of dirt and place them around the base of a newly planted tree. As the ritual at the graveside involving a shovel of dirt signifies an ending to the physical life, the shovelful of dirt for the tree signifies the beginning of life through the gift of memory and the telling of stories.

The genesis for the ritual of planting a tree in memory of a loved one is not new. The Jewish National Fund has linked its tree-planting program and the revitalization of the forests in Israel with the honoring of individuals. Many synagogues have "trees of life" with engraved leaves acknowledging the names of present and past congregants and their families. And trees have been dedicated to Holocaust victims, Righteous Gentiles, and many others. Our tradition embraces the tree as an important image of wisdom and life. We have the tree of knowledge in the Garden of Eden, and the Torah itself is called a tree of life. Moreover, we have many parables, stories, and midrashim dealing with trees.

Accordingly, I find it natural to use a tree-planting ceremony to fill a void felt after the intensity of the funeral and the shivah. There is often a tremendous psychological letdown for the family when the people have left and the services at the home have stopped. Several years ago, I offered to a family the idea of planting a tree in their backyard to honor a father who had recently died. That suggestion was greeted favorably when I related the idea of a new ritual to the above-cited midrash of the old man planting the fig tree. I have now performed the tree-planting ritual for several years and have found that it has become so well received that it is often requested by families who have heard about it from others in the community.

The ritual surrounding the planting of the tree usually involves the story of the fig tree. Then those present are asked to tell a story or to share some particular value of the one who died—one that they believe will provide a continual sense of sustenance and nourishment. Family members are then asked to put dirt around the new tree. A fruit tree is usually planted because it symbolizes continual nourishment by the fruit it bears. After the tree is planted and watered, the Kaddish is recited. *"O seh Shalom"* is sung. Participants often hold hands or just look at the tree in silent remembrance before leaving.

For some families, the tree ritual has been performed to mark the end of the *shloshim* (mourning). For others, it has been timed with another occasion when the family has come together from distant parts. For those with no place to plant a tree or who live in an apartment, trees can be planted at the synagogue, in a nearby park, or at the home of a relative.

This tree-planting ritual has provided a sense of closure for many and an opportunity for personal reflection which they were not ready to express in the public forum of the funeral.

A daughter who had suffered a particularly difficult time with her father buried a piece of paper listing the many issues she had not resolved with him. The ritual was a symbolic gesture of putting to rest many painful issues. In that way, a new relationship could blossom through her memory, and she could appreciate his strengths and see him as a positive contribution to her life.

At another tree-planting ceremony, a son shared that he was too angry to think positively of his mother. As he planted the tree, he remarked that the tree would produce two kinds of apples—delicious apples and rotten ones that would have to be discarded. He then expressed his intent to work through and discard memories of his mother that were painful, so that he could see and appreciate the affirming recollections.

There have been several situations where families have asked me to perform a ritual not only for a recent bereavement but also for other members of the family who had died previously. For them, it became a concrete statement that the memories of loved ones who had died in the past were still a part of their lives. In many cases, the tree planting became a convenient and effective vehicle for teaching children about grandparents. It is not unusual for families to say that the tree planted is now "Grandpa's tree," and its fruit would be referred to as "Grandpa's apple." This connection to a tree in the yard has allowed a living presence, so that parents can more easily tell stories about loved ones.

The planting of a tree can also connect us to God as the creator.

It reminds us that we are partners with God in the ongoing act of creation. As God planted the first trees, we also plant and nurture trees. As God has given each of us the ability to remember, the presence of a tree dedicated to memory serves as nourishment for us and for our children.

Yizkor: The Unending Conversation

Barry Freundel

There is no more poignant time of the year than the moment of Yizkor (the memorial service for the dead) on Yom Kippur. Never are there more people in the synagogue, and rarely, if ever, is there a moment of such high emotion. Yet a measure of objectivity would suggest that Yizkor does not belong with Yom Kippur. Yom Kippur is a day of introspection and repentance, not a day of sadness. Wouldn't the prayer make more sense on Tisha B'Av, when we commemorate the sad events of our history?

This question reflects a common misunderstanding of the nature of Yizkor. I would term the experience of Yizkor a conversation with the dead. Now, the phrase "conversations with the dead" is redolent of dark rooms and mediums in mystical outfits. But superstition and television clichés aside, we should realize that we all are part of an ongoing dialogue with the dead.

Many of us who have lost loved ones continue our conversations with them even after they are dead. Frequently, particularly after the pain of separation has diminished somewhat, those who remain seek solace and guidance in conversation with those they have lost. Even if we do not do it ourselves, most of us know people who stop to talk to a deceased parent or spouse each day before going to sleep or when getting up in the morning. These conversations may consist of reports on the status of their lives, questions, or requests for advice. And far from being a symptom of sanity loss, this practice of "touching base" is quite comforting and salutary, if kept within reasonable limits.

Some may find the prospect of such daily conversations ridiculous and certainly not *their* style, but virtually everyone does it at some point in his life. I do not know anyone who, when attending or preparing for an important event such as a bar mitzvah or a wedding, does not picture a lost loved one present and imagine the reaction that he or she would have. This, too, is a form of conversation with the dead.

Even people who have never lost a close friend or relative engage in conversations with the dead. One case in point is the universal impact of a Bill Mauldin cartoon that appeared in many newspapers after John Kennedy was shot. A variation on the Lincoln Memorial, it showed Mr. Lincoln sitting bent over, his head in his hands, crying. The weeping statue conveyed not only the grief of the nation but the profound violation of the values that Kennedy had represented. The embodiment of these values in the statue of our first assassinated president made sense only because we, contemporary Americans, were in conversation with a dead hero from our past.

And as this last example illustrates, the dead answer our call— not in words, but in ways that nevertheless make a difference in our lives. All of us have learned valuable lessons in morality and behavior from those to whom we were close and whom we have lost. In the best of circumstances, they were positive lessons. But even if they were negative, these lessons serve as guideposts for the way we conduct our lives and are thus also part of our continuous conversation with the dead.

Halakhah (Jewish law) is precisely such a process, experienced collectively by each generation. We consult our authoritative books, the most essential of them written by people no longer with us. Yet they serve as our teachers, sometimes even as friends and colleagues, and we converse with them as we attempt to understand the nuances of their words. It is a dialogue between individuals of very different eras, in which we apply our modern categories of thought and understanding to their impressive intellect and traditional wisdom. Only by engaging fully in this dialogue can we find the eternal truths that will guide our contemporary lives.

On an individual basis, too, those who were major influences in one's life speak continuously from beyond the grave. For myself, I know that whenever I accomplish anything even remotely valuable, I sense the presence of my father and his smiling face. So, too, whenever I give a sermon or class that I think is even remotely worthy of my sainted teacher Rabbi Soloveitchik, zt"l, I can feel his approbation. And if I hit a clunker, I can almost hear his vaunted temper expressing itself.

The classic example of this kind of dialogue is the biblical story of Joseph's captivity in Egypt. The midrash (homiletical story of rabbinic origin) tells us that Joseph, when approached for immoral purposes by Potiphar's wife, was actually tempted. However, at that moment Joseph was visited by an image of his father, Jacob (who was not technically dead at that point, but, given Joseph's situation, might as well have been), and no longer responded to the woman's advances. The message of this story is that conversations with those absent from our life keep us honest and on track, sometimes in the face of enormous communal or societal pressure. Many will recognize the experience of finding oneself in an ethical dilemma and not being sure what to do. Inside each of us there speaks a small voice, part of which is a father, a mother, or some other loved one. If we listen to that voice, we get a sense of how to deal with the situation. Thus our conversations with the dead not only guide us, but also reconcile us with the moral decisions we make in an effort to do right.

What happens, however, in those situations where we cannot get approbation for what we do? What happens if we find ourselves truly at odds with the dead in our communications? For the answer we must turn to one of the most tragic of all biblical stories, as told in 1 Samuel 28:5–6. It was the night before King Saul's final battle, and Saul was afraid.

And when Saul saw the camp of the Philistines, he was afraid, and his heart greatly trembled. And when Saul inquired of the Lord, the Lord answered him not, neither by dreams, nor by Urim [the priestly breastplate sometimes used for communication with God], nor by prophets.

Abandoned by God, Saul took a forbidden step. He summoned a necromancer, a seeker of the dead—an anathema to Torah and to Saul throughout his life—to raise the prophet Samuel from the dead and ask him what to do.

Saul and Samuel, toward the end of the latter's life, had experienced a terrible falling-out over Saul's noncompliance with God's word, i.e., Saul's failure to completely eradicate Amalek, the Jews' worst enemy, as he had been commanded. This created a permanent rift between these two longtime friends and cost Saul his kingdom. Yet Saul, desperately seeking guidance, sought out his old friend beyond the grave.

Unfortunately for Saul, when Samuel rose from the ground he was in no mood for reconciliation. Saul pleaded (1 Samuel 28:15), "I am in great distress, for the Philistines make war against me, and God has departed from me, and answers me no more, neither by prophets, nor by dreams." But Samuel's response offered neither help nor hope.

Why then do you ask of me, seeing the Lord has departed from you, and has become your enemy? And the Lord has done for Himself, as He spoke by me; for the Lord has torn the kingdom from your hand, and given it to your neighbor, to David. Because you would not obey the voice of the Lord, nor execute His fierce anger upon Amalek, therefore has the Lord done this thing to you this day. And the Lord will also deliver Israel with you into the hand of the Philistines; and tomorrow shall you and your sons be with me; the Lord also shall deliver the camp of Israel into the hand of the Philistines (1 Samuel 28:16–19).

What a devastating statement! What a terrible conversation to have with a former friend! Yet despite the harsh words, there actually is some small measure of comfort in what Samuel says. His penultimate words are "Tomorrow shall you and your sons be with me." Even when we are at odds with those in our past and when there is, sadly, no explicit verbal reconciliation, there is at least a sense that we will come to share a final reconciliation. After all, we do ultimately find ourselves in the same place.

Yizkor is the ritual embodiment of our conversations with the dead. Our conversations with the dead provide us with guidance, help us determine where we have been right and where we have been wrong, and reconcile us with our past. There can certainly be no more fitting and appropriate day for these conversations than Yom Kippur, and the recitation of Yizkor probably originated here before also being instituted on the last days of Pesah, Sukkot, and Shavuot.

Sometimes our conversations with the dead are painful, sad and tragic. At other times, they are nostalgic and even comforting. Ultimately and perhaps unexpectedly, they are a celebration of the human capacity to transcend the limits of this life.

The Talmud tells us that no eye has ever seen the world beyond and then been permitted to come back and report what that world contains. But it is also true that some voices carry across that great divide. With Yizkor and our other conversations with the dead, if we listen, our ears can hear what our eyes may not see.

I Am Older Now:
A Yahrzeit Candle Lit at Home

Harold M. Schulweis

The yahrzeit candle is different,
announcing neither Sabbath nor festival.
No benediction recited
No song sung
No psalm mandated.

Before this unlit candle
without a quorum, I stand
unstruck match in my hand.

It is less distant now,
the remembrance ritual of parents deceased.
I am older now,
closer to their age than before.
I am older now,
their aches in my body
their white hairs beneath my shaved skin
their wrinkles creased into my face.

It is less distant now
this ritual
once made me think of them
Now makes me think of me.

Once it recalled relationships to them
Now it ponders on my children's relationship to me.
Once I wondered what to remember of them
Now I ask what my children remember of me
what smile, what grimace
What stories they will tell their children of me.

It is less distant now.
How would I be remembered
How would I be mourned
Will they come to the synagogue
light a candle
recite the Kaddish?
It is less distant now.
Once yahrzeit was about parents deceased,
Now it is of children alive.
Once it was about a distant past,
Now it is about tomorrow.

After the Year, What?

Arlene Rossen Cardozo

If modern grief counselors and researchers are to be accepted as the sages of our times with regard to current knowledge about the human grieving process, then it should be noted that thousands of hours' and dollars' worth of quantitative and qualitative research studies have not yet brought them to the level of understanding of the Jewish sages of centuries past. In the past couple of decades our modern sages have developed grief support groups and "discovered" anniversary reaction and holiday blues, all of which is old news to Judaism. Judaism has for centuries incorporated these and much more into a six-step coping process which recognizes that, while there are indeed stages of grief, some grief goes on forever. Judaism thus wisely developed—centuries ago—a system whereby new mourners are continually welcomed into a community of those who have mourned and who know firsthand what loss and coping with it are all about.

Judaism's six-step structured approach to the grieving process is without parallel in any other religion. It revolves around and takes place within the world's oldest support group: the minyan (the ten or more Jews required to perform the daily services and to say the Kaddish, a prayer of sanctification which mourners recite at the funeral and continue to say at appointed times throughout their lives). This six-step process provides for those coping with either of two kinds of loss, which I call (1) *ordinary loss* and (2) *extraordinary significant traumatic loss*. Ordinary loss is that of an aged parent or a sibling or a spouse who has lived a long, full life—essentially the loss of a part of one's past. Extraordinary loss above and beyond that includes the significant traumatic losses of one's future—when a parent loses a child; or the loss of one's parent by a young child; or the premature loss of a young sibling; or in some instances the loss of a spouse.

The ordinary loss of an aged parent or aged sibling "integrates" with time—usually a year or two—into a person's daily life, and the mourner is able to "recover," "heal," and go on without continuing deep grief. However, the significant traumatic loss of a child, a parent by a young child, or a young sibling cannot ever fully integrate into the survivor's life, because these kinds of loss forever change the life of the survivor. So it is therefore more appropriate to speak of *coping* with that kind of loss, rather than of recovery or full healing from it.

The minyan provides a six-step structured means for this coping, which begins immediately after the funeral and can continue throughout the life of the survivor.

Step 1: Week 1: Shivah. The custom of sitting shivah—with the mourner(s) at home, visited by extended family and friends and in some communities the whole synagogue minyan—enables the mourner to spend the first week following the funeral in the comfort and safety of the home, with the community essentially coming to him or to her. The minyan takes place in the home, and the mourner need not leave the home even to attend the synagogue. By the time shivah is over, the mourner has usually been visited by all those who knew the person being mourned and all those who know the survivors. Those who were themselves close to the deceased come to mourn with the mourners; others who know the survivors but not the deceased come to express their caring for the survivors.

Step 2: Week 2: Entering the Minyan—the caring community. A week after the funeral, the mourner officially reenters the community by literally stepping outside the home and joining the minyan, to continue saying the Kaddish twice a day as he has done during shivah. Only now he is no longer in the sanctuary of his own home, but rather in a different sanctuary—that of the synagogue. By this time the extended family and friends have stepped back into their own daily lives, which have not been effectively altered, while the mourner joins twice daily (morning and evening) with others who are also mourning or who have mourned losses.

Unlike the community of work and civic responsibilities, where the mourner may receive condolences for a day or two and is then expected to perform as usual, the caring community of the minyan recognizes the reality of continuing grief and offers a place for continued solace. Voluntary membership in the minyan for at least the first year can be extremely helpful to the mourner coping with ordinary loss; it is absolutely critical in the rehabilitation of the mourner felled by significant traumatic loss. First, it offers the chance to bond with other Jews undergoing similar trauma; and second, frequently regardless of how terrible one's own loss, one meets others who are undergoing—or who have survived—similar or worse losses. So even in one's own time of greatest sorrow and need to receive compassion, one finds the means also to feel compassion for, and give solace to, others.

Shortly after our precious daughter, Rachel, died three years ago at age twenty-five, my husband, Dick, and I became part of the Beth David minyan in Miami. Our first day there, Philip, who had just arrived as a visitor to the congregation, came up to us after the service. "Welcome to the New World," he said, and then asked whether we had lost a child. "How can you tell?" I asked, wondering if it was as clearly written all over us as I felt it must be. "I just had a feeling," he replied. "We lost our daughter Ellen when she was six, many years ago." As the tears streamed down his face, he told us he was now saying Kaddish for his wife, who had died the preceding month.

Within the first week at Beth David we met Vicki and Bruce, who were saying Kaddish for her nineteen-year-old son, recently killed in a car accident. Bruce, whose mother died when he was eight, led the three of us bereaved parents through those darkest of early days by keeping us continually in motion. While we have other friends from before Rachel's death who are still close, we share a continuing—and deeper—bond with Vicki and Bruce because we four share a kind of loss that goes beyond the experience and understanding of most human beings.

Our daughter Miriam said Kaddish for her beloved younger sister at a synagogue in New York, where she met two young women who were saying Kaddish for their respective fathers. They welcomed Miriam into the fold the day she arrived, and fortunately so. Miriam had returned to New York a week after shivah, still in shock and in profound sorrow, to friends who had no similar experience and to high-pressure, high-profile work in a Wall Street law firm. She was carried through that first year by the support of the minyan group. It seemed fitting that these two women led the dancing at Miriam's wedding two years later when Miriam married a man she met at the minyan.

Step 3: Shloshim. This is the third marker in the six-step grieving process, but unlike the first (shivah), wherein the mourner begins the mourning process with extended family and friends at home, and unlike the second step of joining the synagogue minyan, this third step is a silent marker. It merely means that the first month of mourning is past. In retrospect, on the face of either ordinary loss or significant traumatic loss, a month is but a drop in the bucket of tears of mourning. But at the moment, a month is a long time. It is the first thirty days without one's loved one; the first thirty days of the rest of one's life without that person; the first thirty days of survival in the face of that loss.

Step 4: Yahrzeit. For just short of one year, a direct mourner—one who has lost either father, mother, brother, sister, son, daughter, or spouse—rises and says the Kaddish every day within the minyan. Thereafter, he says it only at specifically appointed times for the rest of his life. Those are on the yahrzeit—the anniversary of the date of death—and at the Yizkor services. For the survivor is then expected to fully engage with life, yet to remember the departed person at special times.

Those in the minyan recognize that the first year, and every subsequent year, the yahrzeit day is a day of sadness and they give additional support to members observing yahrzeit—a squeeze of the hand, an arm around the shoulder. In some minyans it is customary for the person observing yahrzeit to sponsor breakfast following the morning service, both to mark the day and to thank those in the minyan for being there.

In fact, the wisdom of yahrzeit predates by millennia the docu-
mentation of contemporary grief research that "anniversary reactions" are so common as to be considered usual among those who
have lost a close loved one. The whole season can be lousy; whether
it's budding trees or snowstorms or long sunny days or short cold
ones. Every new leaf or snowflake can be a reminder of the time
when one was last together with one's departed, and then of the
death. Thus, the comfort and solace of the minyan is particularly
appreciated on the yahrzeit date and during the yahrzeit season.

Step 5: Holidays: Yizkor. Modern grief researchers have found that
holidays—supposedly happy times—can be perfectly dreadful for
those who have lost a loved one, even years and years later. Most
of the contemporary research on the "holiday season" involves
Thanksgiving, Christmas, and the secular New Year, because it is
secular research. However, the Jewish sages of old knew that holiday times bring back only too well memories of joyful times spent
with departed loved ones. Thus they built specific days of mourning into the holiday cycle, providing outlets for renewed grief during the Jewish year. On the *shelosh regalim*—the three joyous
festivals of Sukkot, Pesah, and Shavuot—as well as Yom Kippur,
Yizkor (remembrance) services are held. These are times when the
community collectively remembers its departed loved ones and,
unlike the yahrzeit date, when all one's departed loved ones are
remembered within the service.

People who live with significant traumatic loss often find that,
if their rabbis lack experience with this kind of loss, they deliver
Yizkor sermons geared primarily if not wholly toward those who
have suffered ordinary loss. Thus sermons are about the loss of
parents who have lived long, full lives, totally ignoring the many
congregants who live with significant traumatic loss. We can hope
that, as more rabbis become sensitized to the need to address the
loss of loved ones of all ages, this situation will be ameliorated.

Step 6: Minyan Forevermore. One is required to say Kaddish for
eleven months, then observe Yizkor and yahrzeit for the duration
of one's own life. Thus the first five steps of the six-step process

are observed by many who suffer loss. Step 6 in coping with grief, however, recognizes that one who has suffered a loss does not need to leave the minyan after eleven months. He or she can stay forever, coming every morning and evening as during the official mourning period; coming regularly but less frequently; selecting one or several times per week to participate regularly; or coming once in a while. At the Beth David minyan, people select from all of these options. What is unusual is for anyone who has been associated with the minyan to stop coming altogether and never be seen again after the eleven months. The minyan is such a close, wonderfully supportive group of people that almost everyone who has been a part of that fold wants to continue the relationship.

Among the core group of our regular morning minyan members are Fritzi, a natural hostess, who greets friend and stranger alike with great warmth and cheerful conversation; preschoolers Joel and Sharon, who come with their father and alternate turns on Fritzi's lap; Irving, who always has a ready twinkle in the eye and a joke on the lips; Sylvia, who radiates comfort and caring; and her husband, Milton, our ritual director who is there for fourteen services a week, and whose compassionate reaching out to each newly bereaved person is beautiful to experience and to behold. Milton had suffered the loss of a sibling as a youngster and the loss of a limb as an adult; he says little and understands much.

Milton closes each morning service with an invitation to "coffee and Danish in the board room," of which all partake. People gather around the long table and enjoy refreshments for which Al and Hy have long been responsible. Hy, who lost his wife several years ago, comes diligently to morning minyan half an hour early to be sure that the coffee is fresh and hot, and the Danish sliced and artfully arranged. Jimmy, also a widower, is another faithful morning minyanaire. His car trunk is filled with all the latest magazines and newspapers from around the world, a perk of his publishing work. He knows just who loves travel magazines, who his *New Yorker* readers are, who prefers fashion magazines, and who specializes in boating and sports, and brings those favorite periodicals to each and all. Newspapers in at least seven different languages fill the hall table outside the chapel, and we have come to take Jimmy, who keeps us literate, so for granted that when he was gone for Pesah this year it seemed we missed not only his interesting conversation and good humor but also our world perspectives.

Alex, who lost his entire family of origin in the concentration camps, comes to minyan every morning in spite of the fact that, when I asked him on Purim this year, "How can you celebrate this festival of deliverance when for your family and all of East European Jewry there was none?" he said, "This I ask myself all the time. Why not for us?"

For many of us in the minyan there was no deliverance either. Not for Rachel, not for Vicki's Andy, killed by a car at age nineteen, nor for Bob and Mildred's son Steven, killed in an accident at forty. Yet Bruce and Vicki and Bob and Mildred are all synagogue members who rarely attended a daily minyan service until they started coming to say Kaddish. Now they all come regularly to the evening minyan and many mornings as well.

I don't ask others, but for me prayer is not the chief reason for coming to minyan. In fact, frequently I quietly slip a book of essays, proverbs, or poetry between the covers of the prayer book during the service. And yet, for me the service is a calming place of solace. The minyan is a truly caring community and an incomparable support group, because it is comprised of other Jews who have loved and lost, yet who laugh, joke, celebrate holidays, and continue to try to live full lives in which they bring happiness to others through playing the cards they are dealt. The minyan is hope personified.

"Welcome to the New World," Philip said to us at minyan that first night. As a man who had lost both spouse and child, he knows all about this New World. It is a New World—whether it's the loss of a spouse, where the widow or widower is now left to totally restructure the rest of her or his life, to fill twenty-four hours a day, seven days a week, in which there was previously a partner, a dinner companion, a best friend, a movie date, someone to wake and sleep with; or whether it's the loss of a child, where suddenly a couple loses the product of their love, the focus of their lives, their future, and future generations.

The minyan is a tremendous help in easing the way into this

New World in two ways simultaneously. (1) It is a place to begin and end the day, where those around you also know grief, where grieving is understood in ways that those who have not experienced a significant traumatic loss can at best give lip service. Thus when I ask Edith, whose husband, a beloved member of the minyan, died suddenly last year, "Did you have a good Pesah at your daughter's?" it's shorthand for "Did you all make the holiday different enough from before and busy enough so that you geared up and got through?" And when Mildred asks me, "How was your birthday?" it's the same kind of shorthand: "Under the current circumstances, did you manage to get through okay? Was it as bad as last year? Have you found a way to go on with celebrations in a different but yet enjoyable way?" (2) The minyan is a place where every day one is witness to many other people who live with significant traumatic loss yet who live their lives in meaningful ways, ways in which they bring happiness to others—caring ways. And further, it's a place to have fun—to share a joke, a laugh. On a weekend after services, a stranger driving through the Beth David parking lot and seeing Bruce and Vicki and Dick and me deep in conversation, or laughing or all vying to talk at once, would presume that none of us has ever had a care in the world. Such is the way of the minyan.

Diary of a Young Widow: A Work in Progress

Gail Katz

THE EARLY YEARS

Think of the Children

"You must be strong for your children,
You must —"
"There are the children to think of:
Remember the children,

Remember —"
"Think of the children."

They half wince when they see me.
"You should only have *nahas* from the children."
Only? Only? I should only have?
May God not punish me, is that all
There is to hope for? Is that to be my only blessing?
What will restore the well of strength
That I may give to their need?
What about me?
Hey, Stan!
Hey, God!
What about me?

"But all the parents are coming. You'll come to school,
won't you?"
So I sit in the back with women who wave to their sons and
husbands at the front tables of the yeshivah dining room. The
fathers snap pictures as the awards are presented. Stan's
camera is a dead weight in my hand.
A restless baby cries out in the women's section; his mother
stands to take him out. From across the room, the father
runs to the cry. Soothed in his father's arms, the child coos
and nestles as the man returns to his seat.

So that's why a kid has two parents.
When one is tired, the other is there.
   Broken, I run from the room.

Losing the ability to swallow life
I have lost twenty pounds
And my sense of wholeness and safety in the world.
I move cautiously
Waiting for the trap door to spring open
Beneath my feet
Or for the *other* shoe to fall.

"But you cannot live like this.
The children need you."

Shhh . . . there is a secret I cannot tell you.
There isn't enough me to give to them. Shhh . . . I'm all
used up.
 used out
 used.
I'm sorry.
I'm sorry I'm not
Nobler
Better.

I'm sorry Abba is dead
Maybe they came for *me* and he said,
"No! Take me!" and they said, "Okay."
Maybe if they took me he would know
How to take care of everything
And organize
and fix
and mobilize
and remarry
And help you live.

Home

My house is darkness
And I
Have to be the light.
It is hollow.

Visionless

And I must find
The molecules of dreams
to light the lights
and I have no strength

left
to me.
My shoulders sigh
and I plod on.

But my children need light
to live
And I must gather the will
to make
the light
to kindle
to nurture the light
that they may live.

Such, such pain
to light their lights
unrestored
alone.

Once
Once I knew who I was.
Once I was soft
And young
And warm
And knew that God was good
And life was good

And now
Now I am lost
And running
because I can no longer pretend
to stay in a world
I once lived in.

Widowspeak

Yes, dear world, I am married
I am married to a man who died,
I am married to a life that died
Our life
My life as I knew me
Who I was —

Life ahead —
Dead
All.
Each.
We —
I —
me —
Dead.

My ring —
His ring —
Our ring is in the bank vault,
Cool steel keeps it in its place below ground.

But I was his. I have his name to prove it.
And now that he is not
I am not.

Don't you see? You shake your head no,
but can't you see?
I was his
And now that he no longer lives
I am —
Nobody's.
I belong to a memory.
I belong with a memory.
I am a memory.

Then who is this person
who leaves for work daily
shielding the kids from the world?
Who is this woman who stretches and reaches
to make time and life go on?
Through nights —
and homemade soups —
Granola / dried flowers / sightseeing day trips —
taxes —
children frightened of the dark —
carburetors —
gravestones —
not-quite-broken arms / appendicitis
field mice / water bugs —
gland lumps —
insurances that won't renew —
twenty-one undone homeworks —
camp trunks / name tapes —
fever —
school-bus accidents

And they say I should only have *simhahs*.

I remember I opened his closet
Three months after he was gone
And placed my hand on the shoulder
of his herringbone brown tweed suit
and slowly embraced the jacket
where his back once used to be —
Fingers moving slowly —
My head pressed to the lapel —
And a moan escaped
From somewhere
Locked deep beneath the pose
of
sanity.

And I stood inhaling his scent
A light warm softness that was him.
Solid.
There with me.
There for me
Of me.
And my hand stroked the empty shoulder
slowly as I wept
until I sank
to the floor
Drained
Lost.

And later
when the wave of sorrow
passed
once again into silence,
I thought of at least three
things I should be doing.
Right away. Right away,
Up, up and away.

Still at midnight
I look through the *Times*.
How often I have fallen asleep
in this chair.
Awake
so tired —
but sitting downstairs
still
unable
to get myself
to
go
up
to my room.

Sleeping alone is impossible
After the years of peace
as one.

He is dead.
Very.
I have stopped
touching
the spot where my ring once was
You know, with my thumb?
Only sometimes
I reach for
what was.

What was
Is not.
Yet I am quite married.
I am married to a life that died.

THE MIDDLE YEARS

Best Foot Forward: The Widow Dates

What shall I wear
That will help him decide
   to call back?
How can I capture his eye
That he will skim the list of one hundred names
   given him
Till he spots mine.
   Me!
Oh, me!
I'm over here!
   Yoo hoo!
I'm different from the others
Choose me

Oh, me
Choose
Oh, choose
   me.

And don't wear those awful shoes
so frumpy, ich —
Buy a boot, for heaven's sake.
And no skirt and blouse
That's date dress for kids
Not
Adults
And his wife was
An adult,
dear,
So it's an adult he's looking for.
A dress or a suit. That's it. A dress
   or a suit.

But—he may come in a sweater, you know.
   It's happened that way before.
No.
You don't know, do you? How could
   you know?
No.
Sooo
A skirt, blouse, and blazer
will juggle me through.
And it should be a blouse
that drapes beautifully.
And I guess I'd better
have my nails done.
Simply.
Colorless
but shining
would be best, yes?

And the right bag.
I'll need a new coat—mine is dead.
It's from another life
That no longer is who I am.
A new coat, yes.
Young —
with the times . . .
Pretend.

Pretend this first date
Is simply to have
A lovely evening
Yes.
That this best behavior careful smiling
neat, supportive, quiet, genteel woman
Is really
me.

Putting my best foot forward
Trying not to let it end up in my mouth.

AND LAST YEAR

Phoenix

Moving
Shaking her feet slowly
    in disbelief
The Phoenix stretched
Her long legs.
First one
Then the other
Shaking off the ashes of yesterday.

Strange, she thought,
Hm —

I would have sworn
   life was over —

I remember
I wanted to jump into the flames
   of yesterday's end
That I
   would
   be
   no
   more. That I would ache
   no more.
That I might die
if not instead of
   then
At least
   with
yesterday.

But —
but
I am
here.

Changed
yes, surely changed
But
yes,
yes
I am here.

She leaned back
and reached out
her neck
Her face
up

beyond the
   ruin.
The sun shone
   above her.
The soft wind
stroked her cheek
   calling her soul,
"Arise!"

Lifting her wings so slowly
she inhaled,
Then sighed —
Then breathed in again
Reaching higher
and higher
To embrace the day.

Oh, dear God —
   there *is* day!
There is *still*
   beautiful new day
beyond here —
Oh, look at the day!

A small movement in the
   clouds above
Held her a moment.
Drawn, she watched an arrow pierce
   the open space.

The geese followed the leader.

Did you know that geese
Mate for life?
For life.

But . . .
Well, but he can lead.
And take care of
And do things well —

But is that enough for a goose?
Silly goose.
It needn't be so —
Silly goose. If you let it be so
   it will be so.

And the Phoenix
stood
And looked at the ashes
   of yesterday.
And kissed them sadly
   with her soul

And,
   turning her face to
      the sun
Arose
   took flight
      to join
         tomorrow.

In Many Houses

Author Unknown

In many houses
all at once
I see my mother and father
and they are young
as they walk in.

Why should my
tears come,
to see them laughing?

That they cannot
see me
is of no matter:

I was once
their dream:
now
they are mine.

Name

Nessa Rapoport

The baby bears an old name, of one who lived for almost a hundred
years. That one is gone; this one will grow, nourished by sepia
photographs and books, hungry to partake of what was treasured
by her namesake. In the mysterious chemistry of love, the child
takes on the attributes of the one who's gone, and bestows upon
the rest of us an arduous happiness.

PART TWO

Questions

Chapter Eight

Is Euthanasia Permitted?

There is no more agonizing question being debated nowadays than that of euthanasia. Pick a side, and I can give you arguments for the other side. On the one hand, is it really life that we are preserving when we keep people on respirators or other complex machinery indefinitely? Does the family or society have the economic and spiritual resources with which to prolong the process of dying when the possibility of any meaningful recovery no longer exists? Is it a favor to the person to draw out the dying this way? But on the other hand, is it not a slippery slope that we step upon when we change the law to permit euthanasia? If we can do it for the terminally ill, then why not for the weak and the feeble and the infirm and the old? And if we can do it for them, why not for those who are no longer productive? Once we start believing that there is such a thing as a "right to die," how will we prevent it from becoming a "duty to die"?

Feelings run very high on both sides of this issue. People think that theirs is the only legitimate moral and spiritual position. I confess that I feel the partial truth of both positions, and I think that the Jewish tradition does too. The tradition stubbornly insists that murder is the ultimate sin, that our bodies do not belong to us and that therefore we have no right to end life—not ours, not anyone else's. But the same tradition distinguishes between acts of commission and acts of omission. And the same tradition contains the story of Rabbi Yehudah's handmaiden, who prayed for his release from suffering at the same time that the sages were praying for his life. The tradition does not judge her wrong.

We understand that the great truths in this world are very often not either-ors but both-ands. And so, out of respect for the partial truth that exists on each side of this difficult issue, we present here a number of different views.

Laws Concerning One in a Dying Condition

A dying man is considered the same as a living man in every respect. He may . . . inherit property, and he may bequeath property. If a limb is severed from his body, it is regarded as a limb severed from a living person, and if flesh, as flesh from a living person. . . .

He may not be stirred, nor may he be washed, and he should not be laid upon sand or salt, until the moment he dies.

His eyes may not be closed. Whosoever touches him or stirs him sheds blood.

Rabbi Meir used to compare a dying man to a flickering lamp: the moment one touches it he puts it out. So, too, whoever closes the eyes of a dying man is accounted as though he has snuffed out his life.

—Tractate *Mourning* I: 1, 3, 4

However, if there is something that causes a delay in the departure of the soul, such as clattering noise near the patient, as if someone is pounding wood, or if there is salt on his tongue, and these delay the soul's leaving the body, then it is permitted to remove the hindrances, because there is no direct act involved but simply the removal of an obstacle that prevents death.

—Shulhan Arakh, Yoreh Deah 339:1

Rabbi Yehudah's Handmaiden

On the day that Rabbi Yehudah was dying, the rabbis decreed a public fast and offered prayers for heavenly mercy [so that he would not die]. . . . Rabbi Yehudah's handmaiden ascended to the roof and prayed: "The immortals [the angels] desire him [to join them] and the mortals desire him [to remain with them]; may it be the will [of God] that the mortals may overpower the immortals [i.e., that he would not die]." When, however, she saw how often he resorted to the privy, painfully removing and replacing his tefillin [in terrible agony], she prayed: "May it be the will [of God] that the immortals may overpower the mortals." The rabbis meanwhile continued their prayers for heavenly mercy. She took a jar and threw it down from the roof to the ground. [For a moment] they stopped praying, and the soul of Rabbi Yehudah departed.

—The Talmud

The Maggid Rediscovers Music

The "Yehudi," the tzaddik of Pzhysha, once saw with the eyes of his mind that the maggid of Koznitz, who had fallen ill, was now in danger of dying. Immediately he told two of his faithful men who were excellent singers and players to go to Koznitz and gladden Rabbi Israel's heart with music. The two set out at once, reached the maggid's house on Friday, and were told to welcome in the Sabbath with their singing and playing. When the sounds entered the room where Rabbi Israel lay, he listened intently and his face brightened. Gradually, his breath grew even and his forehead cool, and his hands stopped twitching and lay quietly on the coverlet. When the music ended he looked up as though he had just awakened and said: "The Yehudi saw that I had passed through all the worlds. The only world in which I was not, was the world of melody. So he sent two messengers to lead me back through that world."

—A Hasidic Tale, from *Tales of the Hasidim* by Martin Buber

I Want a Choice

Joseph Levine

My wife died of colon cancer, in my arms, on June 1st of this year. That's not the way it was supposed to work out in our lives. I was the one who had the heart attack eight years ago. I was supposed to go first. We had an unspoken agreement that she would see me out and then go on with her life. The statistics for women in general and the genetic line she came from (both parents died in their middle to late nineties) were on her side, we thought.

Elizabeth "beat the odds" by living eighteen months after diagnosis (they told me after she was gone). We were not strangers to death. Both of my wife's parents died after long illnesses in the past two years. I am a rabbi who works as a hospital chaplain at one of the greatest medical-research centers in the world. Over the years we had come to know and love many people who struggled with, and died of, cancer, AIDS, Alzheimer's, and heart disease—not as statistics, but as people who ate in our home.

Together we had come to the conclusion that we would not let nature "take its course" when it came to our dying. Those who speak glibly of the "holy final moments" generally have not experienced prolonged, intense chemotherapy or repeated major surgery.

Perhaps if I share with you this story I wrote seven years ago about a significant moment in our lives, you will get a feeling for the person who made the decision to choose how and when she would die.

During the forty years we had been together, we had struggled and achieved, raised four sons, seen two marry, had one grandchild and another on the way, and were three-quarters of the way through our last mortgage. The kids were all gone—the almost-quiet years. It was a lazy Sunday morning. We were reading in the living room, Bach's Toccata and Fugue in the background.

She was a nest-builder *par excellence*, so it came as no surprise to me when, on the latest of the hundreds of lists she has compiled over the years of "things to do," she casually announced that it was time "to make arrangements—so that the kids won't have that burden." I put the paper down on my outstretched legs. Her tone of voice reminded me of another occasion years ago when something similar had come up on the list. Now, what was it? Something official, a legal thing, papers to be signed, witnesses. I scratched my head. No, wait, that was the second time. The first was earlier, when the kids were small. Same tone, similar suggestion. I knew that I had complied then as I would now. Not that I would have thought of it myself in the first place—whatever it was.

Then I remembered that first time—years before, when we were still in our twenties, long before her hysterectomy and my heart attack, when her parents still referred to us as "the children." She had stated it simply: "What if something happens to us, like an auto accident, and we are both killed? Who will raise the boys? It's not fair to place the burden on our parents. Who can we ask?"

I remembered wondering where she got the idea. After all, I was the one who came out of the New York blue-collar tenements and was supposed to be the expert on life's dangers. She was, by contrast, a serene Cincinnatian, a child of gentle academics. I had often teased her about her Walt Disney perfect-white-picket-fence upbringing. What did she know about danger? By personal experience, nothing. By maternal instinct, a hell of a lot. So we sat down with our little address book that listed family and friends spread all over the country and, after much discussion, picked a name and made arrangements.

That was the first time. The second was ten years ago. There was the lawyer, the notary, the witnesses, "The Will," all done the way it should be, fair and square to all concerned, "so the boys will know where they stand." So what's left, I wondered? I roused myself from my momentary reveries in time to refocus on her quiet voice. She was saying, "If they want to put up a stone, that's up to the boys, but at least they won't have to run around to find a place." I smiled—she would be considerate until the end, and beyond. Thus, we began the process of our negotiations.

It was always the same: she raised the issue, as many times as it was necessary to get and keep my attention. I would procrastinate, delay, make manifold suggestions, and finally commission her to "look further into the situation." That was the process that led to our standing together on this hot August Sunday morning in the deserted cemetery. She led me to the least expensive section and reported what the salesman had told her the week before. She repeated her concern about not burdening "the boys" (now young men well launched in their lives).

As she was earnestly speaking I experienced a flashback to when we had first met. She was eighteen, a college freshman; I, a pipe-smoking, Dostoevsky-reading man of the world at twenty. Where had the years gone? I focused on her face, long gone; the black bangs and ponytail replaced by salt-and-pepper ringlets of a perm she was still trying to adjust to. My Brooklyn pompadour had long since gone to spare thatch and white beard. Yes, her face had changed, but the heart—that wonderful, trusting, loving, caring, giving heart—was still the same. Only the sudden appearance of mourners making pilgrimages to their separate patches of hallowed ground kept me from sweeping her into my arms and kissing her and thanking her, and begging her forgiveness for the times I had hurt her. She was, I realized (as I had always known she would), bringing me safely home into our final harbor.

Holding hands, we went into the office and made the arrangements. And this time it was her turn to be surprised, because I insisted that we look at some of the more expensive plots. "I want you to have a nice view of the trees on the hill."

On our way out of the cemetery office, we walked by a display of sample tombstones. One featured intertwined ivy leaves with the inscription TOGETHER ALWAYS. We smiled and repeated our decision that plaques would be the responsibility of "the boys." But down deep, I knew that those corny words were true.

Clearly, she was a lady who was considerate of others and herself. Our world crashed, the week after her father's death. The emotional roller coaster of going from "well" to "terminal" took two weeks. It was not surprising to me to hear this gentle, sweet, thoughtful creature say, "I want to be able to end it when I choose." She promptly joined the Hemlock Society. I told her I would respect her wishes and do whatever was needed to be done (including going to jail, although I don't think I said it to her at the time).

We did not give up hope. She entered several research protocols, carefully weighing each time the cost/benefit, hope/disappointment possibilities.

Toward the end, she said to me, "I don't have what I need to do it." So we made a list of the medications that filled our medicine chest. I had a short conversation with a friend who checked off two items on my list. When I came home, I said, "We have it." She smiled with relief and gratitude. But, as the cynical Yiddish proverb has it, "Man plans and God laughs." Her colon, lungs, and liver had been repeatedly scanned, but it was a brain tumor, which had gone undetected, that took her life. But it was at home, in my arms, with her sons holding her hands. She died as she had lived, in love and dignity.

So as I sit here writing these words with tears rolling down my cheeks, it is for the loss of my beautiful mate, the mother of my children, and grandmother. But without bitter memories of mean-ingless suffering.

I know she would want me to say, "Give those you love the chance to choose what they want and then support them in death, as you would in life."

Final Entrance

Sharon S. Epstein

People in physical and mental pain deserve our support and help, but not in helping them to die. Such assistance reduces our under-standing of humans, robbing them of a third dimension: the spiri-tual dimension, the one in which we form a meaning to life, the one that makes us human.

In fact, many elderly do not wish to go raging into the night; they wish to live, in part, because it is their very dying process that provides a new dimension to the meaning of their own life and the lives of their families. As the *New York Times* noted, dying patients in Holland in their seventies and eighties are far less likely to ask to commit suicide.

This desire to live does not surprise me, since from my experi-ence many of these people have found value and meaning to life and cling to it as long as possible. One recent experience exemplified the importance of using even death as part of our spiritual search for meaning.

THE FULFILLMENT OF FAREWELLS

About nine months ago, my eighty-year-old mother-in-law died of a cancer which had been in remission fourteen years. She cherished the births and some of the growing years of her four grandchildren. She was aware of her impending death, and she prepared for it by sorting through her papers and talking with family in a non-emotional way, rehashing past experiences.

She told us she didn't want her grandchildren to visit her. Although she didn't say it, we could only assume she felt strongly that she didn't want them to remember their grandmother as she was now. We sympathized with her and were upset. But her dying process did something else for all of us. It expanded our understanding of the preciousness of life and in a sense made us more appreciative of what she gave us and what we could give her. When we brought the grandchildren to see her for a few minutes anyway, she wasn't angry. She became stronger as she reached out to them, caressed them, and smiled. She was getting a reinforcement of her meaning in life by seeing that we cared even at the end. Yet, had we listened to her adamant statement that she didn't want visitors, and had we done something to hasten her death (and alleviate our own pain in seeing her dying), she wouldn't have known how very much meaning she had to us as a mother and grandmother.

I believe that a person who seems not to have the spirit to live can be helped by a caring person to find a focus on life that would make the dying process a more meaningful experience. Euthanasia or aid for the patient in dying is the way out that says, "I give up. I can't get anything more." It's dying in despair without knowing how much purpose and meaning life has throughout its course.

MEANING TRANSFORMS TIME

My views are based on the work of Dr. Viktor Frankl and his practice of logotherapy. In his book *Man's Search for Meaning* he stresses that every person (irrespective of financial, physical, and psychological state) potentially has tasks to perform that will give meaning to life. If family and friends could take a step beyond their own pain and grief, they could perhaps help the dying person focus on some meaning in the current situation beyond pain and despair.

Frankl lived in a seemingly hopeless situation in several concentration camps. He could have said: "I can't stand the horror of these conditions. Let me behave in such a way that the Nazis will end my life." He'd have given up. Instead, the pain strengthened him. He thought about his life in the future. If he could survive, he had a book to write and family to be with if they also survived. Everyone has such a mission to find a purpose and meaning in life.

My mother-in-law's death taught me more about the importance of life. My own acute pain in seeing her body wasting away in pain each day did several things to strengthen the spirituality in my life. I regret I can't thank her directly, but I can thank her through my own life tasks.

Her dying process helped me deal with an emotional fear of death that had been pent up inside me for nearly thirty years. When I was fourteen years old, my own father died from a stroke which put him in a coma for several weeks prior. From age eight on, I had grown up always knowing that his heart condition was serious, always in fear that any day death would come to him, always afraid of that death. Emotionally, as a child and as an adolescent I wanted to run away from that sickness and impending death.

As my mother-in-law lay dying, however, something drew me there to be with her. I still had mixed feelings about death, yet I knew that by being with this lady, who had lived a full life, I could do something important for her by letting her know I cared. She helped me understand death as a natural part of life. As an adolescent I was too scared and inexperienced in life to mourn my father's death emotionally, but now my mother-in-law's dying process allowed me to finally mourn his death.

WHAT I LEARN FROM MY ROUNDS

I also discovered my mission in life through the active participation in the dying process. One month after the death, I began doing volunteer work at the Stony Brook University Hospital in the ALC (alternate level of care) program. Here I visit patients in long-term care who are usually waiting to be placed in a nursing home. Some may die in the hospital before they even get to a nursing home. Most are elderly.

When I visit elderly patients who tell me that life might as well be over for them because they are useless and a burden to family, I listen sympathetically, patiently, and eagerly to their stories of the past. Maybe they just need to know someone wants to listen to them. Maybe they are tired of being lonely. If they still insist that they feel useless now, I stress how I get so much from them by learning about a past culture through their stories and try to help them see their value at this point in their life in educating others firsthand about a lost past and a lost culture. I thank them for this opportunity and really mean it. (I can't even describe the inner spiritual warmth I get from them. They teach me to appreciate life and people.) I hope this is one way for them to find some meaning and purpose to life in the declining days and to die in peace, not in the despair produced when one gives up.

One man in his nineties is confined to bed, unable to move, breathing with a respirator. I can't carry on long conversations with him because it is hard to read his lips. Yet I feel as if I know him and continue to learn more about him with each visit. He is alert and content when he talks proudly about his eighty-year-old wife and his three children and their accomplishments. His pride in his family makes him smile in spite of the objective circumstances of his situation. One son ran for a political office this election day, for example. The father was so proud of this that he told me with an enormous grin on his face that he had voted by absentee ballot in the election.

Each day of life is one more chance at a final entrance into life's meaning.

Long-Term Dignity

Yaffe Ganz

During the last few months of her life, my mother, *a"h,* suffered. Even when she was not conscious, I think she suffered still. Surely the people around her suffered, both for and with her.

Yet every moment we had was precious. Each hour meant another smile, another squeeze of a hand, another bit of love. I cried for her suffering, but I was grateful for the moments—for myself, for my sister, and for my children who were with her, loving and helping, until the last few particularly difficult days.

Even in the midst of her suffering and pain and eventual withdrawal from the world, there was an affirmation of life and love and continuity. And when it all came to an end, she returned her soul to her creator in a state of dignity, despite her grievous physical condition.

Hers was a private ending, but not a final one. She was part of a long and holy chain that began with Avraham and Sarah and continues through her great-grandchildren and, *b'ezras Hashem,* beyond them. Her suffering and death were part of the great, unending drama of Jewish life. And when her granddaughter, who was then four, asked if Bubby was ever coming back, I was able to answer, "Yes. Someday. I don't know when, but someday she will be back." Amidst all of the pain, there was Jewish comfort.

The story of a different death comes to mind. While waiting in a doctor's office, I was leafing through a psychology magazine when I saw it. It was about an old man from Appalachia who was becoming senile. He had been an independent, self-sufficient fellow for his entire life and now, in his more lucid moments, he was appalled at his own behavior. He could no longer control what he said or did. He was turning into a bother, a fool, even a danger. He decided to die.

For two months he starved himself, drinking only water. His family agreed not to interfere. They had decided to "allow him to die in dignity." His grandson, a college student, returned to record the process, taking photographs and writing up meticulous daily reports. When the old man went into a coma, the family doctor suggested putting him in the hospital and feeding him intravenously. The family decided that this life-prolonging treatment would run counter to the grandfather's expressed will. They wanted to "honor" his decision to die. The grandson's report and photographs were later published in the respectable, accredited, academic magazine of psychology I was holding.

Nu, I reasoned, fools! This was not a Jewish decision, but then again, these were not Jewish people. I have my own problems to worry about.

But the thing kept nudging me. I couldn't imagine anyone I know acquiescing in such an act. No matter how I rearranged the drama in my mind, the people I knew would have been at that grandfather night and day to get some nourishing chicken soup into him. By hook or by crook, they would have fed that stubborn, frightened old man. They would have tried to show him that they wanted him to stay around, that they loved him as he was, that he was not a "bother."

But it was the grandson who really upset me. To fly home for the sole purpose of recording your grandfather's starvation as an interesting "experiment" in human behavior?? To sit there for weeks at a time and never once attempt to change his mind, to convince him how needed and important he was, how he was breaking your heart, to break *him* down and force-feed him, if necessary? What kind of grandson was this? What kind of subhuman, detached, scientific, unloving human being was he? And even assuming that human beings like this do exist here and there, how could a respectable, civilized, academic magazine agree to publish the story and the pictures (which did not add to the old man's dignity in the slightest)? How could a culture that could sit back and coolly watch this suicide claim any cultural or moral superiority over ancient Sparta, which left weak babies out to die? Was this grandson (and his parents and community) watching human refuse or a human being? The entire episode was highly disturbing.

Our world is all agog over the concept of dying with dignity, but death is hard to dignify. At best, it's a sorrowful business; at worst, it's a mess. Only if one lives with dignity is dignity conferred on one's death as well. Nachum Ish Gamzo, a rabbinic sage, lived with dignity. He lived without arms or legs and, as one of the ten martyrs, he died a ghastly death. But it was all done with dignity. The divine image shone through wherever he went. The living skeletons in the Nazi camps who walked to their deaths with the words of Shema Yisrael on their lips died in dignity too.

But a society that disseminates the message that the sick and elderly are no longer "productive" allows neither its healthy nor its sick citizens to live or die in dignity. It tells them that they themselves have no intrinsic value. There is value to their lives only so long as they are "useful." As soon as they cost more than they produce, they are worth nothing at all; it's better for everyone concerned if they are allowed to "die in dignity."

Dignity begins at one end of the spectrum of life and ends at the other. If an unwanted, unborn baby is disposable, then a sick or elderly person is disposable too. And since we're fast reaching a society of exchangeable parts, where human organs can be reused and human beings refitted, why shouldn't younger, stronger, smarter, richer human beings be given life and health at the expense of those who are obviously not "worth much" anyway? They tell us this is being "humane."

I doubt it. *Brave New World,* that shocking piece of science fiction, seems less like fiction lately. A little more genetic engineering and man will begin to think he's God. It's a scary thing to watch. And like it or not, it affects us. Maybe that's why that Appalachian grandson gave me such a bad case of the creeps.

In all fairness, I suppose he had his own "creeps" to deal with. There is, you see, no way man can live happily-ever-after and escape the darker side of life. The joys, the successes, the accomplishments, all come with a built-in catch. Something can always go wrong (and often does). Life itself is the ultimate imperfection—it always ends in death. We can put off thinking about it, but it won't go away (death seems terribly theoretical to the young). And when you are finally forced to confront it, in yourself or in someone you love, its finality can be devastating.

Even less dramatic daily "deaths" are difficult to cope with. Sickness, heartbreak, failure, divorce, and other disappointments and disasters wait for us at every street corner. I once tried explaining to a young mother that no matter how carefully she planned even the immediate future, she had to take the unexpected into account. The warning registered in her brain, but not in her heart. Who can contemplate the possibility of bankruptcy, cancerous growths, heart failure? Who wants to think of even minor calamities—a child with diarrhea and raging fever, or breaking an arm on the way to Aunty Shifra's wedding?

A nonreligious-on-principle friend once told me, "You religious people have it so easy. Everything is all set up for you. You're told exactly what to do, what to think, how to act. No matter what happens, you think it comes straight from God. You have nothing to worry about."

I tried to explain that there was a slight gap between our "instructions" and our performance and that religious people struggled to understand and accept and find meaning in life, just as she did. But there was something to what she said. We *do* have "instructions"; all we have to do is internalize them, not only in our brain, but in our heart. It's easy for me to look at someone else's troubles and say, "It's a *kapparah,*" an atonement. But if the troubles come *my* way, God forbid, my first reaction is to holler!

Sometimes, I do just that. God is big enough to understand exactly how small I am and how large my problems loom—to me. And so I protest vociferously, and then I cry, and then I whimper, and then I come to the heart of the matter—I pray, and ask, and beg, knowing that this is the only court of appeal I have. And somewhere in this process, if our hearts are open and our intentions pure, a transformation occurs. The protest becomes a prayer and the prayer bestows upon us that ephemeral quality our society calls "dignity." Why? Because prayer implies the existence of God, and the existence of God implies a redemptive reason for our suffering and death.

Isn't it amazing that with a philosophy like that, the Jews, of all the people in the world, are the least reconciled to human suffering? That although they have suffered more than most peoples, they are not inured to suffering? That they are surely the most merciful of all peoples? Mercy is, after all, one of the hallmarks of the children of Avraham.

Belief, acceptance of God's law, the inviolability of life, mercy—these are the ingredients of dignity. I guess they don't always hear about them in Appalachia, or in the psychology magazines.

On Choosing the Hour of Our Death

Yoel H. Kahn

Unetaneh tokef kedushat ha-yom . . .

We acknowledge that this day is utterly holy, that it is awesome and sacred. . . . On Rosh Hashanah it is written, and on Yom Kippur it is sealed: How many will pass away, and how many will be born; who will live and will die; whose life cut short, and whose life lived full. . . .

Unetaneh tokef, attributed to Rabbi Amnon of Mainz on the occasion of his martyrdom in the tenth century, is key to the traditional imagery of the High Holy Day season. While we wrestle year after year with its subtleties and possible interpretations, this powerful prayer boldly asserts a fundamental Jewish orientation toward life and death: the hour of our birth and the hour of our death are in the hands of God; everything in between is in our human hands.

The author of the *Unetaneh tokef* saw in every moment of human history the hand of God, and certainly so the time of death: *who by water and who by fire; who by thirst and who by famine; who by war and who by wild beasts.*

If this text were being composed for contemporary use, we would necessarily add:

who by injection, and who by withdrawal of medication;
who by morphine, and who by barbiturates;

who by subtle acts of omission, and who by deliberation;

who alone, and who assisted by friends, family, or health-care providers.

Increasingly, the time and circumstances of death are no longer entrusted either to chance or to God; unlike ever before, people are planning, preparing, and controlling the circumstances of their death. Dr. Jack Kevorkian of Michigan has assisted more than a dozen people in ending their own life; with much less publicity, many doctors and family members have done the same. In California and Washington, ballot initiatives to legalize physician-assisted suicide were defeated recently. Similar initiatives are expected to appear again on the California ballot and in other states soon.

As liberal Jews, we place great emphasis on seeking guidance about contemporary issues from the teachings of the Jewish tradition. Yet there are often enormous chasms between the fundamental premises of the teachings of our tradition and the philosophical ideas and values underlying much of our contemporary thinking. The attempt to apply Jewish teaching about suicide to the issue of planning to end one's life demonstrates this problem.

SUICIDE IN JEWISH TEACHING

Judaism strongly opposes suicide. Bereshit Rabba teaches that those who take their own life will be called to an accounting before God. Judaism's disapproval is codified in laws that prohibit eulogies, public acts of mourning, and full burial rites for a suicide. The objection to taking one's own life is grounded in the belief that only God can make the determination of when a person should die, and that it is the ultimate act of human arrogance to interfere. Further, Israel's God is called *ha-chafetz ba-chaim* and *Elohim chayim* "the God of life who delights in life" and who therefore is always alienated by death. Within the strict boundaries of the Halakhah, however, there is a very large loophole which reflects the tradition's compassion and its understanding of human circumstances. For a self-inflicted death to be truly a suicide, the rabbis ruled, it had to be voluntary and premeditated. When a person took her or his own life under physical or emotional duress, *me-ones,* this was not legally considered suicide and the proper rites were not denied. The law presumed that anyone who was found dead by his or her own hand had done so involuntarily, unless there was overwhelming evidence to the contrary, evidence that was never especially sought out. Liberal Jewish teachers have emphasized this compassionate dimension of the halakhic tradition.

The culture in which we live generally considers most suicide attempts—whether successful or not—as symptoms of compromised mental health or as calls for help. This interpretation resonates with Jewish teaching about a person acting under duress. So long as the suicide can be linked to emotional duress or depression, historical Jewish teaching about suicide can be applied, whether as a source of binding law or personal guidance. The current debate focuses, however, on people who go to great lengths precisely in order to prove that they are not "temporarily out of control" but are instead carrying out a rational and reasonable decision.

"RATIONAL SUICIDE"

More and more often, well before they are in deep depression or unbearable pain, people are actively talking about choosing and controlling the circumstances of their own death. Hemlock Society founder Derek Humphry's 1991 book *Final Exit* became an instant best seller. Faced with the prospect of terminal illness or severe erosion of the quality of life, or having watched the agony of others with the same disease, people are actively declaring their intention to end their own life rather than allow nature—or modern medical intervention—to take its course. This considered decision to end one's own life is often called "rational" suicide, to distinguish it from "emotional" suicide.

Rational suicide is not an idea the Jewish tradition knows. Judaism assumes that no one in his right mind would ever choose suicide and therefore concludes that anyone who does so has to be temporarily out of control. On the other hand, those who are considering rational suicide explicitly affirm that they are actively choosing a reasonable course of action in the face of unbearable circumstances. What today is called rational suicide—the deliberate, premeditated ending of one's own life—is precisely the kind of suicide that the historical Jewish tradition theoretically condemned but practically could not imagine.

It is hard to seek guidance from our tradition when we do not speak the same language. The quality of life, the measure that has become so critical for us, is not a concept that previous generations talked about. How can the wisdom of Judaism guide us if prior generations never imagined circumstances like ours? Perhaps the rubric of "suicide" as understood by the Jewish tradition is the wrong place to look, and we must seek elsewhere in the Jewish tradition for parallels to our present circumstances. I propose that the traditional categories of *kiddush ha-Shem* and *hillul ha-Shem* can help us formulate an appropriate stance on this issue. *Kiddush ha-Shem* is the Jewish tradition's complementary rubric for the secular value called "quality of life."

Under what circumstances do active steps to end a life stop being "suicide" and become transformed into something else? Most liberal Jews, but perhaps not all, would agree that a person who attempts suicide because of circumstances that are potentially transitory or reversible—depression, loss, pain—should be restrained or rescued. And most, but perhaps not all, would agree that a person who can survive only on a respirator should be empowered to turn off the intrusive and artificial breathing machine, even if death is the sure consequence. But in between these extremes, the demand for a death with dignity or an end to suffering poses additional questions: What constitutes death with dignity? Is there a difference between passive steps, such as refusing medication, and active steps, such as taking an overdose of drugs? When is it right not just to welcome death but to seek it out?

JUDAISM DOES CONSIDER THE "QUALITY OF LIFE"

The fundamental Jewish value is that life itself—regardless of its quality—is sacred and good. The Jewish tradition's extreme valuation of life is reflected in the talmudic instruction urging violation of any of the mitzvot if necessary in order to preserve life (with the exception of the circumstances discussed below). People are moved to consider taking their own life when they no longer believe that life is worth living and have no hope of improvement. Judaism teaches that there is always hope and therefore repeatedly opts for life. Some contemporary teachers insist that Judaism's emphasis on life as inherently good is absolute, regardless of any subjective "quality of life." They argue that in the case of a person who needs and seeks to die, all we can do is ask God for a quick death and an end to suffering—but any form of active intervention is forbidden.

Judaism also teaches, however, that there are rare times when the sanctification of life and God—*kiddush ha-Shem*—is best served by giving up one's life. The continuation of life under such circumstances would be a desecration of the name of God, *hillul ha-Shem,* and death is seen as preferable. In a famous passage in Sanhedrin 74a, the rabbis declared that Jews should allow themselves to be killed as acts of *kiddush ha-Shem* rather than violate the prohibitions against idolatry, *gilui arayot* (sexual immorality), or murder. While the Talmud, in fact, insists that only in these exceptional cases does *kiddush ha-Shem* require allowing oneself to be killed rather than violate one of these mitzvot, Jews since the time of Masada have chosen to end their own life as an act of *kiddush ha-Shem*. As their chronicles demonstrate, many of the martyrs of the First Crusade died in the Rhineland in 1096 by their own hand. At our synagogue's Yom Kippur Yizkor service, as in many others, we remember the Holocaust by reading the letter left behind by one of the martyrs of the Beis Ya'akov school in Warsaw, where ninety-six girls and women killed themselves rather than make themselves available to the Nazis. In this case and in many others in our history, Jews opted for a death with dignity; as they understood their Jewish responsibility, *kiddush ha-Shem* required that they give up their life. Although life might continue, they concluded, it would have led to a desecration of life; they sanctified their life by choosing death, and we venerate their memory. While death is usually associated with desecration and life with sanctification—as the Hallel declares, "The dead shall not praise Yah" (Psalm 115:17)—Judaism, paradoxically, has always valued voluntary death as the ultimate sanctification.

Cannot the distinction between *hillul* and *kiddush ha-Shem* guide us today? Although we may not agree with the three situations that the tradition values as appropriate for *kiddush ha-Shem*, perhaps we can borrow Judaism's teaching that there can come a time when, although the continuation of life is possible, there is no prospect of holiness left. Judaism suggests, and Jewish history has taught, that there can be a time when continuing to live would become a desecration of the source of life and when death is therefore preferable.

LISTENING TO THOSE WHO SUFFER

The members of my congregation and their families face this question continually. Once I visited a dying man and his long-time companion in the hospital. The man was very near death, in pain, and barely able to respond. His partner turned to me and said, "I wish he would die and this anguish would be over." I returned the next morning, and the lover said to me with great joy, "He opened his eyes once and called my name and held my hand. I told him how much I loved him." I asked whether it was worth the night of pain for those moments and he said that for himself it was; he could only guess that for his dying companion it was too. In my congregation, a community devastated by the AIDS epidemic, we are all too familiar with dying and death. I have learned to be grateful for the moments of grace when a smile or a word or a look informs us that the essential personality has not yet been lost, even though it may appear to be as disfigured and eroded as the body it shares.

From time to time, I have seen interviews with people who are considering when they might choose to end their own life: some say they could not stand a disfiguring disease, or an inability to work, or the loss of mobility or vision or bladder control, or the cumulative effect of all of these. These are immeasurable losses; they strike at the heart of one's self-esteem, identity, and control over one's own life. Yet while each of these losses diminishes our ability to live as we have always expected to and depended upon, I do not believe that they diminish the essence of our lives.

Sometimes these successive stages of loss can be accepted and integrated. But much harder, as disease progresses, is the sometimes rapid loss of so much that had been so important. Over and over, among the members and extended family of our congregation, no sooner does a person reach an initial peace with one loss when another organ or system fails, another beloved friend dies, dementia advances, and everyone knows full well that death can only be delayed, not avoided. Dying people ask: Why shouldn't I end my life now, in control, before my friends and family have to exhaust themselves and their resources in care and while I can still be remembered as I lived best?

I struggle to reply: Because dying is part of living. Because there are redemptive moments of grace, ones I have witnessed or been told about, which make hanging on worthwhile. There is the fact that many people do find strength to go on, one day or one hour at a time, when earlier they could not imagine living under just these conditions. If there is a time when we can say that a person's life has been emptied of meaning and extending it would be a *hillul ha-shem,* it does not come early in disease or illness. *Kiddush ha-Shem* is an extreme act, reserved for extraordinary occasions, and it cannot be invoked casually.

HILLUL HA-SHEM: "A MOCKERY OF LIFE"

Judaism teaches that each person, regardless of abilities or intellect or health, is created and lives *be-tzelem Elohim*—in the image of God. When a person has died, Judaism demands that we treat the body with great respect, not because the body is the image of God, but because our personhood is lived through our body. Part of the respect we give to the dead body is not to allow it to remain for a long period in the bed where it lived, nor do we eat or worship in its presence. Such actions are considered essential acts of living, and doing them in the presence of the deceased is called a mockery of the dead, insulting them by emphasizing the characteristics of life which they can no longer enjoy. Is it possible that there are times when a person, though still technically alive, cannot participate in the essential activities of life to such an extent that continuing life has become a mockery of life? As Graham Greene asks, "What happens if you drop all the things that make you I?" When one can only be sustained by machine, when pain has no relief, when every organ and system is failing and death can only be held at bay—perhaps under such circumstances, choosing to end life may truly be an act of *kiddush ha-Shem*.

Perhaps. When I first began working on this subject some time ago, I did not think I would reach such a conclusion, and I remain uncomfortable with its implications. Nonetheless, I have supported and stood by friends and congregants who have made these decisions. For some, the knowledge that they have the choice to make such a decision can enable them to continue the struggle to live. Still, I find I must balance my increasingly strong conviction that choosing to end one's life can be an act of holiness with my own loyalty to a more traditional belief that sustaining life for the sake of what has come before, entrusting our lives and our deaths to the hands of heaven, is also *kiddush ha-Shem*.

Death with Dignity vs. Euthanasia

Leon R. Kass

"Call no man happy until he is dead." With these deliberately paradoxical words, the ancient Athenian sage Solon reminds the self-satisfied Croesus of the perils of fortune and the need to see the end of a life before pronouncing on its happiness. Even the richest man on earth has little control over his fate. The unpredictability of human life is an old story; many a once-flourishing life has ended in years of debility, dependence, and disgrace. But today, it seems, the problems of the ends of lives are more acute, a consequence, ironically, of successful—or partly successful—human efforts to do battle with fortune and, in particular, to roll back medically the causes of death. Although many look forward to further triumphs in the war against mortality, others want here and now to exercise greater control over the end of life, by electing death to avoid the burdens of lingering on. The failures resulting from the fight against fate are to be resolved by taking fate still further into our own hands.

This is no joking matter. Nor are the questions it raises academic. They emerge, insistently and urgently, from poignant human situations occurring daily in hospitals and nursing homes as patients and families and physicians are compelled to decide matters of life and death, often in the face only of unattractive, even horrible, alternatives. Shall I allow the doctors to put a feeding tube into my eighty-five-year-old mother, who is unable to swallow as a result of a stroke? Now that it is inserted and she is not recovering, may I have it removed? When would it be right to remove a respirator, forgo renal dialysis, bypass life-saving surgery, or omit giving antibiotics for pneumonia? When in the course of my own progressive dementia will it be right for my children to put me into a home or for me to ask my doctor or my wife or my daughter for a lethal injection? When, if ever, should I as a physician or husband or son accede to—or be forgiven for acceding to—such a request?

These dilemmas can be multiplied indefinitely, and their human significance is hard to capture in words. For one thing, posing them as well-defined problems to be solved abstracts from the full human picture and ignores such matters as the relations between the generations, the meaning of old age, attitudes toward mortality, religious faith, economic resources, and the like. Also, speech does not begin to convey the anguish and heartache felt by those who concretely confront such terrible decisions, nor can it do much to aid and comfort them. Further, generalization necessarily abstracts from the special and concrete features of each human situation. No amount of philosophizing is going to substitute for discernment, compassion, courage, sobriety, tact, thoughtfulness, or prudence—all needed on the spot.

Yet the attitudes, sentiments, and judgments of human agents on the spot are influenced, often unwittingly, by speech and opinion, and by the terms in which we formulate our concerns. Some speech may illuminate, other speech may distort; some terms may be more or less appropriate to the matter at hand. About death and dying, once subjects treated with decorous or superstitious silence, there is today an abundance of talk—not to say indecorous chatter. Moreover, this talk frequently proceeds under the aegis of certain increasingly accepted terminologies, which are, in my view, both questionable in themselves and dangerous in their influence. As a result, we are producing a recipe for disaster: urgent difficulties, great human anguish, and high emotions, stirred up with inadequate thinking. We have no choice but to reflect on our speech and our terminology.

Let me illustrate the power—and the possible mischief—of one notion currently in vogue: the notion of rights. It is now fashionable, in many aspects of public life, to demand what one wants or needs as a matter of rights. How to do the right thing gets translated into a right to get or do your own thing. Thus, roughly two decades ago, faced with the unwelcome fact of excessive medical efforts to forestall death, people asserted and won a right to refuse life-prolonging treatment found to be useless or burdensome. This was, in fact, a reaffirmation of the rights to liberty and the pursuit of happiness, even in the face of imminent death. It enabled dying patients to live as they wished, free of unwelcome intrusions, and to let death come when it would. Today, the demand has been raised: we find people asserting not just a right to refuse burdensome treatment but a positive "right to die," grounded not in objective conditions regarding prognosis or the uselessness of treatment, but in the supremacy of choice itself. In the name of choice, people claim the right to choose to cease to be choosing beings. From such a right to refuse not only treatment but life itself—from a right to become dead—it is then a small step to the right to be *made* dead: from my right to die will follow your duty to assist me in dying, i.e., to become the agent of my death, if I am not able or do not wish to kill myself. And, because of our egalitarian tendencies, it will continue to be an easy step to extend all these rights even to those who are incapable of claiming or exercising them for themselves, with proxies empowered to exercise a right to demand death for the comatose or demented. No one bothers very much about where these putative rights come from or what makes them right, and simple reflection will show that many of them are incoherent. Some people, for example, claim them as part of a so-called right to privacy or autonomy, yet shamelessly insist that my claim to privacy (or autonomy) ought to *oblige* a doctor to *intervene* in my private life for the sake of ending it. Worse, since *all* of our so-called natural or human rights presuppose our self-interested and self-loving *attachment* to our own *life*—the foundational right, after all, is the right of self-*preservation*—attempts to derive therefrom any "right to die" or a right to be made dead are not only groundless but self-contradictory.

Comparable mischief can, of course, be done beginning with the notion of duty. From the acknowledged human duty not to shed innocent blood follows the public duty to protect life against those who would threaten it. This gets extended to a duty to preserve life in the face of disease or other nonhuman dangers to life. This gets extended to a duty to prolong life whenever possible, regardless of the condition of that life or the wishes of its bearer. This gets extended to an unconditional duty never to let death happen, if it is in one's power to do so. This position, sometimes alleged—I think mistakenly—to be entailed by belief in the "sanctity of life," could even make obligatory a search for the conquest of death altogether, through research on aging. Do we have such duties? On what do they rest? And can such a duty to prevent death—or a right to life—be squared with a right to be made dead? Is not this intransigent language of rights and duties unsuitable for finding the best course of action in these terribly ambiguous and weighty matters? We must try to become more thoughtful about the terms we use and the questions we pose.

Now I am painfully aware that talking about talk looks like a cowardly and unfeeling thing to do in the light of the tremendous burdens people face. I have no illusions about the ability of such reflections to resolve our horrible dilemmas. In fact, I have no intention here even to try to resolve them. On the contrary, I want rather to increase the difficulty by showing the dangers in sloppy and simplistic thinking, which promises, falsely, to set matters right. Before we run off to embrace a new solution—for example, active euthanasia—we should try to get clear in our thoughts about what we are doing and why.

Toward this end, I wish to explore here the relation between two other powerful notions, both prominent in the discussions regarding the end of life: death with dignity and the sanctity of life. Both convey elevated, indeed lofty, ideas: what, after all, could be higher than human dignity, unless it were something sacred? As a result, each phrase often functions as a slogan or a rallying cry, though seldom with any regard for its meaning or ground. In the current debates about euthanasia, we are often told that these notions pull in opposite directions. Upholding death with dignity might mean taking actions that would seem to deny the sanctity of life. Conversely, unswervingly upholding the sanctity of life might mean denying to some a dignified death. This implied opposition is, for many of us, very disquieting. The dilemmas themselves are bad enough. Much worse is it to contemplate that human dignity and sanctity might be opposed, and that we may be forced to choose between them.

The confrontation between upholders of death with dignity and upholders of the sanctity of life is, in fact, nothing new. Two decades ago the contest was over termination of treatment and letting die. Today and tomorrow the issue is and will be assisted suicide, mercy killing, so-called active euthanasia. On the extremes of both battles stand the same opponents, many of whom—I think mistakenly—think the issues are the same. Many who now oppose mercy killing or voluntary euthanasia then opposed termination of treatment, thinking it equivalent to killing. Those who today back mercy killing in fact agree: if it is permissible to choose death by letting die, they argue, why not also by active steps to hasten, humanely, the desired death? Failing to distinguish between letting die and making dead (by failing to distinguish between intentions and deeds, causes and results, goals and outcomes), both sides polarize the debate, opposing not only one another but also those in the uncomfortable middle. For them, it is *either* sanctity of life *or* death with dignity: one must choose.

I do not accept this polarization. Instead, I mean to suggest the following: First, human dignity and the sanctity of life are not only compatible, but, if rightly understood, go hand in hand. Second, death with dignity, rightly understood, has largely to do with exercising the humanity that life makes possible, often to the very end, and very little to do with medical procedures or the causes of death. Third, the sanctity and dignity of life are entirely compatible with letting die but not with deliberately killing. Finally, the practice of euthanasia will not promote human dignity, and our rush to embrace it will only accelerate the various tendencies in our society that undermine not only dignified conduct but even decent human relations.

HUMAN DIGNITY

The phrase "death with dignity," whatever it means precisely, certainly implies that there are more or less dignified ways to die. What would a dignified facing of death require? First of all, it would require knowing that one is dying. One cannot attempt to settle accounts, make arrangements, complete projects, keep promises, or say farewell if one does not know the score. Second, it requires that one remain to some degree an agent rather than (just) a patient. One cannot make a good end of one's life if one is buffeted about by forces beyond one's control, if one is denied a decisive share in decisions about medical treatments, institutionalization, and the way to spend one's remaining time. Third, it requires the upkeep—as much as possible—of one's familial, social, and professional relationships and activities. One cannot function as an actor if one has been swept off the stage and been abandoned by the rest of the cast. It would also seem to require some direct, self-conscious confrontation, in the loneliness of one's soul, with the brute fact and meaning of nearing one's end. Even, or especially, as he must be passive to the forces of decay, the dignified human being can preserve and reaffirm his humanity by seeing clearly and without illusion. (It is for this reason, among others, that sudden and unexpected death, however painless, robs a man of the opportunity to have a dignified end.)

But as a dignified human life is not just a lonely project against an inevitable death, but a life whose meaning is entwined in human relationships, we must stress again the importance for a death with dignity—as for a life with dignity—of dignified human intercourse with all those around us. Who we are to ourself is largely insepa-rable from who we are to and for others; thus, our own exercise of dignified humanity will depend crucially on continuing to receive respectful treatment from others. The manner in which we are addressed, what is said to us or in our presence, how our body is tended or our feelings regarded—in all these ways, our dignity in dying can be nourished and sustained. Dying people are all too eas-ily reduced ahead of time to "thinghood" by those who cannot bear to deal with the suffering or disability of those they love. Objecti-fication and detachment are understandable defenses. Yet this withdrawal of contact, affection, and care is probably the greatest single cause of the dehumanization of dying. Death with dignity requires absolutely that the survivors treat the human being at all times as if full God-like-ness remains, up to the very end.

It will, I hope, now be perfectly clear that death with dignity, understood as living dignifiedly in the face of death, is not a matter of pulling plugs or taking poison. To speak this way—and it is unfortunately common to speak this way—is to shrink still further the notion of human dignity and thus heap still greater indignity upon the dying, beyond all the insults of illness and the medicalized bureaucratization of the end of life. If it is really death with dignity we are after, we must think in human and not technical terms. With these thoughts firmly in mind, we can turn back to the mat-ter of euthanasia.

EUTHANASIA: UNDIGNIFIED AND DANGEROUS

Having followed the argument to this point, even a friendly reader might chide me: "Well and good to think humanistically, but tough practical dilemmas arise, precisely about the use of techniques, and they must be addressed. Not everyone is so fortunate as to be able to die at home, in the company of loving family, beyond the long reach of the medical-industrial complex. How should these techni-cal decisions—about respirators and antibiotics and feeding tubes and, yes, even poison—be made, precisely in order to uphold human dignity and the sanctity of life that you say are so intermin-gled?" A fair question; I offer the following outline of an answer.

About treatment for the actually dying, there is in principle no difficulty. In my book *Toward a More Natural Science,* I have argued for the primacy of easing pain and suffering, along with supporting and comforting speech, and, more to the point, the need to draw back from some efforts at prolongation of life that prolong or increase only the patient's pain, discomfort, and suffering. Although I am mindful of the dangers and aware of the impossibility of writing explicit rules for ceasing treatment—hence the need for prudence—considerations of the individual's health, activity, and state of mind must enter into decisions of *whether* and *how vigorously* to treat if the decision is indeed to be for the patient's good. Ceasing treatment and allowing death to occur when (and if) it will can, under some circumstances, be quite compatible with the respect that life itself commands for itself. For life is to be revered not only as manifested in physiological powers, but also as these powers are organized in the form of *a* life, with its beginning, middle, and end. Or, in other words, life can be revered not only in its preservation, but also in the manner in which we allow a given life to reach its terminus.

What about so-called active euthanasia, the direct making dead of someone who is not yet dying or not dying "fast enough"? Let us begin with voluntary euthanasia—the request for assistance in dying. To repeat, the claim here is that the choice for death, because a free act, affirms the dignity of free will against dumb necessity.

Do the people who are actually contemplating euthanasia *for themselves*—as opposed to their proxies who lead the euthanasia movement—generally put their requests in these terms? Or are they not rather looking for a way to end their troubles and pains? One can *sympathize* with such a motive, out of compassion, but can one admire it, out of respect? Is it really *dignified* to seek to escape from troubles for oneself? Is there, to repeat, not more dignity in courage than in its absence?

Euthanasia for one's own dignity is, at best, paradoxical, even self-contradictory. How can I honor myself by making myself nothing? Even if dignity were to consist solely in autonomy, is it not an embarrassment to claim that autonomy reaches its zenith precisely as it disappears? Voluntary euthanasia, in the name of *positive* dignity, does not make sense.

Acknowledging the paradox, some will still argue the cause of freedom on a more narrow ground: the prospect of euthanasia increases human freedom by increasing options. It is, of course, a long theoretical question whether human freedom is best understood—and best served—through the increase of possibilities. But as a practical matter, in the *present* case, I am certain that this view is mistaken. On the contrary, the opening up of this "option" of assisted suicide will greatly constrain human choice. For the choice for death is not one option among many, but an option to end all options. Socially, there will be great pressure on the aged and the vulnerable to exercise this option. Once there looms the legal alternative of euthanasia, it will plague and burden every decision made by any seriously ill, elderly person—not to speak of their more powerful caretakers—even without the subtle hints and pressures applied to them by others.

And, thinking about others, is it dignified to ask or demand that someone else become my killer? It may be sad that one is unable to end one's own life, but can it conduce to either party's dignity to make the request? Consider its double meaning if made to a son or daughter: Do you love me so little as to force me to live on? Do you love me so little as to want me dead? What person in full possession of his own dignity would inflict such a duty on anyone he loved?

What, indeed, does human dignity require of us, regarding our loved ones, as we grow old, decline, and die? I have thought much about this question. Arguing now against myself, I confess that I look ahead with deep horror on the prospect that I might fall into a protracted state of such reduced humanity—say, with loss of memory, self-control, and the ability sensibly to converse—that I become a burden or even an object of loathing for my spouse and children. Under such conditions, it has often seemed to me that it would be better—indeed, nobler and more dignified—for me to take my own life than to live so as to cause my children to harden their hearts or to harbor secret wishes for my death—a horror to be prevented not for me but *for them.* It is hard to imagine anything worse, parentally speaking, than for a parent *by his very existence* to force a child's heart to turn against him. Suicide for such "altruistic" reasons, unlike suicide to escape from my own pain, would not appear to be base or undignified; it seems to belong, at first glance, in the category of noble self-sacrifice. But there is a catch: to be in fact noble, my suicide would have to be accomplished in full secrecy. No mean feat for the demented and immobile. No suicide *known* to be a suicide bequeaths anything but pain and guilt to his loved ones, the very thing that I would be trying to avoid. But suppose, now, that euthanasia (assisted suicide) were legal. My children—everyone—would be invited to deliberate about, wish for, encourage, and even participate in the death (and killing) of those they love. What a legacy! The very thing I have imagined committing suicide to prevent, the new dispensation will necessarily have brought into being. Can this really be death with dignity?

Of course, the whole thing could be made impersonal. No requests to family members, only to physicians. But precisely the same point applies: how can one demand care and humanity from one's physician and, at the same time, demand that he play the role of technical dispenser of death? To turn the matter over to non-physicians, that is, to technically competent professional euthanizers, is, of course, to completely dehumanize the matter.

Proponents of euthanasia do not understand human dignity, which, at best, they confuse with humaneness. One of their favorite arguments proves this point. Why, they say, do we put animals out of their misery but insist on compelling fellow human beings to suffer to the bitter end? Why, if it is not a contradiction for the veterinarian, does the medical ethic absolutely rule out mercy killing? Is this not simply inhumane?

Perhaps inhumane, but not thereby inhuman. On the contrary, it is precisely because animals are not human that we must treat them (merely) humanely. We put dumb animals to sleep because they do not know that they are dying, because they can make nothing of their misery or mortality, and therefore because they cannot live deliberately—i.e., humanly—in the face of their own suffering or dying. They cannot live out a fitting end. Compassion for their weakness and dumbness is our only appropriate emotion, and given our responsibility for their care and well-being, we do the only humane thing we can. But when a conscious human being asks us for death, by that very action he displays the presence of something that precludes our regarding him as a dumb animal. Humanity is owed humanity, not humaneness. Humanity is owed the bolstering of the human, even or especially in its dying moments, in resistance to the temptation to ignore its presence in the sight of suffering.

What humanity needs most in the face of evils is courage, the ability to stand against fear and pain and thoughts of nothingness. The deaths we most admire are those of people who, knowing that they are dying, face the fact frontally and act accordingly. They set their affairs in order; they arrange what could be final meetings with their loved ones; and yet, with strength of soul and a small reservoir of hope, they continue to live and work and love as much as they can for as long as they can. Because such conclusions of life require courage, they call for our encouragement—and for the many small speeches and deeds that shore up the human spirit against despair and defeat.

And what of nonvoluntary euthanasia, for those too disabled to request it for themselves—the comatose, the senile, the psychotic. Can this be said to be in the service of *their* human dignity? If dignity is, as the autonomy people say, tied crucially to consciousness and will, nonvoluntary or "proxy-voluntary" euthanasia can never be a dignified act for the one euthanized. On their own view, the situation is beneath dignity. Indeed, it is precisely the absence of dignified humanity that invites the thought of active euthanasia in the first place.

Is it really true that such people are beneath all human dignity? I suppose it depends on the particulars. Many people in greatly reduced states still retain clear, even if partial, participation in human relations. They may respond to kind words or familiar music; they may keep up pride in their appearance or in the achievements of the grandchildren; they may take pleasure in reminiscences or simply in having someone who cares enough to be present. Conversely, they may be irritated or hurt or sad, even appropriately so. And, even nearer bottom, they may be able to return a smile or a glance in response to a drink of water or a change of bedding or a bath. Because we really do not know their inner life—what they feel and understand—we run the risk of robbing them of opportunities for dignity by treating them as if they had none. It does not follow from the fact that *we* would never willingly trade places with them that *they* have *nothing* left worth respecting.

But what, finally, about the very bottom of the line, say, people in a "persistent vegetative state," unresponsive, contorted, with no evident ability to interact with the environment? What human dignity remains here? Why should we not treat such human beings as we (properly) treat dumb animals and put them out of "their misery"? I grant that one faces here the hardest case for the argument I am advancing. Yet one probably cannot be absolutely sure, even here, about the complete absence of inner life or awareness of their surroundings. In some cases, admittedly extremely rare, persons recover from profound coma (even with flat EEGs), and they sometimes report having had partial yet vivid awareness of what was said and done to them, though they had given no external evidence of it. But beyond any restraint owing to ignorance, I would also myself be restrained by the human form, by *human blood,* and by what I owe to the full human life that this particular instance of humanity once lived. I would gladly stand aside and let die, say, in the advent of pneumonia; I would do little beyond the minimum to sustain life. But I would not countenance the giving of lethal injections or the taking of other actions deliberately intending the patient's death. Between only undignified courses of action, this strikes me as the least undignified—especially for myself.

I have no illusions that it is easy to live with a Karen Ann Quinlan or a Nancy Cruzan or the baby Linares. I think I sufficiently appreciate the anguish of their parents or their children, and the distortion of their lives and the lives of their families. I also know that, when hearts break and people can stand it no longer, mercy killing will happen, and I think we should be prepared to excuse it—as we generally do—when it occurs in this way. But an excuse is not yet a justification, and very far from dignity.

What then should we conclude, as a matter of social policy? We should reject the counsel of those who, seeking to drive a wedge between human dignity and the sanctity of life, argue the need for active euthanasia, especially in the name of death with dignity. For it is precisely the setting of fixed limits on violating human life that makes possible our efforts at dignified relations with our fellow men, especially when their neediness and disability try our patience. We will never be able to relate even decently to people if we are entitled always to consider that one option before us is to make them dead. Thus, when the advocates for euthanasia press us with the most heartrending cases, we should be sympathetic but firm. Our response should be neither "Yes, for mercy's sake" nor "Murder! Unthinkable!" but "Sorry. No." Above all, we must not allow ourselves to become self-deceived. We must never seek to relieve *our own* frustrations and bitterness over the lingering deaths of others by pretending that we can kill them to sustain *their dignity*.

The present crisis that leads some to press for active euthanasia is really an opportunity to learn the limits of the medicalization of life and death and to recover an appreciation of living with and against mortality. It is an opportunity to remember and affirm that there remains a residual human wholeness—however precarious—that can be cared for even in the face of incurable and terminal illness. Should we cave in, should we choose to become technical dispensers of death, we will not only be abandoning our loved ones and our duty to care; we will exacerbate the worst tendencies of modern life, embracing technicism and so-called humaneness where encouragement and humanity are both required and sorely lacking. On the other hand, should we hold fast, should we decline the principle of autonomy and its deadly options, we will learn that finitude is no disgrace and that dignity can be cared for to the very end.

Not Through Yet

Rami M. Shapiro

Shirley was a woman in her middle sixties. She was bright, attractive, and seemingly in control of her situation. Her husband, who was six years her senior, had died a few months earlier in a car accident. Two weeks later Shirley was diagnosed as terminally ill.

She related all of this to me with little if any emotion. It was as if she were talking about someone else. Shirley wanted two things from me: information on committing suicide, and my blessing for doing so. I explained I could not help her with the former and asked if she would mind my talking a bit about the latter. She agreed. In essence this is what I said:

I can understand how a person can contemplate suicide. Who hasn't thought of escaping the struggles of life with a quick and easy exit? There is nothing demonic about this. It isn't evil, and we are not bad to think it. In fact, it may be crucial to our sense of personal autonomy and dignity to know that we can control at least that one part of our destiny.

Viktor Frankl, noted psychotherapist and Holocaust survivor, writes that one of the key elements of survival in the Nazi death camps was the knowledge that one could escape the horror through suicide. Knowing this gave the inmates a sliver of power from which to resist the Nazis by surviving.

We need to know that we can die. Not simply at the whim of chance or the decree of nature, but by our own volition, by our own hand, by our own will. Knowing this gives us a sense of dignity and control over our destiny. Having this knowledge obligates us to use it responsibly. Using it responsibly means that we are absolutely sure that death is the proper response to what life has given us. Yes, you can choose to die whenever you wish, but is this really the time to do so? Knowing that you can leave whenever you choose, should you choose to leave just now?

Not only do I support your right to die, I'm willing to sit with you as you do so. If you find in me someone who could help ease your passing, I would do what I could. It is, in fact, a privilege to be asked. Few things are as intimate as dying. And to share a person's final moments is an honor greater than most.

But supporting your right to die and advising you to die at this time are two very different things. Is this the time to die? Are you feeling ill? Are you in insufferable pain? Are you incapacitated? Is there nothing left for you to do with your life? Have you accomplished all you can? Have you said all that needs saying? Have you explored other medical opinions? Have you investigated other therapies and treatments? Are you losing the battle or have you simply refused to fight it?

It is one thing to know life is through with you and quite another to say you are through with life. Not disgusted or angry or despairing, but through.

We all have moments of anger, disgust, and despair, but can you say you are truly through with life? In what sense are you through with life?

We are all terminal; we are all dying. The horrible and senseless death of your husband underscores the fragility of life and the reality of death. The only difference between your death and his is that you know it is coming, while he could pretend his was not. The only difference between your death and my own is that I too can pretend to a future. But who knows? As the Talmud says: We did not choose to be born, nor do we choose to die. The only choice we have is what to do with the days in between.

There is always something to do. And there is always time to die. Take your life into your own hands by all means. All means! That means taking your dying into your own hands, and knowing that you can die whenever you choose. That means taking your living into your own hands, and living until there is no living left. Make of your dying a statement of living. Show those whom you love how to face their own death by living in the midst of your dying. Live no longer than you should. Die no sooner than you must.

Die when you choose, but first consider what else needs to be done. Treat yourself to life, and then when you are ready, treat yourself to death.

I stopped talking. I was drained. Had I said too much? Had what I said made sense? Who was I to say anything at all?

Shirley's face was unreadable. She said nothing. Suddenly she stood up, thanked me without emotion, and left.

About a week later I received a card in the mail:

Dear Rabbi,
I guess I'm not through with life just yet. I'll let you know when. Thank you.

Shirley

Chapter Nine

How Shall We Mourn the Stillborn?

There are new spiritual questions with which our young people are now grappling. As one of them said to me ruefully, "We spent years trying to prevent pregnancy, and now we spend years trying to become pregnant." My consciousness has been raised to an awareness that there are many who want to have children but are unable to do so. I no longer tease young couples and say, "Nu?" Now I see how many of them go from one medical center to another, from one kind of difficult treatment to another, trying to become pregnant, and I realize how insensitive I have been to their pain.

And I am now aware, as I never was before, of the pain of those who lose a child by miscarriage or at birth. We used to know what was appropriate at such a time. The social worker would say: Don't see the baby, don't take a lock of its hair, don't get attached, for it will only add to your pain if you do. And the rabbi would say: Don't give the baby a name, don't sit shivah, don't say Kaddish, for it will only add to your pain. Now we know better. Now we know that, although they meant well, this advice was faulty. Now we realize that listening to this kind of advice only repressed the pain; it did not heal it.

And so now a new generation of social workers and rabbis grope for ways in which people can acknowledge and cope with this kind of loss. It is not enough to tell the parents that the mourning rites are not necessary, as if the rites were an onerous burden from which we are trying to spare them. The mourning rites are a therapy, not just a burden, and we do sufferers no favor if we excuse them from them. The tradition did not provide for full burial and mourning rites in these cases, perhaps because such losses were so common in the past.

Modern rabbis have resisted the plea for some kind of mourning rites for another reason. We were afraid that there is an inconsistency between saying a fetus is not a person when it comes to the abortion debate, and then saying that a fetus is a person when it comes to mourning laws.

But life is stronger than logic and so, as you can see in this chapter, rabbis are beginning to respond to the pain and the needs of people who are suffering such losses. We now understand that the pain of the parents is real and deep, that husbands hurt as well as wives, and that the community has to reach out and help those who are going through this pain. We realize now that some of the things that people say, such as "You're lucky that it happened early" or "You're young, you'll have another one," are clichés that irritate and do not help. And so, just as the custom of having a baby-naming service for girls developed spontaneously all around the country, so the awareness that there is a need to do something for those affected by miscarriage or stillbirth is being acknowledged all around the country. Some of the people who have helped make us conscious of this need speak in this chapter.

A Yizkor Prayer for Stillborn and Infant Deaths

Ira F. Stone

May God remember my son/daughter
—— bat/ben ——
who has gone to eternal rest.
Her/his life was but the briefest flicker of a flame,
extinguished before it had time to shed its light on the world
but not before sharing its warmth with me.
Through the months of his/her gestation
I prepared to nurture and to love her/him.
For the time that he/she lived
I gave to her/him everything a parent could have given
and received everything I could have expected.
May the memory of the joy she/he brought to me

in the short time that we were together
strengthen me, and may God count that joy
as the weight of a life filled with such blessing,
binding through that love and joy
—— bat/ben ——
in the bonds of eternal life.
For the gift of his/her life without transgression,
I pledge to do acts of righteousness and *tzedakah*
that she/he may merit eternal life
and that I may find comfort in this world.

I Lost a Child But Did Not Mourn Her

Ron Wolfson

I have been bereaved, but I have not yet been a mourner. As contradictory as that sounds, it is true. I have lost a child, but I have not mourned her.

Susie and I were married for three years before we "got pregnant." I say "we" because throughout the uneventful pregnancy, I felt as close to the baby-to-be as a father could. I marveled at every stage of development during the nine months, especially when the baby moved. What an amazing feeling it is to touch a human being *in potentia* within the womb! A leg or an arm would push out from Susie's belly, seemingly anxious to come out and play.

Pregnancy is a time of great excitement and wonderful dreams about what will be. Will it be a girl or boy? Will she look like Susie or me? What will we name him? How will having a child change our lives? We had taken Lamaze childbirth classes and awaited the due date. Despite the superstitions about setting up a nursery, we had ordered the basic furniture and bought a few toys. We hadn't thought for even an instant about the possibility that something could go wrong, terribly wrong.

Our first child was born full term on the afternoon of May 6, 1974, and died thirteen hours later. The baby had become stressed during a prolonged labor and Susie was rushed into an emergency Caesarean section. Due to the stress, the baby had ingested contaminated embryonic fluid, a medical condition known as meconium aspiration. Despite the valiant efforts of a team of neonatal specialists throughout the night, there was no way to save her. The baby had been rushed from the delivery room to the neonatal intensive-care unit of Children's Hospital, across the street from Barnes Hospital where Susie remained.

Susie's parents stayed with her and I waited through the night at Children's with my parents. The doctors and nurses were superb, bringing us updates on the baby's condition, but holding out little hope. At one point, a social worker suggested I see the baby. It was a heart-wrenching moment. I spent most of the night crying, thinking about Susie and how devastating this loss would be for her.

Susie had spent the night recovering from the operation in the last room at the end of the hall on the maternity floor. The first inkling she had that something was wrong came when a nurse walked into the room and took down several decorative pictures of smiling mothers holding their newborns. I talked to her by phone, admitting that there was a problem, suggesting that she try to rest from the ordeal of the labor and operation. Early in the morning, an intern, a terrific young man who had worked all night on the case, came into the waiting room to give me the news, but his crying eliminated the need for words. The shock overwhelmed me, even though I knew it was coming. I literally ran across the street to the hospital wing where Susie had been taken. "She died" were the only words I could get out before collapsing into her arms. We cried together for a long time at this most unhappy ending. Little did I know that the ordeal had just begun.

No one knew how to handle this tragedy—no one. The nurses moved Susie from the maternity floor to the urology ward to "save her" the pain of hearing the sounds of babies. The obstetrician came to say he was sorry and then warned us that, because he had had to do a C-section, he would have to add $350 to his fee. Our parents, expecting their first grandchild, were devastated. Our friends rushed to the hospital to offer comfort, but most only exacerbated the hurt with comments like "You're young. You'll have other children"; "It'll be okay." Well, it was definitely not okay.

Jewish tradition failed us, too. What should have been a

moment of supreme joy had become the ultimate nightmare. Instead of rejoicing as new parents, we were plunged into intense grief as mourners. Except, according to Jewish law, there was no mourning for our baby.

As incredible as it seems to the modern mind, traditional Jewish practice stipulates that there is to be no official mourning for an infant who dies before reaching thirty days of maturity. There are historical reasons for this. In the Middle Ages, large numbers of infants did not survive birth. To the legal authorities of the time, relieving parents of the obligation to mourn a stillborn or an infant less than a month old was viewed as lifting a great burden from them. But, to us, it was a great robbery—stealing the traditional forms of bereavement at the precise moment we needed them most. There was no funeral—the cantor arranged for the mortuary to take the baby to the cemetery for burial. There was no shivah—even though many friends and family came to our home to offer their condolences and support. There was no gravestone—she was buried in a tiny unmarked grave in a special section of the cemetery. There was no yahrzeit, no Yizkor, no memorials. It's as if the tradition wanted the memory of the experience to be wiped out completely, as if it never happened.

I bought it. My reaction was not to mourn. "Let's forget about this and look ahead to the future," I reasoned. "We'll get pregnant again. We're moving to Los Angeles. We'll make a fresh start." For Susie, the loss was overwhelming. She was plunged into enormous grief, anger, and pain. Despite the assurances of doctors, social workers, and me that we would recover, Susie felt unheard and abandoned. And Judaism offered her no vehicle for her grief, no status as a mourner. Ironically, for a tradition that is so wise in most matters of loss, its answer for the death of an infant was hollow and unhelpful.

We moved to Los Angeles and came under the care of a wonderful doctor specializing in high-risk pregnancies. It took two years for us to get pregnant again—two years of unresolved mourning for Susie and two years of denial for me. After a very carefully monitored pregnancy, we celebrated the birth of Havi

Michele. Two years later, Michael Louis was born. Seven years after the death of our first baby, Susie joined the first support group for mothers experiencing neonatal death ever held in Los Angeles and finally began to resolve her grief. To this day, I feel I have never truly mourned the loss of our first baby. Perhaps, just perhaps, if the tradition had offered me some way to mourn, I might have been able to cope with this loss in a healthier way.

Neonatal Death

Susan Knightly

I had been diagnosed with cervical cancer. One day, during my fifth month of pregnancy, I was taking a short walk and sneezed. Immediately, I knew the baby was in trouble. I got back to the apartment and called 911. When we got to the hospital, I went into labor. Fifteen hours later, I gave birth to Joshua, ten inches long and one pound, who died during the descent through the birth canal.

This was our third miscarriage in thirteen months. It's amazing how much bonding occurs in those first months. We had been feeling the baby kicking for about four weeks. Leonard would come home and "kiss" the baby. Of course, from the minute you hear you're pregnant, you endow the baby with a personality. We already imagined the baby playing the cello and fingerpainting! What people really don't realize is that very early on, you have this kind of bonding with the baby. From the moment we conceived, I felt I was inviting a soul into my body.

"Please, can I hold the baby?" After I gave birth, I wanted to hold Joshua. We had a wonderful nurse who was very empathetic. She brought the baby to us, dressed in a diaper, a shirt, and a blanket, and I got to hold him. He was a beautiful little boy; he had my husband's features. The doctors were just blown away by this; they couldn't cope with it. They were completely unavailable to me emotionally. Fortunately, the nurse stayed five hours past the end of her shift to be with us.

When I held the baby, the reality of this loss hit Leonard. For him, it had been very exciting to anticipate the baby, but obviously it wasn't the same as it was for me. But when he saw me holding the baby, it became clear that this was a real person, this was his son, this was a life. It gave him license to grieve.

The hospital gave us two choices concerning what to do with the baby; we could leave the baby there for research purposes or bury him in a mass grave. We wanted neither. I'm a convert to Judaism and Leonard grew up in a traditional Jewish home. So we called our rabbi to ask about the protocol. "There is no protocol," he replied. We decided to have a Jewish burial. We made several midnight calls to Jewish funeral homes and found one that was very understanding. In fact, they offered their services for no charge at all. They recommended a cemetery near us in Brooklyn that had a section for premature babies and small children.

Just before the funeral home came for the baby, we decided to say Kaddish in the hospital. We prepared the body ourselves. Leonard wanted the baby buried in his bar mitzvah tallit, so we wrapped him in it, along with some baby's breath and a small rose. Then we said Kaddish.

We arranged a time for a graveside service, alerted our close friends and synagogue community, and two days later held a funeral service for Joshua. The rabbi said a few of the traditional prayers, and Leonard and I each read eulogies we had prepared that let our friends hear what this process was like for us and described our hopes and feelings about Joshua. We had asked our friends to bring readings they felt would speak to the moment, and several of them read poems and shared a few words. We each shoveled earth into the grave until it was completely filled. It was quite beautiful and an important moment of closure for us.

Then we sat shivah. Friends arranged meals for us, each night we had a minyan service, and we were surrounded by community. It was crucial for us not to be alone. We had to give ourselves permission to grieve. We knew if we did not experience our feelings now, we would later, and it wouldn't be healthy. The ritual allowed us to cry, and saying Kaddish enabled us to focus on our grief.

There were friends of ours who had grown up in traditional Jewish homes who were skeptical of our sitting shivah. But once they saw how this was allowing us to deal with our grief, they understood how important it was to have the community around us. There is a real emphasis in our community, particularly among women, on re-creating the ritual to speak to us. We had conversations about what we were doing throughout the shivah, and I think that helped people understand.

Every step along the way has been hard. Leaving the hospital was very hard, burying the baby was very hard, the end of shivah was very hard. But each step has been a bit of closure for us. For several weeks, someone from the *bikkur holim* committee of the synagogue made sure that someone came to the house at lunch. I also get a call almost daily from the National Jewish Women's Organization Pregnancy Loss Peer Support Network. Every day, I got to tell the story. The telling of the story allowed us to talk our way out of the shock.

Today, our grief continues, but we feel very whole, very healed. I can't help but compare how I feel now to how I felt after my two earlier miscarriages, when I had no permission to grieve over my loss. I was very ill for weeks afterward. After this experience of expressing my feelings, rather than feeling ravaged and destroyed, I feel cleansed. I've even recovered physically very well.

I'll tell you something even more amazing. My mother had suffered from depression for many, many years and as a child I never knew why. When this happened to me, she said, "You know, when you were three years old, you had to leave me for six weeks. I lost a baby. It was a premature baby who lived only two days. My greatest regret is I never got to hold that baby. Every time you graduated, every time you had a date, every step you took of initiation into anything, I thought about that baby." Of course, I knew she was sad about something, but I never knew why. She was so thankful that I had so much support. She said to me, "Thank God you're Jewish and you have something to get you through this."

Baby Brother's Gone to Heaven

Anne-Lynne Keplar

The morning after, Adam came to see me at the hospital. A couple of months shy of his sixth birthday, he crawled up in my bed next to me.

"Adam," I said, "we have some very sad news. Your baby brother died last night."

For a moment, we sat quietly as Adam tried to absorb what my husband and I were telling him.

Adam had been eagerly awaiting the birth of his baby brother. The night before, driving to the hospital with us while I was having contractions, he had asked, "Is it October? I want my baby brother to be born in October." That's when Adam had been born, and he had hoped that this would be the first of many things he would share with his brother.

But Adam's brother was stillborn. Rather than tell him that night, we had decided to seek the advice of a psychologist in the morning and then talk with our son.

When Adam wants to talk, the psychologist advised, listen. Adults become so consumed in their grief that all too often they don't listen to their children. And, the psychologist said, let Adam gain "closure." Take Adam to the funeral so that he will know where his brother will be.

So, after telling Adam that his little brother had died, we listened. *How did he die? Where is he? Can I see him?*

We had decided that we would stay together, as a family, this day. Adam needed us. And, we quickly discovered, we needed him, too. He learned from us that day and we from him. His blunt conversation was startling at times, but a helpful jolt of reality. At one point, dear friends who had been through similar tragedies approached our room with their ten-year-old son, Jared. "I have some very sad news for you," Adam said to his young friend in the hallway. "My brother died."

We found it was just as important for Adam to have a friend to talk with, to share his grief with, as it was for us adults. Jared listened to Adam when he wanted to talk and played when he didn't. Adam spent the next day with his godparents and asked Jared to come to play with him.

That first night, at the hospital, we had another tough conversation. The next day, we would go to the cemetery to bury his little brother.

He had many questions and one special request: Can I give my brother my teddy bear?

At the cemetery, Adam sat quietly as the rabbi conducted the service. The rabbi read a note I had written and then asked Adam to place it on the casket. Adam lay down on the ground and placed the card on the casket. Then, without a word, he put his teddy bear into the vault.

Two men began to shovel dirt into the grave. Adam took a shovel and started to fill the grave. As the other men alternated, Adam continued, shoveling dirt until the grave was completely full. As some of the adults began to filter away from the grave site, Adam continued. Next, he took some cut roses he had brought from home and stood them in the dirt. "Mom," he said, turning to me, "these roses don't have roots. We need roses with roots."

That afternoon, we went to a nursery and bought a rosebush— "roses with roots." We returned to the cemetery, where Adam dug a hole and planted it. Then he placed a card atop it: "Welcome to my new baby brother, Adam." He then asked us to take his picture by the flowers.

Later, I asked him why he had to fill the grave with dirt rather than allow the workers to do it. "Because he's *my* brother."

Adam was scheduled to return to school the next day, so I called ahead and talked to the director, telling her what Adam had been through, what he might tell other youngsters, and how he was behaving.

When he arrived, he was hugged and loved. The teachers, school director, parents, and children were wonderful.

"I want to tell the class why I'm sad," he told his teacher. As the other children sat in a circle on the floor in front of him, he told them exactly what had happened. He told them about the tiny box they had put his brother in. "That box went into a bigger box. I put my teddy bear into the box because I didn't want my brother to be alone."

Then he explained how he helped fill the grave with dirt. "It was very hard work but I had to do it." He told them about planting the roses without roots and planting the "roses with roots."

"Where did the baby go?" one child asked. "To heaven," he said.

"What part of the baby goes to heaven?" another child asked. Adam looked at the teacher with a wide-eyed look. She explained about the soul and told the children that God had chosen Adam's baby brother to be one of God's helpers. For Adam, that was extremely helpful, because being a helper at his school is a big honor.

"Did you cry?" another child asked. "No, I had to be strong for my mommy and daddy."

Adam's teacher made a special journal for him, a book with blank pages on which he can express his thoughts by drawing pictures. At the bottom of each page, we write what he wishes to say about each picture. In one picture, Adam's brother is an angel in the sky with God, and he is on the ground. "I wish I could get a new baby brother," his teacher wrote at the bottom of the page. In another, God is in the sky, and he and his little brother are on the ground. "I wish that my brother came back alive," his teacher wrote.

Adam continued to deal with his brother's death honestly. He asked us to buy a baby doll for him. He fed it, dressed it, and slept with it. He even reenacted the cemetery one day, pretending to bury the doll. Most of the time, he loved it, hugged it, and cared for it.

When I was a child, children were rarely included at funerals. Death was not discussed. The person who died just went away.

Our experience was a valuable lesson for me about the importance of allowing a child to work through grief. Adam is sad his brother died, but he knows he has a brother and where he is.

Three Responses to Miscarriage

At the time Jewish law was being codified, when there was no prenatal care as we know it and miscarriage was commonplace, a baby was not considered a person until after it had lived for thirty days. Therefore miscarriage and newborn death required no unique rituals. Today, though the number has decreased, those who do experience a miscarriage expect help and guidelines from the Jewish and secular communities.

Rabbis Blank, Eilberg, and Goodman share their experiences and viewpoints on this issue.

Debra Reed Blank

A friend once observed that there are two tragedies involved in a miscarriage: the most obvious is the loss of the potential child and the ensuing grief of the couple; the other, less obvious, is the community's abandonment of this couple during their time of grief.

In the aftermath of my own miscarriage, which occurred in the second trimester after a battle with infertility, I realized that the friend was only partially correct. The third facet of this tragedy is the lack of guidance from Jewish tradition. Judaism provides rules for coping with virtually every aspect of life. Yet there are no such guidelines for dealing with the emotional and physical trauma that accompany the unhappy ending of a pregnancy, no rituals to enable the couple to channel and express their emotions, and no guide for communal involvement.

While I was trying to come to terms with my own miscarriage by conceptualizing a legitimate Jewish response, the question of miscarriage was presented before the Rabbinical Assembly's Committee on Jewish Law and Standards, which establishes a modern code of Jewish Halakhah. The committee studied responses as diverse as the sitting of shivah—an extreme and inappropriate response—and immersion into a mikvah—a completely personal response which lacks communal involvement and acknowledgment. I submitted a paper to the committee, which was accepted after discussion. It put the response to miscarriage within the guidelines of the mitzvah of *bikkur holim* (visiting the sick).

Maimonides writes in his *Mishneh Torah: Bikkur holim mitzvah al hakol* (Everyone is required to fulfill the commandment of visiting the sick) (Hilkhot Avel 14:4). A person who is a *holeh* (fem: *holah*)—the legal status of one who is sick—requires the attention of *bikkur holim*. These are responsibilities that cannot be left solely to the rabbi of a community. No rabbi can bear that burden alone.

The mitzvah of *bikkur holim* is not only for those instances of extreme, serious illness. Even allowing for concerns that *bikkur holim* not be abused, there are many illnesses that, while not life-threatening, are traumatic, painful, and enervating for the *holeh* as well as for his or her family. These times merit *bikkur holim*.

For the category of *bikkur holim* to be appropriate to miscarriage, the term *holeh* must be applicable to the woman who has just miscarried. Moreover, her husband may also be technically considered a *holeh*. If they are *holim,* they are entitled to the "benefits" due a *holeh* in Jewish law. Frequently, a woman who has miscarried has suffered a physical trauma. Complications might even threaten her life. For the woman, there is no question that she qualifies as a *holah* on the basis of her physical condition alone. But what about the father? Does his mental anguish qualify him as a *holeh?* Halakhic literature recognizes the interdependence of physical and mental health, so the father can also be described as a *holeh.*

Since the category of *holeh* and the mitzvah of *bikkur holim* do apply to miscarriage, we can now specify their application. However, the workings of *bikkur holim* are dependent upon the couple's willingness to make their situation public. Their rabbi and friends can help identify those people with whom the couple might share their loss.

Soon after the miscarriage, a *mi shebayrakh* (a *t'fillah*—a prayer— said during the Torah service requesting God's blessing for one who is sick) may be recited at the synagogue. The *r'fuat hanefesh* (emotional healing) as well as the *r'fuat haguf* (physical healing) of the wife and her husband should be considered when saying this prayer.

After the woman has physically recovered, she can recite *birkat hagomel* (a *brakhah*—a blessing—recited by one who has recovered from illness and who is called to the Torah), pausing a moment from her grief to give thanks for her return to health. Both of these prayers publicly, yet discreetly, remark on the recent experience.

Many have found that combining these prayers with a visit to the mikvah—a symbol of new beginnings—helps to channel and express emotions in a ritualized response. A positive reaction to these rituals depends to a great extent upon the facility and sympathy with which the rabbi explains them. But the rituals alone do not provide comfort and support in response to the grief of the couple. It is here that the community becomes involved by way of the mitzvah of *bikkur holim*. *Bikkur holim* can be just as much an expression of grief as it is a wish for health. Just as a visit to a dying friend is more to grieve the inevitable loss than it is a futile wish for health, a visit to people who have suffered a miscarriage offers an opportunity to share in their grief.

Close friends and relatives should be available to attend to the couple's immediate needs. More casual friends should visit later. Others who have had the same experience might share suggestions for reading materials or other activities they found helpful, when the couple is ready. The standards for *bikkur holim* in the Shulhan Arukh stipulate that one should check whether a particular need could be met (Yoreh Deah 335:8). Too often people couch their offers to help in general, noncommittal language and consequently they are declined. The Shulhan Arukh prods us to make specific offers, such as "I am on the way to the grocery. What can I bring you?" It is important to remember that a telephone call is never a substitute for *bikkur holim*.

Care should be taken so that visits are not burdensome—either too early or too late, or with unwanted advice. The needs of the couple are paramount. The traditional prayer for physical and emotional recovery—*Hamakom yenahem aleihem b'tokh holei Yisrael* (May God show compassion to you with the other *holei* of Israel)—could also be recited by the visitor.

The category of *holeh* and the mitzvah of *bikkur holim* provide us with guidelines for an appropriate and flexible response to the emotional impact and physical trauma of miscarriage. They also provide ways for the couple to channel emotions and for the community to acknowledge the loss. Though no ritual, behavior, or prayer can totally remove the feelings of grief, these responses help a couple to come to terms with what has happened.

Certainly, before these guidelines become the natural and automatic response to miscarriage, much work needs to be done. People have to begin to lose the discomfort and shame associated with miscarriage. Rabbis must educate their congregants about *bikkur holim* and its applicability. If the model of *bikkur holim* is followed, those experiencing a miscarriage would not be overwhelmed by day-to-day responsibilities in a time of great stress, want for sympathetic ears, or sense their loss unacknowledged by either their community or their religion.

Amy Eilberg

Some years ago, in my work as a hospital chaplain, I met a nurse whom I will never forget. In the course of a brief conversation I asked how many children she had. Instantly she responded, "Four. Well, that includes one I lost by miscarriage." This had been a first-trimester miscarriage suffered fifteen years earlier, yet the woman still counted the lost fetus as one of her children. I carry this experience with me as I work with parents who have suffered miscarriage. These people know that while the loss of a fetus is different from other losses, it is a very real loss.

In hospitals around the country, nurses, doctors, social workers, and chaplains understand that a woman who has miscarried and her husband are grieving. What they need most is acknowledgment of the reality and profundity of their loss, and support in their grieving process. When the fetus is of potentially viable size, families are often encouraged by these professionals to choose a name, to hold him or her, to save hair, blankets, or hospital gear, to plan a memorial service, or to keep a memory book. Even secular medical professionals have come to understand the need for ritual to give expression to this powerful and often misunderstood grief. The response of many people is to create their own simple, heartfelt rituals. Jews in this situation desperately want to hear that Jewish tradition, as it evolves in our day, understands their pain.

Jewish law has a superbly developed approach to bereavement. Jewish rituals affirm the essence of grief which needs to be acknowledged immediately after a loss. Just as contemporary bereavement professionals agree that coming to terms with pregnancy loss may take up to a full year, age-old Jewish tradition conveys the wisdom that grief requires time, support, and ongoing acknowledgment to be resolved.

Although for some, traditional bereavement rituals might have been helpful at the time of pregnancy loss, the Committee on Law and Standards has rejected this approach because of its conflict with the issue of abortion. I suggest, perhaps, a modification of the practices of *aveilut* (Jewish mourning rituals) for pregnancy loss. I believe that a rabbi might prescribe some established rituals in response to the needs of each grieving family: *keri'ah,* the symbolic tearing of a garment; a modified burial service if the fetus is large enough to require burial; and a *se'udat havra'ah* (meal of healing). Some might be helped by observing one day of private shivah. Yet others might be comforted by reciting Kaddish for thirty days when the grief is particularly acute.

Such ritual responses would distinguish this loss from the death of a living person but would admit that the loss is real and that the Jewish community understands and wants to provide support as the bereavement process gradually unfolds.

Marvin Goodman

As a rabbinical student, I learned that according to Jewish law a baby is not "viable" and therefore not to be mourned until it has lived thirty days past its nine-month period of gestation. This first encounter with the subject of miscarriage and stillbirth gave me a sense of relief. In intellectualizing this issue, Judaism was in touch with the "modern world."

In the fall of 1981, my wife and I learned that the baby we were expecting had died *in utero*. The following day, labor was induced, and as my wife lay in a drugged state for fifteen hours, I sat waiting. Knowing that the results of this labor would be a stillbirth, I was personally confronted by issues that I had studied only in an academic sense.

Initially, when the doctor asked if we would want to see or hold the baby I concluded that, since a dead body is ritually impure, Judaism dictated we not touch the baby. Even viewing the baby seemed questionable. Later in the day, a doctor who worked with terminally ill children suggested that my wife should be given the choice to see or hold the baby, since it was she who had felt it move and grow. The doctor felt that these acts were necessary to help us confront our grief. At the end of the labor, my wife decided that, without a doubt, we should see the baby. I am glad we did.

The trauma of that day is indescribable. Moreover, the ensuing days, weeks, and months made me realize that the same tradition which ten years earlier had left me relieved by characterizing the "viability" of a baby, now gave me no format to mourn one that was not.

The Halakhah, for its part, is very simple and straightforward. Intellectually, I could rationalize its advice. Emotionally, I could not accept its lack of prescribed action.

After four months, I was still very depressed and knew I was at a crisis point. Together with my wife, I decided some short-term therapy might help. During our meeting the psychologist commented that, just as rituals had helped me deal with the recent death of my father, my wife and I might use ritual as a way to mourn the baby. Although it seemed "wrong" from a halakhic point of view, I was ready to try anything.

We considered many ideas. Finally we decided to buy a single unopened rose each Friday and to read something about or by children before our erev Shabbat meal. I had very much looked forward to blessing our child at this time. Instead, this simple ritual was a public reminder of our loss and provided me a process through which to work out my grief.

Faith Learns to Fill a Need

Barry D. Cytron

My actuary friends might have labeled it a fairly typical statistic for a religious community of our size. Three funerals in one week, the average age of death being sixty.

The week, however, was anything but routine. Two of the funerals were for individuals who had each just turned ninety. The third was for a three-day-old infant, a girl given the name Isabel. Born with major pulmonary underdevelopment, she was doomed from the moment of her entrance into the world. Nothing but a miracle could have rescued her.

Though one was not forthcoming, a different sort of miraculous moment did occur. For her parents were both wise and unselfish in deciding how best to confront their enormous loss. They asked if we might arrange for a funeral—with all the proper rites and prayers—just as we had for those ninety-year-olds. In so doing, Isabel's parents allowed their child's brief span to touch indelibly not only their own lives, but those of their family and friends, too.

The graveside service, held in the middle of a radiant, late-autumn day, was simple and understated: an opening psalm, a set of readings spoken in unison by the hundred or so in attendance, the lowering of her tiny casket into the soft soil of a cemetery hillside, and the shoveling of two dozen spadefuls of earth by Isabel's parents and family, sufficient to close up that broken spot on the landscape. We concluded by reciting the mighty Kaddish, the traditional words spoken by generations of Jews over the centuries to mourn their losses with words affirming God's sanctity and the goodness of life. The entire service had taken less than a half-hour.

On multiple levels, that afternoon was of singular dimension. To begin with, there was the uncommon grief for a child taken even before life could truly begin. For those gathered there, this was a moment to share in a lament for unrealized expectations, to grieve with Isabel's parents their empty arms and shattered hearts.

Then there were the prayers and readings selected for that particular funeral service. What sense, after all, would it make to rely on the standard liturgy? How could I possibly read Psalm 90, for example, with its language of a life "of seventy years, or by vigor, blessed to eighty"? Clearly, other prayers would have to be substituted if the service was to ring true to the emotions of that moment.

Perhaps the most remarkable aspect of what happened that afternoon was that there was a funeral service at all. At one time, many religious communities steered away from bestowing the faith's complete burial rites at the time of a stillborn or infant death. Certainly mine did, probably for many reasons. Such reluctance might have been prompted by uncertainty about the status of a life that had not survived even a bare month. Perhaps it was because neonatal death was so ordinary. After all, in a more primitive world of medicine, in which the death of infant children was an everyday occurrence, forgoing the demanding rituals of mourning might have been the tradition's way of relieving parents of what could have seemed an untold burden.

Whatever the explanation, until recently standard practice for a newborn death was to inter the body with the simplest of procedures: an immediate burial, usually private, sometimes without even family in attendance. Today, it is different.

Thanks in large part to the impact of feminism on religious practice, during the last decade religious communities have begun to rethink how best to help families deal with such loss. For a faith such as Judaism, defined as it is by deference to the past, doing so has been a major challenge. In my own denomination, for example, women rabbis have worked hard to sensitize their male colleagues to the palpable needs of parents at these times. They have mounted a sustained effort to get our national organizations to redefine the mourning requirements and renew the liturgy.

In turn, poetic voices have shaped new prayers that speak to the needs of the hour, with words such as these, based on ancient biblical images: "God, be with these mourners in their grief, until hope breaks through like dawn at the end of night. Teach us to be with them, too. Let their sorrow break against us. Help us to place our arms about them."

In large measure, to be sure, the service for Isabel that day bespoke both the courage and sensitivity of her parents, who were able, in the midst of their own pain, to invite others into their lives. It was also a testimony to the wisdom of those who have urged that ancient rites must be refashioned, and that with such renewal, religious faith, despite the secular temper of our world, can still continue to nurture and guide those in need.

Chapter Ten

How Does One Survive the Loss of Children?

My favorite verse in all the Bible is Genesis 4:24. Adam and Eve have two children, Cain and Abel. And one day the two fight. There are lots of different guesses in the Midrash as to what it was that they fought about. One sage says it was about property, another says it was about a woman, another says it was about religion. Ultimately it doesn't matter what they fought about. What counts is that one killed the other and then was forced by God to run away into exile.

Where were Adam and Eve when this took place? The Torah doesn't say. They are offstage somewhere during the fight. And when they come back they find out that in one fell swoop they have lost both their children. One is dead; the other is a runaway whom they will never see again.

What would you do, what would I do if, God forbid, something like that happened to us?

Now comes the verse that means so much to me: "And Adam made love to his wife *again* and she gave birth to a child." I love that word "again." In Jewish tradition, Adam is called "Adam Ha-Rishon," Adam the First, but that is simply a chronological fact, not a spiritual achievement. Anyone can begin. Our libido drives us to do that. The real wonder of Adam and Eve is that they loved and lost and *began over again*. The Midrash says that that was not easy to do. At first they were filled with nausea and disgust. Is this the way life ends? If so, why should anyone want to go through all the travail of childbirth and bring a child into the world? The Midrash says that they separated from each other for years and that God had to implant an extra measure of desire within them in order to persuade them to come together once again.

But they did. They never forgot the two children they had lost;

no parent ever does. Eve mentions the two of them in the very same breath in which she names the new child: "She called him Seth [which means "gift"] because God has given him to us as a gift, in place of Abel whom Cain killed." She never recovers from the loss of her two children. But she somehow found within herself the courage and the capacity to risk again. She chose to bring a third child into this world, knowing how dangerous that could be.

And it is a good thing for us that she did. Otherwise, we would all be descended from either a murderer or a victim. Now they are our uncles, and we are all descendants of Seth.

Adam and Eve are the models for all the losers in the world. And who is not at some time in his or her life a loser? They got up off their knees and started over again, and for this we must all be eternally grateful.

In this chapter three people who have suffered the same excruciating loss that Adam and Eve did tell their stories. There is no loss more devastating than the loss of a child. Nothing strains our faith and saps our strength as much as such a loss. No one can blame the person who never recovers from it. But here are the testimonies of three human beings who somehow found the capacity to start over again after this kind of loss. Starting over again does not necessarily mean having another child. One of these women did that; the other two find different ways in which to rebuild their lives after the crushing blow. But each of them somehow learned how to begin over again—wounded forever, but still capable of living and loving.

I have no explanation of where this resiliency comes from. All I know is that they did it, and that Noah and his wife did too, after they lost everything, in the flood. And Jacob did it too, after the loss of his true love and favorite son. And Aaron did it, after the loss of his two children on the day of his coronation, on the day that should have been his day of glory.

The story of the death of Aaron's sons is brief and tantalizingly cryptic in the Bible. All we know is that, on the day of the installation of Aaron as high priest of Israel, they died—and all the pomp and pageantry of the coronation suddenly turned to ashes. There are all kinds of guesses in the Midrash as to what went wrong. To a parent it doesn't really matter why they died. To a parent all that matters is that his two children are dead.

Then the Bible says that "Aaron was silent," and a few pages further on it speaks of how he returns to the divine service in the sanctuary. The Bible, which does not usually waste words, records that silence of Aaron. What lesson is it meant to teach?

What were his choices?

He could have blasphemed, and that must have surely been a tempting option. But if he had, whom would he have hurt—God or himself? He could have gone on with the divine service, mouthing the words of praise, but he would not have meant them. And God is not so impoverished that he needs the praises of those that do not mean them. So instead he withdrew into himself and nursed his wounds; then, when he was able to, he came back to the altar. I am sure that the service he offered when he came back was different from the kind he offered before, because he was different now. It was probably a more mature service of God, a more chastened one, but the wonder is that Aaron, like Adam and Eve, like Noah, like Jacob, loved and lost and began over again.

There is a line at the end of the Book of Job that fascinates me. The story itself is familiar. Job has health, wealth, and children, and then Satan persuades God to permit him to test Job, to see if his faith will endure. Satan takes away Job's health, his wealth, and all seven of his children. Job stays firm, demanding to know from God why he is suffering. And in the end, God appears and humbles him by demanding to know who Job thinks he is, challenging the creator of heaven and earth.

That is the story, as we all know it. But there is a footnote to the story that is usually overlooked. At the end of the book it says that God "restored the children of Job." Most Bible scholars think that this is an appendix, pasted on by some pious editor who wanted to give the book a happy ending. But Archibald MacLeish, who wrote a profound play on the Book of Job, *J.B.*, offers a different explanation. I once heard him say that for him this line is the real climax of the book, that what it means is not that God performed a magic trick and brought the dead children back to life, but that, having lost all his children, Job somehow, from somewhere, found within himself the courage to bring more children into the world. According to MacLeish, Job did what Adam and Eve and Noah and Jacob and Aaron did: he learned how to get up off his knees and begin life over again.

Here are the testimonies of three women who have traveled that road from defeat to survival. Each describes in her own way how she learned to endure and how the resources of her faith helped her.

The Story of Rabbi Meir and Beruriah

It happened that while Rabbi Meir was teaching in the house of study on a Sabbath afternoon, his two sons died. What did their mother do? She put them both on a couch and spread a sheet over them.

At the end of the Sabbath, Rabbi Meir returned home and asked, "Where are my sons?" She replied, "They went to the house of study." Rabbi Meir said, "Really? I looked for them there and did not see them."

Then she gave him the cup for *Havdalah,* and he pronounced the blessings. Again he asked, "Where are my sons?" She replied, "They went to such-and-such a place and will be back soon." Then she brought him food. After he had eaten, she said, "My teacher, I have a question." Rabbi Meir said, "What is it?" She said, "My teacher, a while ago someone came and deposited something with me for safekeeping. Now that person has come back to claim what he left. Should I return it to him or not?" Rabbi Meir said, "My daughter, is not one who holds a deposit required to return it to its owner?" She said, "Still, without your opinion, I would not have returned it."

Then what did she do? She took Rabbi Meir by the hand and led him upstairs to the chamber and brought him to the couch. Then she pulled off the sheet, and he saw his two children lying there dead. He began to weep and say, "My sons, my sons, my teachers, my teachers! My sons in the ways of the world but my teachers because you illumined my eyes with your understanding of the Torah."

Then she said to him: "My teacher, did you not say to me that we are required to restore to the owner what he gives to us in trust? 'The Lord gave, and the Lord has taken back. Blessed be the name of the Lord' [Job 1:21]."

—Midrash Proverbs 31:10

Plutarch to His Wife After the Loss of Their Child

Let us bear our affliction with patience. Since she gave us so much pleasure while we had her, so ought we now to cherish her memory, and make that memory a glad rather than a sorrowful one.

Let us not ungratefully accuse Fortune for what was given us, because we could not also have all that we desired. What we had was good while we had it, though now we have it no longer.

Remember also how much of good we still possess. Because one page of our book is blotted, do not forget all the other leaves whose reading is fair and whose pictures are beautiful. We should not be like misers who never enjoy what they have but only bewail what they lose.

And since she is gone where she feels no pain, let us not indulge in too much grief. The soul is not capable of death. And she, like a bird not long enough in her cage to become attached to it, is free to fly away to a purer air. Since we cherished a trust like this, let our actions be in accord with it, and let us keep our hearts pure and try to keep our minds calm.

Not on Merit, But on Mazal

Rava said: Length of life, children, and sustenance depend not on one's merit, but on one's *mazal* [star]. Consider Rabbah and Rabbi

Hisda. Both were saintly sages—when one prayed for rain, it came; when the other prayed for rain, it also came. Yet Rabbi Hisda lived to the age of ninety-two, but Rabbah only to the age of forty. In Rabbi Hisda's house, sixty wedding feasts were celebrated; in Rabbah's house, sixty bereavements. In Rabbi Hisda's house, there was bread of the finest flour even for dogs, and it went to waste; in Rabbah's house, barley bread was for human beings, and even that was hardly to be had.

—The Talmud, Moed Katas 28a

We Will Get Better, We Must Get Better

Rookie Billet

Shouts of "Mazal tov! It's a girl! She's beautiful!" and she's right here near my heart and I close my eyes as the tears flow freely, because she is whole, and she is beautiful, and I thank Hashem for bringing me to this day, and for watching over her till birth, and I can't help thinking: Hashem, You've done Your job, and now You've entrusted her to me.

We name her after two grandmothers we knew and loved. Miriam and Ruth were not just names to us, but representative of the grandmothers who lived into our lifetimes, gave us beautiful times as children, and then were called from this world. I tell you all of this because you have to understand the utter joy and thankfulness I had been coming from when I suffered my loss. The tremendous joy and gratitude that I had felt upon her birth made my pain all the deeper at her death. So just as she began to grow, to fill out her small Stretchies, to need a larger Pamper, to smile at her Ema and turn her head at her name, she died, less than three months old, in her sleep. An unexplained sudden infant death. My beautiful baby.

In the emergency room they asked us: Do you have a rabbi we can call? My husband and I looked at each other, because he is the rabbi. We who had comforted others—now we were bereft. Amidst the terrible crying, the searing pain in the heart that felt like it would never go away, came the practical questions. How could we tell my parents, my husband's parents? How could we tell the children? What were we to do? We had to plan a funeral, a burial, a shivah and then we would pick up the pieces of our shattered lives.

So many questions tear at the person who is suffering. What did I do to deserve this? I must be a terrible person. Why did this happen to me? Can I be angry at Hashem? If I am angry at Him and I express my anger, will He only reach out to smite me some more? Why was this beautiful little soul denied a chance to live, to love, to learn? Surely she was completely pure. Then it must be a punishment to me, the errant adult.

As I return to the outer world from the inner one, I ask: How will I handle being the object of pity? How can I accept comfort when there is no comfort? I've lived a good and happy life. Can I ever be the same person I once was? Can I ever dance with a full heart at a *simhah?* Will every family photo from now on have that awful emptiness? Can I go back to the supermarket and walk down the Pamper aisle without crying? Can I watch the peers of my baby as they grow from infancy to toddling to childhood to young adulthood? Can I run the risk of another child? Can I ever watch, handle, feed someone else's baby?

What will I say when they ask how many children I have? I *have* three, but I *had* four. She existed; her life made a difference; how can I deny her? Yet can I burden an innocent questioner with my tale of sorrow? What shall we do with her clothes, her room, her untouched gifts, her little personalized picture frames and socks? Why didn't I take more pictures? Maybe it's better I have so few—maybe it's not healthy to keep looking at them and bursting into tears.

We made some decisions. We go home from the emergency room to tell the children. We tell them we love them. We tell them we *can,* we *must,* still be a happy family. We tell them we have suffered a terrible, irreversible loss, but no one is to blame. We all loved her so dearly and completely, and our pain is indescribable, but we *will* get better, we must get better. We will never forget her, but neither will her life, nor her death, be the center of our lives. There will be times over the next months when Ema or Abba will cry. That happens when someone we love dies. Crying is good—it helps us let out our feelings. We'll try not to cry too much, but if you kids want to cry, that's okay too. No, you will not die too. Most people die when they're old. Some people die younger. When you die, your soul goes up to Hashem. Your body rests in the ground, in a grave. We put a stone on a grave to express to ourselves and to the world who the loved one was and what he or she meant to us.

We're going to bury Miri here, but we're going to reinter her in Eretz Yisrael before the *shloshim* is complete. Ema and Abba planned to be laid to rest in Eretz Yisrael after 120 years. You children will choose your own places. But Miri will never have a husband to be buried near. She only has us—and just as in life we would have tried to give her the best, in death we will give her a fine resting place on a sunny hilltop in Eretz Yisrael, right next to where Ema, Abba, Bubbe, Zaide, Grammy, and Grampy bought their graves.

Another decision. Both Abba and Ema will say a *hesped* [eulogy] at the funeral. We will have a graveside funeral—simple—for a pure and simple soul. No one knew her as well as we; no one knew her as well as I. I speak of my love for her, of the death of potential, of not knowing what her first word would be, where her first step would take place. I speak of the way she looked at me as she paused in her nursing, and I can see any mother who ever held and fed her child and experienced that simple social behavior imagine a little what such a loss is like.

The pain of the soul. The physical pain, from ending the nursing so abruptly. I cry and cry during shivah. Friends I have not seen for ages, reaching out as my head is filled with pictures of the baby. Talking, listening, trying to make people feel that they've comforted me, trying to reach every person who comes in with the message that their visit was appreciated, their visit served some purpose. Trying to find comfort from what people are saying. Trying to sort out the occasional stupid remarks and discount them. Wondering all the while what I will ever do when shivah is over.

The people, the troubles that crawled out of the woodwork. The incredible revelations of people who looked happy, looked elegant, gave charity, danced at weddings, yelled at their children. There were those among them who had also suffered, who had loved and lost, who had borne the deepest of pain. Could I too emerge from my pain and be my old self again, so that a stranger who had not known me in 1982 could meet me sometime later and not read from my countenance what I had suffered? Could I possibly resume walking the streets of the world unblemished, without a sign of my loss, like an ordinary person? It seemed hard to contemplate, yet there walked those others, who, looking well and wonderful as they crossed the threshold of the mourners' house, spoke of the same unspeakable pains as I was feeling, but in the past tense.

For us, my husband and me, this was the beginning of a new understanding of *tzaros rabim chatzi nechamah,* "suffering shared by many is a partial comfort." We had asked ourselves: What can that mean? Why should I be comforted by the fact that others have suffered? Why would the suffering of others make me feel any better? The answer is that seeing those who have suffered, and who have also made a recovery, resumed their lives, survived—*this is* the *nechamah!* To see yourself a few months, years, down the road of life as you see those who have suffered and come back to a measure of themselves, this is the partial comfort. The knowledge that the road back from the loss can be scaled—it is not impossible—is the first inkling that there is a measure of comfort out there to be acquired.

Words that had meaning, words that gave comfort. The friend who had lost her beloved father a short time ago spoke of the question she found in a hasidic *sefer.* How will we recognize those we loved when we meet them after 120 years in the world-to-come? If they died young, will they have grown old? If they were hurt or wounded, will they have healed? How will we know them, how will they know us if we have changed or aged? The answer is that we will know them, we will recognize them because they will be clothed and cloaked in the good deeds we do in their name. I could relate to this. I could see my baby come toward me in the world-to-come draped with the *tzedakah* and *chesed,* the acts of charity and kindness that I would do in her name, we would all do in her name. I would no longer feel that half my life, or my whole life, for that matter, had been snuffed out. Now I would live for two. I would do all the good deeds and the mitzvot for myself, and I would also do the ones she had not lived to do.

I could appreciate the beautiful days fully, for her as well as for me. I would dance on joyous occasions myself, but with an extra measure for what she would have danced, had she lived. Through my life, I would give her life. There had to be *some reason* why she had lived, however briefly, why she had entered my life and left it so abruptly, so painfully. And as much as I would sometimes feel, as a mother does, *mir far dir,* that I should have gone in her place, there was some unfathomable reason why I still lived, why I was still blessed with life. And I was going to use it, to cherish it, to live it as fully as I could.

Another friend mentioned the story, reprinted in Rav Zevin's *Sipurei Chassidim* (*Tales of the Hasidim*), of the baby born to a loving, fine Jewish woman, who lived two years and died suddenly. The mother went to the rebbe who had given her the blessing for the child, and he told her a strange story of a certain Jew who grew up to be an outstanding member of the community who, unfortunately, had been lost among other nations for several years during his youth. It was only through a special spark that this unique soul possessed that it was able to renounce its foreign background and return to Judaism. The story tells us that when this soul was reunited with its maker after 120 years, Hashem felt that the soul, as wonderful as were the deeds it had achieved on earth, lacked one thing. For two years it had been nursed by a stranger. So the special, beautiful soul had to return to earth, to a fine, caring Jewish mother, for two years. And this soul was her baby, the one that had lived two years and died.

I had never thought much about the transmigration of souls, but I understood that the teller of the tale was trying to tell me that mine, too, was a special home to whom a special soul had been sent for a short sojourn, a small *tikkun* or mending on its way to *olam habah,* the World-to-Come. The storyteller wanted us to feel special at having been chosen. And though I found it hard to believe, in my heart of hearts I said that stories such as these are not told without reason. I was happy I had nursed the baby almost exclusively, and I found a small comfort in thinking that perhaps there was something special about my baby's soul.

Another friend sent me the story of King David and his first child with Bas-Sheva. She reminded me of David's behavior while the child was ill. He wore sackcloth, he fasted, he prayed, he spoke to no one. Finally the child died. Everyone was afraid to tell David because if he had mourned so while the child was still alive, while there was still hope, they feared for his life if he learned the child had died.

David began to realize they were shielding him. He asked outright and learned that the child had died. To everyone's shock, he removed the sackcloth, got up, got dressed, and asked for something to eat. When the servants questioned him on his bizarre behavior, he explained, "While the child was alive, I prayed, I fasted, I humbled myself; there was still hope. Now that death has won this round, I shall go to him—he shall not return to me. While he still lived, there was work to be done."

In the work of the poet, there are "miles to go before I sleep—miles to go before I sleep." And those miles must be covered through good deeds and good works.

It was not so easy. I knew all these things in my mind. But to have your mind overpower the source of tears, to have your mind overpower the source of pain, to have your mind force yourself to greet your public, to go to school, to shul, to meetings, to business as usual—that is another thing.

There were times when I said to myself it would be easier to just have a breakdown—retire to a hospital for a month or two. But in thinking it through in more lucid moments, I began to take a very practical attitude. What feelings, thoughts, actions are productive, useful? And what feelings, thoughts, actions are wasteful and unproductive? Clearly, guilt is a very damaging and unproductive feeling. I was lucky. I knew I had been a good and caring mother. I had read in all the literature that Sudden Infant Death Syndrome, or SIDS, was neither predictable nor preventable and that I had nothing to feel guilty about because nothing I could have done would have prevented my baby's death.

And yet, the question remained. What if I had checked the baby earlier? If I had found the baby before it was too late, I could have begun CPR while there was still time. Like any mother, sometimes I had let the baby cry. I could feel guilty about that too. But I began to pull myself together and say: Will it do me, my husband, my baby, *O"H,* may she rest in peace, my remaining children and family any good if I devour myself with guilt? Will it help anyone in this entire world if I end up in an institution? Of course not. I had to do what was practical, what was valuable to the living. I had to get better. I had to discharge any negative, useless guilt feelings and apply all my energy to being normal, being the kind of wife, mother, daughter, teacher, friend I always had been. I had to take charge of my life.

Shortly after I came to this conclusion in my heart of hearts, I came upon a wonderful essay that my husband's rebbe had written some years earlier and it crystalized for me in beautiful, poetic Hebrew the exact feelings I had had. As I read it, I couldn't help feeling that my having thought of it myself cemented its meaning for me. Had someone external just told me about it, I might have said: That's easy for *you* to say. But the rebbe's words confirming my own thoughts gave me great strength.

In speaking of Job and the terrible *tzaros* [suffering] that befell him, the essay discusses the age-old philosophical problem: Why do the good suffer? The *Rosh Yeshivah* identifies two different kinds of personalities: *Adam HaGoral,* man of fate, is tempest-tossed by bad things, by troubles. In these brutal waves he is torn, battered, as he goes whichever way the winds and storm blow him. *Adam HaYiud,* man of destiny, is different. He too is tossed and battered by troubles. But he doesn't accept his fate passively. He gathers his strength and steers himself through and above the storm, and changes his *fate* into his *destiny*. He understands that his goal must be to change his fate into his destiny.

Other thinkers speak of individuals who changed their fate to their destiny, who *did something* at this point in their lives to say: I must give meaning to this event by changing my life in some way. Some do it by becoming active in organizations or support groups for the victims of their particular problem. Some do it by giving lots of charity, or doing research on the medical problem that affected them; or by writing a book, or by changing jobs, or realigning priorities. But each is characterized by a firm conviction—to change the fate into destiny. Somehow this event was not a scourge but a crisis to be weathered, a turning point to be cherished, an opportunity to do something that would otherwise never have been done.

It was not clear to me at that moment precisely what I would do, but I think that from then on, I took charge of my life. I would go back to work. I would try to have another baby as soon as Hashem would give me the gift—not to replace, but to fill my empty arms, to respond to death with life. And I would share. I would have, unfortunately, many chances over the next five years to give strength to families who lost babies. People would call and lead my husband and me to bereaved families. I would listen, I would talk. I would call, I would be there, I would share. I would help them understand that their feelings were normal. I would say aloud for them what they were afraid to say aloud, lest it be considered crazy or "out of sight" by the blessedly uninitiated.

I could tell them about how we decided what to write on her tombstone, words that would help us say when we visited the grave: "Yes—that is what she was. This is how we felt about her."

Miriam Rus, daughter of Yitzhak Tzvi and Rahel,
Precious girl, pure soul
We loved her with a deep love
She was taken away with a kiss
on the 17th of Tevet 5742

We wrote MIRIAM RUS, DAUGHTER OF YITZHAK TZVI AND RAHEL— both father and mother, because we both felt the need to be joined with her memory through the stone. I would tell them how I put away the crib after shivah, how I packed the boxes of beautiful unworn gifts and wrote on them "with *mazel,*" as a mother who had lost a child to SIDS thirty years ago told me she did. I would tell them how I looked at her picture and cried, not wanting to torture myself but somehow needing to.

I could tell them what others had told me in their turn—that the statement made at the end of the *shivah* call—"May you be comforted together with all who mourn Zion and Jerusalem"— was not a wish or a blessing or a hope that the bereaved will be comforted, but a charge and a statement of irrefutable fact: Hashem *will indeed* comfort you. Just as all those who have loved and lost before have eventually been comforted, so too will you. It has to be that way.

I can tell you. I've been there. But you have to help yourself. "He who comes to be cleansed, the Almighty helps him." We have the concept of *hishtadlus* [effort, or determination]. We have to try. We are in charge of our life, of our destiny. We have to spare no effort to put our mind in control of our emotions. If you desire it, it won't be just a fable—it will be real. If we will it, it can happen. And I believe in the power of the mind, of the intellect, to assess the situation and say: What is the best response? What is the response that will be most noble, most practical, most helpful to myself, to my family, to those I love and live for?

Once we decide upon that response, every fiber of our being has to go into implementing it. Even when I wake up in the morning and feel like going back to sleep for two weeks, I have to rise, dress, look my best, do my work, meet my public, get through that day. We are helped by talking things through with whatever network of support we have built for ourselves—a husband, a wife, a parent, dear friends, a trusted rabbi, doctor, or therapist.

I was very blessed. I had a strong marriage, supportive parents and in-laws and good friends who helped to smooth the way. My prayers were answered, and my determination to respond to death with life fulfilled. Before our baby's yahrzeit, I had a beautiful little son. It was a tension-filled time. There was so much riding on this child emotionally for both my husband and me.

We named him very significantly, we felt, Moshe Hillel, for the memory of our Miriam Rus *O"H*. Moshe—because Miriam watched over her little brother Moshe in the bulrushes, and our Miriam would watch over Moshe from *shamayim* [heaven]—and Hillel for our own Hallel [the psalms of rejoicing], our rejoicing, and because his *bris* was on Hanukkah, when the complete Hallel is said each day, and also because we light candles each night in a pattern that is *mosif v'holech:* our light and our joy is multiplied progressively, as was the ruling of Bais Hillel.

We chose to have the baby put on an infant-monitoring program, which meant that whenever he was asleep he would be attached by electrodes to a small machine that watched his breathing and heart rate, and would send an alarm if anything was irregular. For me, this was not a reflection of any lack of faith, but an affirmation that I believed with a full heart that this child would make it. But I also felt that it was my responsibility as a parent to do the best I could. Just as I would always buckle my children's seatbelts, no matter how short a distance I rode, I would always attach the monitor because I had to do my part—to use all the technology available to be a partner with *Hakadosh Baruch Hu* to protect my baby and try to guarantee him life through my *hishtadlus* [effort].

Every aspect of the baby's birth became a déjà-vu experience for me. I relived in my mind bringing home the baby that we lost, her first feeding, her first trip to the doctor. The first three months were the most difficult; my joy in him was tempered by the memory of my joy in Miriam and how that joy was doomed to be cut short so abruptly. And yet, the awe and wonderment and the profound gratitude for the great miracle of his birth were even greater.

When we heard during his naming at his *bris,* "*Kayem es hayeled hazeh* . . . Preserve this boy for his father and mother," and the blessing "*Zeh hakatan gadol yehieh* . . . May this little one grow big," I cried very real tears, knowing that these prayers were not just words but true supplications for life and longevity. But the baby survived, his parents survived, and he brought a tremendous amount of joy into our lives. He did not *replace,* but helped to *restore.* To this very day we find him to be a special little boy with a *lev tov,* a good heart.

The story doesn't end here. We were blessed with a little girl whom we named Shira Nomi—also for Miriam Rus—because Miriam went out and sang *shira,* a song, and we also wished to exult in our new baby girl, to sing *shira;* and Nomi, for her [Naomi's] love and devotion to Rus [Ruth]. We had another little girl less than two years later, and I feel that these children have enriched our lives immeasurably. Our three older children still speak of the baby we lost and they have made her name familiar to the younger ones, integrating Miri's memory comfortably into the fabric of our family life.

Over the years we have given *tzedakah l'iluyi nishmas,* charity in the name of Miriam Rus, my husband and I have delivered public *shiurim* [classes] and dedicated them and other learning to Miriam Rus and to the memory of other *kedoshim* [pure souls]. Our friends at the shul dedicated the *shtender* [lectern] in the new *bais medrash* to the baby's memory. Although at first tears came to my eyes each time I saw the beautifully embroidered letters "In memory of the soul of the child Miriam Rus," I now can look at it and feel that it is an expression of the love and empathy our friends felt for us. And it is an indication of our involvement in *talmud Torah* for her, as I said earlier, an attempt to live *for her* as well, to do the good she did not live to do and give meaning to her short life through deeds and study done for her sake.

Though the chapter is concluded, the story is not over, because the human mind is such that we continue to live with our memories. I am no longer cut to the quick by the thought of Miri or the magnitude of what I lost, but I experience twinges of pain at different moments in life—on the 9th of Av when we mourn the destruction of both Temples and the millions of children killed in those and subsequent holocausts; at the time of a family *simhah,* when people ask how many children I have; when I pray on Rosh Hashanah and Yom Kippur and say "who will live and who will die," and remember how I prayed on the High Holy Days I was pregnant with Miri, little knowing that by *Shabbos Bereishis* I would have a perfect baby and by the 17th of Tevet she would have died.

But I have lived with all this. I also have a stronger recognition than ever before of how much I am blessed. I don't think of what bad I must have done to deserve a *tzarah* [pain] such as this, but I gear my daily soul-searching to being the best kind of person I can be. I don't believe that *cheshbon hanefesh* or soul-searching introspection should be geared to searching for the particular sins that might doom us to particular punishments. Our sages tell us that rewards for mitzvot and punishments for sins are all settled in the world-to-come. In this world we have to live a good and ethical life for its own sake. There is not a day that goes by that I do not say the prayer *Modeh ani* with a whole heart and extra concentration: Thank You, Hashem, for each day that dawns afresh in a beautiful world.

I have stronger intimations of my own mortality now than I had then; I am aware of what death is. I have seen it. I am still frightened of it, because of the great pain it causes the survivors. But I am less frightened at the prospect of my own death. I want to live long and fully, of course, but I am more sure that something awaits me after I have "crossed the bar." The death of my child has strengthened my belief that there is a world-to-come. With our limited vision or narrow perception, we find it hard to imagine a world beyond our own world. But they exist. "Yes, I believe that there is a world-to-come," the song goes.

So with what, then, do I conclude? I have been struck, but I have survived. Losing a child is one of the most terrible and painful things that can happen to a person. And yet the person who lives through this can still go to visit Eretz Yisrael and speak to family after family who lost grown children—tall, beautiful sons whose potential had already begun to see fruition—and say: I can put my own tragedy in perspective. Far greater tzadikkim [righteous people] than I have experienced *yesurim* [suffering] and the Talmud does speak about something called "suffering out of love."

Though the initial pain of my loss seemed to be unbearable, I have borne it. Though the loss itself was irreversible, I have, thank God, three subsequent children who have been a source of enormous joy and who make life very full. Mine was not the kind of tragedy you continue to live with every waking hour. For this I am deeply grateful. I have walked away, and I have not been smitten again and again, God forbid. My life, my soul, my self, my family, my relationships with people, my relationship with the Almighty have all been enriched by Miri's life.

To answer the question I asked myself at the outset—"Could I ever again be the person I was before the tragedy?"—I have to say: Yes, I am the same person I once was, and yet I am not. I can once again be happy with a full heart, as I never thought I would be able to be. But I have a different kind of vision now than I had then, a greater clarity of purpose, a more finely tuned sense of what is important, of how to help those who have suffered.

On Being the Kaddish

Patricia Z. Barry

Thus, even when they are gone, the departed are with us. . . . We remember them now; they live in our hearts; they are an abiding blessing.

—*The New Union Prayer Book*

Gregory, our firstborn son, was killed in Lebanon on June 9, 1982, the third day of Operation Shalom HaGalil. It was not yet called the War in Lebanon. The operation began on June 6, but in the sunshine of early summer in North Carolina, I convinced myself that I was not worried. We did not learn of his death for nearly a week. I remember that week: even in the middle of it, before we knew, I remarked that I felt as though I were in the eye of a hurricane. I lied to myself, believing that he was on border patrol; I did not think of him in combat; I told myself that, statistically, he was safe—most soldiers go into battle and emerge living, if not unscathed.

It was graduation week at our local high school; my youngest son, Neil, was graduated on the day Greg was killed. That was Wednesday. As the week wore on, terrible things happened in Chapel Hill. Tony, an old friend of Neil's, tried to kill himself; Randall, an extraordinarily promising fellow in the graduating class, killed someone while defending his friend in an uninvited brawl; a graduating senior was killed in a wreck; three young graduates, close friends of Neil and sons of friends of mine, were lost on a stormy night on the Haw River, which had been transformed from a lazy southern stream into a dangerous maelstrom. They were found after a long night of panic. The news from Israel was bad, an ominous background to a schizophrenic week of parties and tragedies. I joked that sons were probably safer fighting in Lebanon than graduating from Chapel Hill High. Now I think that deep inside I knew that Greg was dead, though my mind never admitted the possibility. My energy level dropped to nearly zero by the end of the week; I left my office, canceled all my social engagements, and occupied myself for hours with needlework.

The following Tuesday, June 15, at 10:00 in the morning, the rabbi knocked on my office door. John Friedman is an amiable fellow; nothing in his demeanor alerted me that something was amiss. He closed the door and said, quite simply, "Greg has been killed." I just screamed. I don't know where it came from; I am not a screamer, but I screamed. I howled at the top of my lungs. *NO!!! NOOOOOOOO!!* I screamed at the rabbi, I told him he was wrong, I screamed at God, I screamed at Greg, I howled in rage and protest as women before me have, until I was spent. I did not cry; after the screaming, I was ice.

I called my second son, Alan, who was in California with his father (from whom I am divorced), and called my own father, who told my mother. I could not. At home, friends met me and helped me pack; by 4:00 that afternoon, Neil and I were on a plane to New York to make a connection to Israel. We were met by my brother and his wife and son; my brother Michael bought a ticket and came with us without even a toothbrush or a change of underwear. Alan stayed with his father in California. We arrived in Israel on Wednesday afternoon and were met by people from Kibbutz Gazit, where Greg made his home. They, too, had learned of his death only that morning and were in a state of shock and despair. Nevertheless, we were enveloped in love and shared grief by everyone: the kibbutzniks (already my friends from a previous visit); Dorit and Judy, Israeli friends who met us at the airport and never left my side until we departed thirty-nine hours later; and people from the army, each of whom helped in a dozen ways, thoughtfully, with great sensitivity and kindness.

On Thursday, at 3:00 in the afternoon, the traditional burial time in Israel, we walked slowly to the kibbutz coffeehouse. Greg's body arrived from wherever it had been housed and lay in state in a flag-draped pine casket as all the adults in the kibbutz gathered outside. At 3:30, the casket was loaded into the back of a jeep and we walked slowly in silence behind it, some two hundred mourners, to the cemetery, a distance of about a mile. The sun shone and the wind blew through the pines, and I was conscious of his spirit everywhere. We buried him in a traditional military ceremony. The kibbutzniks shoveled the earth into the grave; my brother helped. Eight women soldiers, not yet in their twenties, laid flowers on the grave. Rifles were fired three times in his honor. Afterward, we all felt lighter, relieved. We left Israel the next morning.

We were home by Friday evening, met by Alan, my parents, and the rest of my brother's family. On Sunday there was a memorial service at our synagogue, the temple overflowing with friends and associates, young people with ashen faces and glazed eyes, mothers with wet cheeks and fathers with tight mouths and profound sympathy in their eyes. We sat shivah and knew the comfort and unimagined wellsprings of community support. I was comforted by the certain knowledge of the presence of Greg's spirit, which had surrounded me and given me strength throughout my hours in Israel, and which was still palpably present through that week. My spiritual awareness has always been stirred by the daily miracles of life itself—by leaves and flowers and bugs and bird-songs. That week, all things small and alive stood in contradiction to the terrible thing that had happened.

Rabbi Friedman visited. We sat on the deck in the sunshine, and he said, "You know, now you are the Kaddish. Usually the child is Kaddish for the parents, but you are his Kaddish." I did not know what he meant: the Kaddish is a prayer, not a person. Having been brought up as a Reform Jew in a family that was highly assimilated, and having been relatively untouched by death in my family (my grandmother died at a hundred and two later that summer), I had never heard the term Kaddish used as the rabbi was now using it. "What do you mean?" I asked. He told me that it is the responsibility of the Kaddish to keep the memory of the dead person alive, to not forget, not to let others forget.

In the weeks that followed, I cried, but not yet to the depths of my crying. The prospect of that kind of crying, of the uncontrolled and uncontrollable letting-go, was terrifying, for that would mean facing the images of death I carried with me, thinking of Greg's having been killed without me there, without my being able to comfort him, remembering him as he was—tall, handsome, burst-ing with life and passionate love for Israel, embracing experience with his whole being. How could I face the total, permanent sepa-ration that all my crying would signify? To really cry would be to sink into grief so profound that there might be no way back from it. I was seized by terror at the merest glimpse of the abyss of despair that would surely swallow me if I let go; I was too fright-ened to admit the tears. Better to back off, to travel, to embroider, to visit with friends, to return to work, to "get back to my life." And I was moderately successful. In Israel they had told me to be strong, and I was strong.

Gregory had gone to Israel to work on a kibbutz immediately after his graduation from high school. He fell in love with the country and its people and found there a purpose for his own life.

Israel gave him the opportunity to contribute as an adult to something he believed in. A year later, he became an immigrant, and by the time of his death he had lived there nearly three years. In October of 1982, I returned to Israel to begin the sabbatical year I had planned before he died. Friends met me at the airport at Lod and took me to Haifa, where Greg and I had spent a week together when I had visited him in 1981. Now, winding up the mountain, I was flooded with memories, and I began to cry in earnest. I was not thinking of his death so much as of the time we had spent together here. Here we had stopped to look at the harbor, here was the little sculpture garden where we picnicked, here was the Merkaz HaCarmel, which, as he told me with a touch of awe, was the most expensive shopping area in Haifa. Each memory brought a new flood of tears. My friends were concerned. I assured them that I was fine, that I was only remembering. And as I explained, I began to understand: the crying was helping. Each tear a memory, permitting yet another memory, still more tears.

I cried all the while I was in Israel. I cried on city buses in Haifa where I lived, I cried on buses between cities. I cried on the kibbutz and I cried in Jerusalem. The more I cried, the more I remembered about Greg—and the more I could focus on other things when I was not crying. I came to welcome the tears, to believe that they were the source of my strength. It was wonderful to be in Israel, closer to the memories, near people who understood loss, and my loss, and I was strong. I taught at Haifa University, made friends, learned Hebrew, studied, and remembered.

I had been in Israel four months when I received a letter from Claire, one of Greg's high-school friends and a friend of mine. She wrote that his old gang had spent several evenings together during the college winter vacation, but that they had hardly spoken of Greg, for they were afraid to upset each other. And finally I recalled the words of the rabbi and understood them: to be a Kaddish is to be willing to suffer the grief of remembering.

Judaism teaches that the spirits of the dead live in eternal peace.

But further, the prayers of mourning adjure us to remember the dead in order that they may live. In *The New Union Prayer Book* we read, "Now we know that they will never vanish, so long as the heart and thought remain within us. By love are they remembered, and in memory they live." And, "Thus, even when they are gone, the departed are with us. . . . We remember them now; they live in our hearts; they are an abiding blessing."

The Kaddish prayer, recited at the end of every religious service, is a ritual that assures that we remember the dead whenever we gather together to worship. Recitation of the Kaddish is a mitzvah, a commandment. Again from *The New Union Prayer Book*:

> [The Kaddish] possesses wonderful power. Truly, if there is any bond strong enough to chain heaven to earth, it is this prayer. It keeps the living together, and forms a bridge to the mysterious realm of the dead. One might almost say that this prayer is the . . . guardian of the people by whom alone it is uttered; therein lies the warrant of its continuance. Can a people disappear and be annihilated so long as a child remembers its parents?

Remembering the dead, then, is an injunction. It is the means by which the dead continue to live, and, more than that, it assures the survival of our people.

But to remember—really to remember, to remember in detail—brings with it nearly intolerable anguish. We suffer through the remembering, and wonder how long it will last, wonder, as time goes on, whether it may be without end. We long to be free again, the grieving behind us. As the prayer book itself warns, "If we dwell too long on our loss we embitter our hearts and harm ourselves and those about us."

But I have come to realize that to grieve is not merely to dwell on our loss. Yes, we cry for that—but also for the life that has ended. If it was a young life, we cry because the flower has fallen before fully bloomed. If the manner of death was painful or protracted, or abrupt and violent, we cry for that. There are tears of longing that are different from the tears of self-pity, and there are tears of regret for business unfinished, and of remorse for injuries real or imagined that are now beyond repair. And there are the tears that come with the simple rememberings, the memories pleasant and dear that happen to us when a song or a glance or a smell reminds us of the loved one who has died.

The observer will see the tears and think they are all the same, that they all mean pain, will not know that the tears are the waters that soothe the pain and that they lubricate our memories. The observer will not know that if we seek to remember, we must be prepared to cry. That is what it means to be the Kaddish for another who has died, who is dead.

Or is Greg never to be mentioned again by his high-school friends? When they meet years from now and reminisce, will his life be taken from him yet again? Am I, his mother, to fear to speak of him lest others feel uncomfortable? Is his memory not available as a delight because it may also be a sadness? Surely Greg deserves more, better—he who was so energetic a participant in life, he who was so often the cause of joy. The fact of his death must not be allowed to take precedence over the fact of his life. The years of his young life are not less worthy, less worth remembering than the years of the others, Greg's brothers and friends, who have not died.

For a whole year, I could not rid myself of the imagining of the manner of his death. It haunted me until I cried my way into remembering, from my own childhood, *Life* magazine pictures of World War II, soldiers dying in battle, then war games my brother played with his friends, memories that brought terror—and detoxified the thoughts of my own son, shot. I am no longer haunted as I was; my work at remembering has moved me beyond the anger and beyond the terror, has enabled me finally to forgive Greg for dying and thereby hurting me so, has permitted me to move back, to the time before his death, to his life.

Greg's old friends are stiff with me, resent me as a reminder of their loss, perhaps also of their vulnerability—to loss, to death. I wish I could help them, for their sake and also for my own. They know so much about Greg, the everyday kinds of things I so want to hear about.

I have begun to ask friends and relatives what they remember. Usually it is very little, unless I persist, and then, as they shed their own tears, they begin to tell me wonderful things—anecdotes, trivia, the bits and pieces that linger—and trigger my own memories, permit me to recover more and more about Greg and his life.

It is more than a year and a half since Greg was killed. It is still difficult and likely always will be. I sometimes sense a pull to be depressed forever, that to feel myself fully happy would be a betrayal. But that, of course, is nonsense, for depression and sadness are only a small part of the grieving, of its purpose.

Which is to heal, and to live. That is what I have learned; that is what it means to be Greg's Kaddish. And that, finally, is what it means that his memory is a blessing. *Zichrono livrachah.*

Firepower in Mitzvot

Agnes G. Herman

Among the family pictures that paper the walls of our home, one face appears again and again: Jeff with a beard and without one; Jeff in a white shirt, a red shirt, a blue one; Jeff with nephew Matthew, with sister Judi, with his beloved Alex, and, of course, with his dad. On the bulletin board in the kitchen there is Jeff as a toddler, happy and healthy.

Why so many? AIDS wrenched our precious son from us on December 11, 1992. Jeff's voice and the stages of his growth are stored in my memory. The pictures keep his face, his big hugs, and hearty "Hi, Mom" in sharp focus.

I was furious with God when Jeff died; he was only forty-three. Less than two years before, he was robust and symptom-free, although HIV positive. None of us had any idea how quickly the virus that causes AIDS would destroy his health and steal his life.

Ten years earlier Jeff was suffering from diverse and vague symptoms which could have been mononucleosis, influenza, hepatitis—or AIDS. AIDS had just appeared on the scene, inexplicable, insidious, frightening. Our family doctor examined Jeff. He tested HIV positive but was told to come back in three months since the tests were far from definitive.

We panicked and wrapped ourselves in denial. Jeff did not go for retesting and we did not insist. We donned rose-colored glasses and colluded in his benign neglect.

My husband and I tried not to pry into our son's relationships. But periodically I could not resist the question, "Do you know how to protect yourself?" With studied patience, he responded, "Of course, Mom, don't worry."

When Jeff entered into a relationship with Alex in the mid-1980s, it became a commitment that was monogamous, loving, and forever. I had hoped for that; I did not like either of our children living alone. Our son had found someone he deeply cared for who reciprocated his love. It was many years before I understood the full depth of their devotion.

Later on, when Jeff became ill, Alex seemed to withdraw from us. The greater Jeff's distress, the more defined Alex's withdrawal. "Alex is afraid you are going to move in and take over, or worse, try to take me home with you," Jeff explained. We assured him we had no intention of breaking up their home. I shared my own devastating memory—my frustration and anger—of battling my mother-in-law for control when my husband was hospitalized on our first visit "home" in 1946. We reassured Jeff and Alex of our respect for their independence and our joy in their love for one another. We expressed our admiration and appreciation for Alex's loving care—he was indeed a guardian angel.

What, then, was my role in Jeff's illness? In the mid-1980s I was invited to become a member of the National AIDS Committee of the Union of American Hebrew Congregations and the Central Conference of American Rabbis. Its mission is to alert and educate congregations to the growing epidemic, and to remind us how our Jewish values and responsibilities inform the roles we must play in combating this plague.

My learning curve rose dramatically as I rubbed shoulders with doctors and counselors, rabbis and educators, researchers and laboratory technicians. The more I learned, the more my concern grew for Jeff and Alex. Secret fears and private worries became my realities. Nightmare scenarios invaded my thoughts. I inundated our boys with literature, wishing knowledge could transform the awful truth.

After both their diagnoses were confirmed, they read, became more informed. In search of a healthier and less frenetic life, they moved from the city to beautiful Clearlake in northern California, which gave them a perfect, peaceful setting. They became involved in an AIDS support group, raised money, distributed blankets.

It soon became obvious that Jeff and Alex were in trouble. Our son's fatigue, lack of energy, and escalating aches and Alex's pneumonia were ominous symptoms. Never complaining, they seemed dedicated to helping us keep our illusions. Jeff, who had the knack of thinking positively, developed a litany of survival: "I am not going to let this thing get me. I will live long enough to enjoy the cure." He never wavered. His hopeful attitude was contagious when his dad and I were with him, but elusive when we were apart.

Even when Jeff sat paralyzed and mute, debilitated by AZT, the antiviral AIDS medication, he continued to plan for energy-filled tomorrows. He wanted to live until the moment he died. During the last days, when he could not eat or drink, he still managed a smile, responded to us with his eyes.

Jeff's life was an inspiration. When near the end I asked if he was afraid, he mouthed, "Of what?" Sweeping his good arm across the beautiful vista of lake, mountains, and sky that was his daily companion, he seemed to be saying, "With all this beauty, what is there to fear?" His spirit kept ours alive.

As parents we were supposed to be his role models, yet it was he who taught us to be brave, to accept reality and keep going. "We are all going to die," he had reminded us earlier. "It will just be sooner for me."

Our Jeff was special, as all children are to those who love them.

AIDS cut him down, deprived us of each other too soon. But before it did that, it inspired the best that was Jeff. Even as he was able to find the patch of blue in an otherwise gray sky and say, "It will be a beautiful day," so was he able to shake his fist at AIDS and wage war with hope, courage, and trust.

In early December Jeff lay in bed, no longer able to sit. My husband and I took turns stroking and loving him; he could not respond. One day with enormous effort he lifted himself up and threw himself into my arms to hug and be hugged. The strength he mustered gave me renewed courage to continue through the horror with him.

Each evening during Jeff's final week, before returning to our hotel my husband and I kissed our son and said, "Good night, we'll see you tomorrow." Each morning, emaciated and weak, he found the strength to awaken. On Friday evening Jeff's total exhaustion was evident. Separately, his dad and I sat with him, took him into our arms, and said, "Goodbye, son." Thirty minutes later, he died.

If Jeff was angry at his fate, he never expressed it. In contrast, my husband and I were furious. At first we found no target for our feelings, but when Jeff died we believed God had failed us. How could a compassionate creator have allowed this?

Tired of hearing from friends that now God would take care of Jeff and soothe our pain, and time would heal our hurt, our rage overflowed. It attacked our peace of mind, threatening to destroy us. We struggled to examine our faith and discover what Judaism had to teach us.

In time we relearned who we are and what our responsibilities are on this earth, that God is not the decision maker in our lives but our inspiration for day-to-day living. We renewed our belief that we are responsible for what takes place in our lives.

We reminded ourselves that we should daily reflect God's goodness and love, that we are obligated as Jews to perform the divinely inspired mitzvot, to extend our hands and hearts to others in pain. We agreed we are not allowed to sit back and lick our wounds. And we stopped blaming God for Jeff's death.

It was difficult to admit that it was we who had failed, not God.

We had been passive and silent when there was foot-dragging by our government, when the President would not even utter the word AIDS. We stood by for years when there were insufficient research dollars, blatant bigotry, inadequate health care and education, bickering among scientists, and overpriced medication. Our own silence and passivity—and yes, even our bigotry—contributed to the disease's spread. God did not deserve our fury; society is to blame.

As a result of our wrestling, we have committed ourselves to be active participants in the war against AIDS. We believe we can validate hope and trust by counterattacking, by touching the lives of those who have it, by reaching out to the families who care for and suffer with them. We have firepower called mitzvot: we act out our Jewish values.

We must put a Jewish face on AIDS. Judaism teaches us to respect the dignity and feelings of others, to empathize, not criticize, to make the world better. Each of us must reach out with help, support, and advocacy. We may not shun or isolate the sick. We must sit with them, feed them, take their hands into our own, stroke a fevered forehead, let them know they are not alone.

When I wrote my first article concerning Jeff, I knew that our family had linked arms and emerged from the closet together. Today I know Jeff's ever-present photographs cannot bring him back. I know too that his hand is in mine, and I can hear his voice: "Go for it, Mom. Tell the story. We have to beat this thing!"

Note: Alex died in June. We lost another son.

Chapter Eleven

Do We Believe in an Afterlife?

In a sense, this chapter is an act of resurrection, for it revives the rich heritage of Jewish thought about life after death that has been repressed, denied, disclaimed, or ignored for so long. It seeks to make this part of the Jewish heritage accessible to a new generation.

It is true that in the Bible itself there is hardly any mention of afterlife, a line here, a hint there, a reference to Sheol on occasion, but not much more than that. The reason for this is that the Bible was given to Israelites who came out of Egypt. The whole cult and culture of Egypt was essentially death-centered. Those who have seen the magnificent exhibit of the treasures of King Tut when it toured this country some years ago will understand what we mean by saying that Egyptian religion and society were death-centered. The gold and the diamonds, the lapis lazuli and the feldspar, the colored glass and the benches of ivory and ebony, the alabaster bowls and jars, the bejeweled scabbards and scimitars, the amulets and the statuettes that made up this exhibit were simply dazzling. To think that all this art went with King Tut into the grave in the hope that it would help him bribe the guards and bring him safe passage into the afterlife!

The Israelites who left Egypt were appalled by all the opulence that was made only for the grave. The treasures buried with King Tut would have been more than enough to feed a whole province of Egypt for years. And this is why the Torah that was given to the people who left Egypt is so reticent about afterlife, so totally different in tone and content from the Egyptian Book of the Dead or the other sacred writings of Egyptian society. The silence of the Torah on this subject is a response to the religion of Egypt.

But post-biblical Judaism is more explicit. The sages made their faith in resurrection very clear: They make us affirm it *five times* within the second prayer of the Amidah and in many other places in the liturgy as well. They taught that there there is more than just this world, that there is a world-to-come, in which God will bring justice and bliss to those who suffer in this life. And post-Talmudic Judaism continued this affirmation down through the centuries in two main streams. The rationalists, the medieval Jewish philosophers, expounded this doctrine in one way and the Kabbalists, the mystics, expounded it in a different way. But for both schools of thought it was clear that this belief was central to Jewish self-understanding. Every time a Jew is called to the Torah he or she recites a blessing that declares: *"Eternal Life* He has planted within our midst" and every time the Yizkor prayer is said, we hear the affirmation: *"In Gan Eden* may he find his rest."

Then came modernity and crushed out our sense of wonder about this life and our capacity to hope and trust in another life. The idea that there could be anything more than just this world seemed antiquated, naive, a remnant of the past, to the nineteenth century rationalists. But as a wise man once predicted: "The next generation is going to spend much of its time and energy fishing out of the wastebasket the ideas, values, and truths that the previous generation discarded."

All of a sudden, there is a new openness to the idea of afterlife, as this chapter demonstrates. It comes out of the Jewish renewal movement, which is restoring a number of questions that were once thought settled back on the agenda of Jewish life. There is a new understanding of cosmology, a new curiosity about mysticism, a new tentativeness about the definition of matter and energy, and all these things have come together to bring about a new interest in this topic.

In this chapter we bring together a number of very different voices. Some of them sound like descendants of the rationalists; others as continuers of the Kabbalists. What unites them is that they do not speak as historians or as archeologists, digging up the beliefs of the ancient Jews; they speak as pathfinders, pointing the way for those who want to believe.

What is the most appropriate language of discourse for a discussion of this topic? We have not limited ourselves only to right hemisphere thinkers who argue with the canons of logic but have chosen to include poets and parable makers as well. For this is a topic on which no one can speak with dogmatic certainty or prove their case with theorems, and perhaps poems and parables can reach beyond the level that logic can go.

In the World-to-Come

In the world-to-come, there is neither eating nor drinking nor procreation nor business dealings nor jealousy nor hate nor competition.

But righteous men sit with their crowns on their heads and they enjoy the splendor of the Divine Presence.

—Rav, in the Babylonian Talmud, tractate Berakhot, 17a

And what is the meaning of the sages' statement "they enjoy the splendor of the Divine Presence"? This means that the righteous attain to a knowledge and realization of the truth concerning God which they did not know in this world, while they were confined by a murky and lowly body.

—Maimonides, "Laws Concerning Repentance," Code 8:2

The Birth

Y. M. Tuckachinsky

Imagine twins growing peacefully in the warmth of the womb. Their mouths are closed, and they are being fed via the navel. Their lives are serene. The whole world, to these twins, is the interior of the womb. Who could conceive anything bigger, better, more comfortable? They begin to wonder: we are getting lower and lower. Surely if it continues, we will exit one day. What will happen then?

Now the first infant is a believer. He is heir to a religious tradition that tells him that there will be a "new life" after this wet and warm existence in the womb. That is a strange belief, seemingly without foundation, but one to which he holds fast. The second infant is a thorough skeptic. Mere stories do not impress him. He believes only in that which can be demonstrated. He is enlightened and tolerates no idle conjecture. What is not within one's experience can have no basis in one's imagination.

Says the faithful brother: "After our 'death' here, there will be a great new world, a whole new realm of being. There we will eat through the mouth, not the navel! There we will be able to see for great distances, and we will hear through these two things that we have on the sides of our heads! There our feet will be straightened and eventually we will learn how to walk upon them! And our heads will be up and free, rather than down and boxed in!"

Replies the skeptical brother: "Nonsense. You are straining your imagination again. There is no foundation for this belief. It is only your survival instinct, an elaborate defense mechanism, a subterfuge. You are looking for something to allay your fear of 'death.' There is only this world; there is no world-to-come!"

"Well, then," asks the first brother, "what do you think it will be like when we leave here?"

The skeptical brother snappily replies, with all the assurance of the certain, "We will go with a bang. Our world will collapse and sink into oblivion. No more. Nothing. Black void. An end to consciousness. Forgotten. This may not be a comforting thought, but it is the only logical and realistic one."

Just then the water inside the womb bursts. The womb convulses. There is upheaval, turmoil, writhing. Then there is a mysterious pounding. Faster, faster; lower, lower.

The believing brother exists. Tearing himself from the womb, he falls outward. The second brother shrieks, startled by the "accident" that has befallen his brother. He bewails and bemoans the tragedy—the death of a perfectly fine embryo. Why? Why? Why didn't he take better care? Why did he have to fall into that terrible abyss?

As he is thus lamenting, he hears a head-splitting cry and a great tumult from the black abyss, and he trembles: "Oh, my! What a horrible end! Just as I predicted!" he says.

Meanwhile, as the skeptical brother mourns, his "dead" brother has been born into the "new world." The head-splitting cry was a sign of health and the tumult was the chorus of mazel tov's sounded by the doctor, the nurses, and the attendants, all thanking God for the arrival of a healthy child.

The Ship

David (Mickey) Marcus

This parable comes not from a theologian or a philosopher but from a soldier. It was found on the body of the American Jewish soldier Colonel David Marcus, who was one of those who helped to form the first army of the state of Israel and who died in the defense of Jerusalem.

I am standing upon the seashore. A ship at my side spreads her white sails in the morning breeze and starts for the blue ocean. She is an object of beauty and strength, and I stand and watch her until at length she is only a ribbon of white cloud just where the sea and sky come to mingle with each other. Then someone at my side says, "There! She's gone!" Gone where? Gone from my sight— that is all. She is just as large in mast and hull and spar as she was when she left my side, and just as able to bear her load of living freight to the place of destination. Her diminished size is in me, not in her, and just at the moment when someone at my side says, "There! She's gone!" there are other voices ready to take up the glad shout "There! She comes!" And that is dying.

Is There Life After Death?

Blu Greenberg

Not entirely trusting myself to deal with this topic, slightly fearful of it, and wishing to gain some distance on something so intensely personal, I decided first to interview several friends and relatives on their views of an afterlife. Below is the condensed version of two informal interviews. The first is of L., an Orthodox Jew, fifty-plus years old, a successful entrepreneur and highly intelligent man, and the father of three grown children:

B: Do you believe in *olam habah* (the world-to-come, the hereafter)?
L: Of course.
B: How do you understand or envision it?
L: (*Long pause*) Now, that's a different story. I am not really sure.
B: Well, let's give it a try.
L: I see it in two ways. One, a place where the good people go, or rather, where their souls go after they leave this place; and second, the way I say it every day (in the daily prayers)—the resurrection of the dead at the end of days, whatever or whenever that is.
B: Let's go back to the first idea. So you believe there is some kind of universe where the souls of the righteous "live," so to speak?
L: Well, not exactly. When my father died (in his sixties), I thought his soul surely went to "heaven," that he lived on after his physical demise. Because he was such a good person, he should have lived another twenty years, so at first I couldn't accept that his life was over. Naively I kept thinking he was going to come back. But, of course, he never did. . . . So I picked the most available concept, *olam habah,* and that is what I told myself. And that is what I told my kids, and that is what they believed—and maybe still do, though come to think of it, no one has mentioned "Grandpa in heaven" in a long time. But I believed it myself. Even now sometimes I believe my father knows what is happening on earth, what I'm doing, but only rarely do I think so. I certainly don't imagine there is a whole society of souls out there conversing with one another. I don't think my father's soul meets every day with [the souls of] his cronies from his old shul. On the other hand, my mother says she talks to my father, and when she dies, God forbid, I think she will be reunited with him. But I suppose that contradicts what I just said [about souls getting together]. . . . I'm not sure how the whole thing works. I suppose I should study it. Who has written about this?
B: So, in other words, except for your mother's and father's souls

reuniting, the main activity of a life after life, or a life in the world-to-come, is communication with those still in this life, a vertical form of communication connecting the two worlds, rather than a horizontal one with all of the good souls living on in *olam habah* and constituting a society of good souls?

L: Yes.

B: Am I putting words into your mouth?

L: No. That's exactly what I was saying.

B: What, then, does *olam habah* mean?

L: Something for the philosophers and halachists to deal with.

B: Let's go back to the personal for the moment. When you die, God forbid, and you pass the test of righteousness and warrant a place in *olam habah,* do you think your soul will live on?

L: No worry. I wouldn't pass the test. I'm an ordinary mortal.

B: But if you did?

L: I don't know, really; I just don't know.

B: Would you like it to be so?

L: I'm not so sure about that either. On the one hand, I am curious about people. It might be interesting to look on and know what is happening on earth, to keep tabs, to see how the kids and eventually the grandchildren are doing. On the other hand, I think a clean break between life and death might be good. I don't really know if I'd want to live on. Life is great, but when I die—hopefully not before another thirty years or so—sooner if I'm sick—when I reach eighty, I'll probably have had as much as I can stand. Besides, as I understand it, there's no food, clothing, and no sex, so what good is it? Just kidding; don't quote me on that.

B: Well, this is all anonymous.

L: Okay, then. Just kidding!

B: How about resurrection at the end of time? What's your personal view?

L: An even deeper mystery. Though I know it's one of our basic beliefs, physical resurrection is not central to my personal faith. I suppose this is why I have mixed feelings about autopsies. [L. believes, contrary to the view of many Orthodox rabbinic opinions of our time, that autopsies should be performed to help science advance in the task of saving future lives.] . . . But perhaps

I'm too young and too far from the end of time and enjoying the good life here and now to answer those questions. . . . I guess in the ultimate economy of things . . . [these concepts are] necessary to human faith.

B: But why? In what way?

L: They give people an anchor or a dream that life isn't over when it's over.

B: But you just said you wouldn't necessarily want to live on.

L: Yes, but as I understand it, resurrection means the whole thing, physical bodies and all. And as I understand it, you don't have to pass any tests. Everyone will be restored to life, and goodness will reign, and there will be no evil or war, and people will be good and moral. And the *yemot hamashiach* [messianic times] is a good vision to have, something to hope for, better times.

B: Do these concepts have an impact on your personal life?

L: (*Long pause*) I don't think so. Occasionally it has occurred to me that when I want to do something I know I could get away with that is evil, something that is truly evil, not just paying in cash with no sales tax, but something like murder or stealing or violence, that I will be punished for it in another life. But even then it's more a matter of God watching me now and holding me accountable. Still, I am not going to take any chances. So, I guess you could say it does have an impact in terms of preventing me from doing something really terrible. . . . But then, I'm probably unique in this, because if people in general understood this notion of punishment in the next life, there wouldn't be as much evil and violence, raw evil, in the world today.

The second interview was with G., an Orthodox woman in her early forties, extremely intelligent, a mental-health professional, and a mother of seven. It is presented here in abbreviated form:

B: Do you believe in *olam habah*?

G: Well, I know it is one of the thirteen Ikarim (Articles of Faith). Therefore, I have to believe in it.

B: What is it you believe?

G: In my naive way, I believe it is a place where souls are basking in the splendor of God, not in a corporeal way but in a spiritual sense.

B: Does it have an impact on your personal life?

G: Yes, though not in a conscious way. Or perhaps I should say I'm conscious of it in the abstract. I understand it as a reward, a reward for living the proper Jewish life. . . . I also like to believe that at some point dear ones will be reunited in some way with their loved ones. . . . But I don't believe it is only the righteous, only religious people, who will [merit this] . . . but all people leading a good life, the right kind of life, will live there. By that I mean people who do their best to live a good life. . . .

B: Is there a connection between this world and that, a consciousness between the two worlds?

G: It could be. I really don't have a sense about this.

B: Have you ever discussed the idea of *olam habah* with your kids?

G: I have on occasion talked to them about *olam habah,* but in terms of reward and punishment—no!

B: When you die, God forbid, and you qualify for a place in the next world, how do you conceive of it? What do you think it will be like?

G: I haven't come to terms with it. It doesn't have a subjective quality for me where you go, where the souls go, if one doesn't make it, what the relationship is between heaven and hell— these are things I haven't grappled with.

B: Is there any connection between heaven and hell?

G: I imagine there must be, but intellectually I can't grasp that concept. It's too simplistic to think there's one place for the good people and one place for the bad ones. It's far more complex than that.

B: What about *Tehiyyat Ha-Metim* (resurrection of the dead)?

G: I don't have any idea.

B: Do you think your soul will live on?

G: If it does, it won't be in the form of a continuation of myself, not me functioning as a human being, as I do now or as I am

now. Rather, it would be some distilled, clarified spiritual
essence of myself. . . .

However, it seems to be in vogue now to believe in some kind
of a concrete hereafter. I find it shocking, and very telling that
recently one of the soap operas on TV featured a whole group of
people in an afterlife. A few people died, and then they were in
heaven, dressed in white, orchestrating what was happening here
on earth—such as whether to avoid an accident that would kill
someone, etc. Something like *Oh, God* [the movie]. . . ."

Coming back to what I said before about basking in the splendor of God, I believe there is some connection between learning
Torah and that existence . . . that it will be some kind of spiritual existence. Maybe it will be so distilled that it will be just
basking.

B: Just there, lolling around?

G: Yes, but I think there will be some sort of Torah enterprise,
Torah emanations. If Torah is only for this world, then it
wouldn't be so, but if, as I believe, Torah is something more,
then whatever aspect of Torah is transcendent and beyond this
world will be pursued in the other world.

I think it will also be some sort of perfect communal existence. I suppose the reason I say this is because of the midrash
"tzaddikim nehenim miziv hashechinah," a picture of tzaddikim sitting at the table, learning Torah and basking in the splendor of
God. Part of that is the image of tzaddikim not being able to flex
their arms and therefore unable to feed themselves so that each
one feeds the other across the table. To me that symbolizes a
perfect communal existence.

These ad hoc, unschooled, though very thoughtful eschatological
opinions reflect more or less the views held by other respondents:
a diffuse understanding of the tradition on matters; a range of
belief and disbelief in the hereafter—the odd combination of
remoteness and immediacy, ambivalence and affirmation; and
finally, a very tenuous acknowledgment of the impact of such con-

cepts on one's actions in the present life. Moreover, these informal
findings parallel those of others who have looked at the state of
contemporary belief.

Had I been similarly interviewed on the subject, without benefit of preparation, as was the case for my respondents, I believe I'd
have made quite the same statements—ambivalent, hesitant,
uneven, of piecemeal knowledge. And this despite that I know the
concept of the afterlife is a staple of the faith system I fully
embrace, high up on the list of the top ten or thirteen principles
the philosophers and halachists select for their primary lists. It is an
elemental belief I liturgically affirm with regularity and without a
second thought, or to be more accurate, without a thought altogether.

However, when one is forced to take a long, directly focused
look—which writing forces one to do—one learns something else
about one's self. In the course of working on this chapter, I was
surprised to find how powerfully I hold a view of an afterlife and
how deeply and profoundly it influences so many of my decisions
and actions.

Having said that, I must convey the other, which is also true—
that despite its deep and pervasive impact, the idea of an afterlife is
not something I think about systematically or coherently or speak
about very often, if at all. This raises a curious question, and then
a second one:

Is it possible for one's actions to be informed by so inchoate a
value, one not even close to the surface? Yes, I believe so. It is a
value that is deeply internalized, securely embedded in the psyche;
thus, it is ever ready to influence deed and thought. Nor is it mere
rationalization to say that this is perhaps the most healthy way of
incorporating such a belief. Were it ever present in consciousness,
it would border on the morbid and exert a paralyzing effect. One
should stay focused on this life and not become detached from it.
To do otherwise would be to suggest that this life is unbearable;
fantasies of an afterlife would then serve as ropes thrown over-
board. Not surprisingly, as one chronicles through history the idea
of an afterlife, it becomes quickly apparent that, when Jews (or

Christians, for that matter) felt the noose around the national neck, concepts of afterlife and resurrection took on more prominence than in better times, when such ideas fell from dogmatic eminence.

Next question: If my thoughts of an afterlife are so diffuse, so far from surface consciousness, how is it possible for me to know that they affect my very life? One way is that this concept comes to the surface periodically, reflexively, intersecting my here-and-now life at strange times and in unexpected places. And it feels quite comfortable; I never fight it, never deny it.

One such example, an incident that occurred many years ago when I was a student at HILI yeshiva, comes to mind now. My ninth grade *chumash* teacher, Mr. Levy, had previously taught us: The whole world is like a vestibule. Prepare yourself in this world so that you may enter the world to come (*Pirkei Avot* 4:21). I do not remember my initial reaction, but it wasn't something stunning. Probably I tucked it away quite matter-of-factly, as philosophically passive teenagers of yesteryear were wont to do.

Several weeks later, in one of those irreverent acts that thirteen- and fourteen-year-olds commit against vulnerable authority figures, we girls planned a mock wedding. When Mr. Levy turned the knob and walked through the classroom door, we surprised— no, shocked—him with shouts of "Mazal Tov" and a hail of confetti all over his dark blue serge suit. I see his face before me even now, the rounded features, his eyes opened wide in disbelief. The generally mild-dispositioned and slow-spoken Mr. Levy turned quite furious and then quite pale. For a brief instant, I feared he would die of a heart attack. Then the thought disappeared from my mind. But, through my tears of riotous laughter, I felt a momentary pang of remorse.

In five minutes, it was back to business as usual. Except for confetti all over the floor, smudges of wiped-off lipstick around our mouths, the bride's and groom's paraphernalia resting on a back desk, we were docilely back to the study of sacred texts. But I had had a flash of insight. I remember looking all around me. Was this room my vestibule?

I do not know whether this was the first time I experienced a glimpse or glimmer of an afterlife. Given my upbringing, I tend to doubt it, for surely, I, like L.'s young children, had had death explained to me in terms of an afterlife. Nor do I know how often thereafter I experienced my life as a vestibule. Certainly it was not a recurrent pattern, but I do know that every once in a while a palpable feeling that there is a real world beyond my immediate one is summoned from the recesses of my being and then returned to a quiet resting spot until summoned forth once again.

What triggers thoughts of an afterlife? A variety of experiences. When I hear of someone who has successfully made a *shiduch* or when I labor in the matchmaking field myself, I not only rejoice in the new couple's happiness but instinctively note that the matchmaker will be rewarded with a place in the world-to-come. When I make special effort to study Torah under pressured circumstances, I'm aware that my efforts will be rewarded with a place in the afterlife. When my mother-in-law, who survived her husband by fifteen years, would speak of her conversations with him, and then toward the end of her life speak of joining him, I would listen to her with wonder, not doubt.

Yet I must acknowledge that my most powerful and frequent thoughts of the afterlife arise from a different source. It is not the view of the afterlife as reward nor as image of a place for souls to be rejoined that trips the eschatological switch. Rather, the notion of an afterlife serves as an inhibitor of harmful, dishonest, or evil deeds, actions I might otherwise try to get away with, acts that I would not be held accountable for on this earth, things that no one would know but God and me, and which perhaps not even the heavenly computer is tallying at this very moment. There are situations where I could steal, not only outright theft, but where someone has given me too much money or has added up the columns incorrectly, and no one would know if I didn't speak up; situations where I could take revenge on someone who has hurt me and that person would never know it was I who had harmed him or her; or more base feelings—fantasies of wanting to murder someone and no one would suspect me because of the fine station in life or particular reputation I enjoy. Unlike L.'s case, the immediate consequences of my actions (such as fines, jail, or embarrassment) seem less significant than the consequences to my life after life. And unlike G., who doesn't think in terms of reward and punishment, I think of final judgment, tipped scales, divine retribution, full disclosure, total accounting. It is not that I am consumed with contemplation of a place in the world-to-come or even that I envision and long for it, but rather that I don't want to be unworthy of it; I don't want to fail the test for entry—I tremble at the very thought.

So I have admitted it: my primary and recurrent association with afterlife is its inhibition over my baser instincts, the fear of being found out at the end of my days. I am not necessarily proud of this, for I am aware it is a more primitive, less sophisticated, less mature view. Yes, I know we should exhibit virtuous behavior for its own sake, out of pure love for God and humanity, and not out of fear of punishment. Nevertheless, I am grateful that even an inchoate vision of the next life keeps me relatively "clean," free of moral stain, in this one. It is not totally foolproof, and happily my base instincts are less rather than more. Still, a final accounting before crossing into the afterlife is an important accessory to a large set of ethical laws for the here and now. Given the penchant for some evil in ordinary people like myself, there would surely be greater incidence of breach. Similarly, when I perform a good deed that goes unnoticed or unrewarded—as do many good deeds in life—a quiet awareness that this act will eventually be counted makes me feel good.

A second powerful association with afterlife comes when I am forced to confront death or injustice—even more so, when these two forces converge, such as in the untimely death of an unusually good person. Perhaps *olam habah* is not an immediate answer, nor even a fully satisfactory one; yet here, too, the image of an afterlife gradually assimilates itself into the subconscious and from there surfaces every so often.

Last year a dear friend died very suddenly. I felt a massive grief at his loss not only because I loved the man but also because of his death at this particular time of his life. Simmy, age seventy-four, had recovered from a nasty bout of shingles two years earlier. After years of urging by his wife, Anne, he finally agreed to semi-retirement from his busy law practice in Boston, which meant he now worked only twelve hours a day. They had recently purchased an apartment in Jerusalem, directly across the street from their younger son, daughter-in-law, and four young grandchildren. The last were very close to him and, like their father, called him "Dad." Simmy and Anne planned to spend several months a year in their Jerusalem apartment.

Simmy was a true tzaddik, albeit in bon vivant's clothing. Courtly and polished, he could also be opinionated and contentious. Beneath that colorful exterior, beneath even an occasional goddamn and what in hell, lay the gentlest, tenderest of souls. He did more acts of *chesed,* more favors for people, than anyone I've ever met. Any of his acquaintances who ever encountered an underdog would instinctively advise, "Go ask Simmy G. for help." And somehow he always managed to find a way to avoid even the merest thanks. He could have called in one-tenth of his personal IOUs—which he never had anyone sign—and lived out his years, unto one hundred and twenty, in luxury and dignity. Yet just as he was poised at a moment when he could finally enjoy a most happy time of life, it was snuffed out. He should have had another fifteen years, ten at least. I wept for a solid week after his funeral. I grieved for his wife, for his children and grandchildren, as did the many hundreds of people who attended his funeral and walked in his cortege, the great and famous rabbis who eulogized him, the bank clerk who burst into tears a week later upon learning of his death. For weeks and then months I grieved at the premature end of his life and could find no consolation anywhere inside of me.

More than any saint I've ever read or heard of, Simmy deserved a place in *olam habah;* by dint of a single act of *chesed,* the scales of the heavenly court would have been tipped, and he would have been sent express to the world of the righteous. Yet in the weeks and months immediately following his death, this did not once occur to me. He was dead, very dead. If he was not here, he was nowhere. It was totally unfair, unjust.

But my system simply could not handle that. It rebelled against so blatant a violation of fairness. In recent weeks, as the pain has become a bit less raw, as time has given a small measure of respite, I find myself occasionally thinking that Simmy is probably arguing and cajoling his way through heaven, helping a few helpless saints. And I've heard his extremely bright and sophisticated twelve-year-old grandson Noah say, "I talked to Dad . . ." All of this doesn't take away the sadness that he's not here, but somehow it makes it more manageable. Otherwise we might just throw up our hands in total bewilderment. . . .

These, then, are my primary associations with an afterlife. Still I have not answered for myself the question: why do I believe? Rational skeptic that I am, why should a matter so thoroughly unverifiable, so defiant of laws of nature, have penetrated my consciousness and exert such power over me? . . . I who read with great suspicion reports of those who have "been there and back," glowing whiteness, lightness, pervasive love. . . .

One reason, I am certain, is because I was schooled that way. *Olam habah, Tehiyyat Ha-metim* [resurrection of the dead], *bet din shel ma'alah* [the Court on High]—these are prominent features of rabbinic literature, of liturgy, of Halakhah and *agadah*. Educated as I was in Orthodox institutions where these concepts were—are—taught quite matter-of-factly and are never challenged, I simply took it all for granted. Mr. Levy's classroom appeared to me to be a vestibule because Mr. Levy had transmitted the message of the sages that it was so. G.'s vision of tzaddikim feeding one another across the table was her association because she had encountered that particular midrash. When I tell a joke, I am mindful of the halakhah that requires me to give proper attribution to its author. When I see a letter lying in a drawer and am curious about its contents, I remember the ban: one who eavesdrops or reads another's mail loses a place in the world-to-come. Such a simple act made so explicit reverberates in my mind when I am faced with the opportunity or desire to commit an even larger "crime." Just as I have accepted the commanding voice in other areas of Jewish living and belief, so, too, here.

The second reason I believe is that I think I must. For me, as for many other people, the idea of a hereafter serves a cosmic need. There is simply too much injustice in the world, as the old Yiddish proverb "God runs the world but not like a *mentsh*" attests. If God is omniscient, omnipresent, omnipotent, there has to be something else beyond this moment in time. Hitler now in his grave and Jewish children now born to the second generation are not enough. Hitler deserves something more terrible than inert death, and the second-generation parents' one hundred cousins who didn't survive deserve something more than our memory of their truncated, traumatic lives. Nice guys should never finish last. And I have seen righteous people neglected and their children begging for bread, and I know something is terribly amiss.

The reader might question how I can give the second reason, cosmic need, when I have just given the other, that I would not have come to the idea on my own had I not been educated to believe. Perhaps there is inconsistency here, yet both are true. After having been educated to believe in *olam habah,* I find it natural to apply that concept as an answer to questions that others who were not a priori disposed to that idea would try to answer in some other way.

Up until now, I have told you I believe life doesn't end when it ends. I have also described what triggers a mental association with afterlife. Finally, I've attempted to explain how I came to such a belief.

But the original question was: what happens after we die?—a question that challenges me to conceptualize "life" on another plane of existence. The truth is that here I am not at all sure what

I envision. Let me reflect on the matter a moment. It could be that only the soul lives on, embodied in some kind of vaporous matter. But, no, I don't think so. On the other hand, if souls are reembodied, flesh upon bones, at what state of physical development, or decay, does this occur? Surely our bodies are not resurrected in the state they were at death. . . . Who would want that? And, if it is bodies—as my nephew Nachie once asked, "Where's there enough room?"—and, if the next world entails resurrection in bodily form, why do I feel no fear that I might exist in the world-to-come as a blind person because of the eye donor card in my wallet? I find myself in agreement with those halakhists who legitimate selective autopsies as long as they meet the conditions that the body parts are treated with dignity and then given proper Jewish burial and that the accumulated knowledge will increase and enhance life on earth—for the honor of the living takes precedence over the honor of the dead. Yet who knows?

Will the bodies of those who die in the *galut* roll through subterranean channels until they reach the Holy Land and from there be restored afresh to a future life? Who is my late neighbor with now? Is he rejoined with his first wife who predeceased him by thirty-one years and who now lies next to him in the burial plot they purchased long ago through their synagogue, or will he ultimately be with his second wife of thirty years, whom he also adored?

Is the next world a parallel world, with communities or hierarchies—or is the only hierarchy the one that exists between heaven and hell? Is there gender equality? I wonder. Are people's feelings hurt? Does Noah work out the entire conversation, or is Simmy actually talking to him? Are my Uncle Isaac and Aunt Ceil, who were married, not too romantically, for almost fifty years and died within a few hours of each other and traveled together in short twin caskets from Seattle to Jerusalem, still bickering and still caring for each other? Is corporeal revivification a total impossibility?

And who gets in? Is it all Israel, except for a few sinners, or is it all the righteous of the world, including even those who believe in many gods yet affirm the afterlife?

And what activities abound in *olam habah*? Is it primarily Torah learning? Is my mother-in-law busy all day long acting as a *melitz yosher,* an intercessor on behalf of her numerous kin? Are there children running about, and are their youthful souls wafting about more energetically than the oldsters'? Is there eating and drinking? Can you taste a persimmon in the afterlife? Can there ever be a life without dieting?

I have a thousand questions, but only at this very moment. Otherwise I simply never bother to envision this realm. I can agree with almost any scheme that has been presented, as well as with its opposite. Through my interviews, I came to understand that this is true for others as well. Geniuses that the rabbis were, they constructed a philosophy of afterlife offering something for everyone—images to appeal to different personal world views and engage very different souls. Rejecting one eschatological scenario, an individual can find his or her resonant images in a different traditional source. The rabbis advanced a fundamental teaching that somehow remains responsive to personal packaging and to very individual taste. The only requirement, it seems, is that one affirm the idea. Beyond that, it is open season.

And that suits me quite well, for I am certain that what may have been an appropriate vision as a child no longer suits a mature adult. In fact, I would categorize my conception of life after death as a sliding scale of faith. As Arthur Cohen has suggested, belief in the hereafter is a "doctrine of trust, neither pressed upon others nor denied by ourselves."

All of which brings me to my final comment in this chapter, though not likely my final thoughts on the matter: Perhaps I feel so little concern with detail and so much engagement with concept because the major impact of *olam habah* is on my life here and now, not in the sense of rerighting the scales of justice but rather as a paradigm for this very life. What the concept of revivification, resurrection, afterlife says to me is that you can fall down and rise up again. You can hit bottom and turn around. You can suffer depression and reversal—and spring back. Life inevitably has its swings, and just as some sort of physical life and the life of the soul can come back after death, so can life on this earth. It is no coincidence that in the *Shemoneh Esreh,* the blessing for resurrection incorporates concepts of lifting the fallen, healing the sick, freeing the trapped: it is the blessing not only of life after death but of optimism for better times in this life. Not only can God restore life after death, but the Holy Blessed One can lift us up, over and over again. And not only God, but you, I, can restore, renew, refashion our lives.

For that alone a belief in life after death is worth holding on to. Besides, the rabbis say, who does not believe in it will find no place in the world-to-come. I'm not willing to take any chances. I believe. I believe.

Permission to Believe

Marc Gellman

The only question is Why do the righteous suffer? And the only answer is the *olam habah,* the world-to-come. That is my teaching when the reality of suffering presses in upon us. I place great stress on the value and truth of this authentic but often-overlooked Jewish belief which we have given to Christianity and then abandoned ourselves. This dream, this faith in life after death can quell the storms of despair and fear that grip us all when we look without blinking into the face of our own mortality or the mortality of those we love.

Olam habah not only saves our hope in the face of death; it also saves our faith in God in the face of the world. The essential and defining belief of our faith is that the world was created by an all-powerful and benevolent God, and unless there is a world-to-come, that belief simply makes no sense. Without a world-to-come to even out the scales of justice set so askew in the world-that-is, we simply cannot believe in a God of justice. Without a world-to-come where goodness is rewarded and evil punished, we simply cannot believe in a God of goodness.

The poet Archibald MacLeish stated with haunting simplicity the dilemma of evil in a world with an all-powerful and good God in his play *J.B.,* a modern midrash on the Book of Job. He has the character called Nickles, a popcorn seller in the circus who represents the devil, taunt J.B.: "If God is God He is not good, / if God is good He is not God; / take the even, take the odd." The choice posed by this dilemma is powerful and very depressing: an impotent but well-meaning God or an all-powerful God who is a bastard. Take the even, take the odd.

Aristotle took the even. He voted for a God who was all-powerful but totally removed from all human affairs—in his words, "thought thinking itself." Mystics, existentialists, and Buddhists take the view that God is not all-powerful and that goodness is evanescent.

Normative Judaism takes the only way out, and that way is straight into the world-to-come. I offer you this Jewish way out of Job's dilemma. In tractate Horayot 10b, we learn:

> R. Nahman b. Hisda comments on the observation in Ecclesiastes 8:14 that often we see good people suffer and evil people thrive. On the contrary, he asserts, "The righteous have the lot of the wicked only in this world; in the world-to-come it is reversed." Then Rabba replied, "What about the righteous who do not suffer in this world?" (He apparently knew both of the righteous people who did not suffer.) To Rabba, Rav Nachman replied, "Blessed be those who are able to enjoy both worlds."

In this passage the simple and powerful solution to the suffering of the righteous and the prosperity of the wicked is affirmed: there is another world where everything crooked is put straight. The suffering of the righteous in this world is of no consequence when measured against an eternity of bliss in the world-to-come, and the transitory pleasures granted to the wicked in this world are nothing compared to their utter annihilation in the world-to-come. Indeed, Rav Josiah chimes in with other reasons why the wicked might prosper in this world. They might repent. They might still be moved to do a mitzvah or two in their lifetime, or they might have children who would become righteous. But the main reason for the prosperity of the wicked is clear to the rabbis. God is clearing out any rewards due to the wicked in this world so that they might be utterly annihilated in the world-to-come.

The Greeks had a motto "The mills of the gods grind slowly, but they grind exceeding fine." The *olam habah* is the Jewish equivalent of that hope. We need to know whether John Demjanjuk was or was not Ivan the Terrible, was or was not a concentration-camp guard at Sobibor. We need to know whether he was just an illiterate Ukrainian who landed in Cleveland, a city with a famous hospitality to illiterate Ukrainians. We need to know, and it seems at this juncture of the legal process, that we cannot know. For the Israeli Supreme Court to release John Demjanjuk was one of the great acts of judicial courage in our time. A just court must always release the accused if guilt cannot be proved beyond a reasonable doubt. That is the way with courts in the world-that-is, but what we must believe—what we must know—is that the courts in the world-to-come will know who John Demjanjuk is and what he did, and he will receive the perfect justice in that world which he could not receive in this one. Not to believe this is to believe that even genocide does not reach the notice of a moral God.

It is also important that we keep up the pressure to find the killers of Yankel Rosenbaum. For me and for every Jew and for every person of good will, this is not an old news story. The killers of Yankel Rosenbaum must be brought to justice, but if the code of silence in the black community of Crown Heights in Brooklyn, New York, is so strong that no witness will ever summon up the courage to step forward and say, "I was there that night. I saw it all and these are the people who put him down"—even if that immoral code of silence thwarts the search for his killers in this world, it is critical to believe that in the world-to-come his killers will find themselves taken and judged in an instant. Not to believe this is to believe that even pogroms do not reach the notice of a compassionate God.

Our belief in the moral equilibrium in the universe absolutely requires a belief in a world-to-come. Our belief in a good and powerful God demands the belief that this God will not be forever silent in the face of cruelty and evil. Our belief that justice can be delayed but not denied cries out for a world-to-come where the scales of justice will be evened out by God. It is the only way that the mills of the gods can grind exceeding fine; it is the only way that God can put back the shattered pieces of our hopes and dreams that goodness has an edge in the universe over evil. This is the essential point: God and the world-to-come are not two ideas. They are two parts of the same idea. They are two facets of the same diamond, two sparks of the same fire and the same hope that bring the only enduring light to the dark night of our souls.

Nickles was right. The devil is right. In this world, the riddle holds. If God is God, he is not good; if God is good, he is not God. Take the even, take the odd. In this world, justice is not only delayed but all too often denied. In this world, the motto that drives people is Do unto others before they do it unto you. In this world, bad things happen to good people and good things happen to bad people. The only answer is that this is not the only world.

But perhaps there really is nothing. Stare for a moment into the terror of nihilism, which is the only coherent alternative to this belief of Judaism. Looking at nothingness is a necessary spiritual exercise before you can firmly accept a belief in the world-to-come.

We all know that there is either something after death or there is nothing. Let us consider the possibility that there is nothing. Let us examine the possibility that death is the true and final end of us in every way—no heaven, no hell, no soul, no eternal life, no God. Just blackness and nothingness. Let us consider this charming, heartwarming, hope-inducing prospect. I was taught by teachers trained in the traditions of European existentialism who were big fans of nihilism. Let me offer you just one of their descriptions of what you can expect if there is no *olam habah,* and then ask yourself just one question in response: "Can I live with this?"

Richard Rubenstein, my first Jewish teacher, wrote:

I am convinced that I have arisen out of nothingness and am destined to return to nothingness. All human beings are locked in the same fatality. In the final analysis, omnipotent nothingness was lord of all creation. Nothing in the bleak, cold, unfeeling universe is remotely concerned with human

aspiration and longing. . . . Only death perfects life and ends
its problems, and God can only redeem by slaying. We have
nothing to hope for beyond what we are capable of creating
in the time allotted to us. . . . In the final analysis all things
crumble away into the nothingness which is at the beginning
and which is at the end of creation.

I was once convinced by these words. I was once swayed by the
nihilism of this brilliant teacher and atheist rabbi. He was my first
Jewish teacher, and I was naked in the face of his brilliance. In fact,
I remember my first day as a rabbi in the shadow of his words. I
was just twenty-two years old, and already waiting for me in my
new office at Northwestern University Hillel Foundation was a
young man with a question. He asked me straight out, "Rabbi,
what will happen to me after I die?" I looked at this troubled man
who had come to me for comfort from the wellsprings of the wisdom of Judaism and I said to him, "After you die, I believe that the
worms eat you." He left sobbing deeply. (Many rabbis now call me
for advice. I tell them all, "Answer only trivial questions for the
first ten years of your rabbinate.")

Since that day I have grown older, grayer, heavier, and wiser. I
found the courage to speak the words of faith and hope that my
parents and God had placed within me from my childhood. Since
that day I have seen thousands cope with death or be defeated by
death, and from each of them I have learned. I have learned that
there is something—not nothing—out there waiting for us, something wonderful and loving and peaceful and joyous. I have learned
this by watching hundreds of people die. I am a good watcher, and
what I have seen is this: people who believe in the *olam habah* (even
if they have never heard the phrase or studied the texts that teach
it) die with infinitely greater serenity and peacefulness than people
who do not believe in the world-to-come. People who face a death
conceived of as utter annihilation cannot be serene—they are torn
and bitter, and they die in anger.

Since that day I have seen dying husbands tell their already
deceased wives and dying wives tell their already deceased husbands that they were coming, and I know that they were not

speaking to nothingness. They were speaking to somebody. My friend and teacher Father Richard Neuhaus told me of his first day as a chaplain at Nassau Medical Center. A Jewish man named Harry lay dying before him and then suddenly awakened from his coma, looked at Richard—who was crying—and said, "Don't worry, don't be afraid. Everything will be all right." And then at that moment he died. You don't have to believe in out-of-body, near-death experiences of tunnels and bright lights to learn that there is something after death. You just have to watch people die, and then you will know that Harry was right. Like my friend Richard, I have watched people die, and I know for certain that the ones who die like Harry, with serenity and grace, with hopefulness and quietude cannot be wrong.

Since that day long ago when I poured the salt of nihilism on the wounds of my young interlocutor, I have watched and learned from dying people. Their wisdom has given me the wisdom and courage to offer sincere spiritual counsel to hundreds of frightened people that their loved one is all right, that his soul is resting peacefully in the world-to-come, and that in time they will be reunited with him. I know these words bring solace, but I would not say them and I did not say them until I knew them to be true. I wish I could find that chap who came to me my first day as a rabbi with his very good question, to which I gave such a very poor answer. I would read to him from the third chapter of the Wisdom of Solomon, a work of the early rabbinic period:

> The souls of the righteous are in the hand of God, and no torment will ever touch them. In the eyes of the foolish they seem to have died, and their departure was thought to be an affliction, and their going from us thought to be their utter destruction, but they are at peace.

This is the truth and the answer. Believing that death is not the utter extinction of those we love is the only hope strong enough to help us leave the gravesite and the only hope strong enough to help us cope with the cruelty of the world. However, this truth cannot be learned from a book or a professor or a theologian. It must be learned from life and from a teacher: perhaps a rabbi, perhaps a parent or grandparent or friend—from someone who believes that it is true. And I believe that it is true! Any comfort I have ever been able to bring to the hearts of the sorrowing is driven and sustained by my faith in the *olam habah,* which is essential and true, mysterious and wonderful, gentle and sure, challenging and comforting.

We will be together again in that place. Turn right beyond the green pastures just beside the still waters, and you will find me. I will find you. I will be teaching Torah or golfing—one of the two—and you will say, "How could we ever have doubted that such a place was real?" And I will say that I understand.

I understand that in life you saw so much wickedness in the world, that it was hard for you to believe that the good in the world could win. I understand that when you saw someone you loved more than life itself taken from you, it was hard to believe that anything that had been so cruelly taken could ever be given back again, that anything that had withered and died could ever put forth new green shoots and blossom again into the sun of a new day. I understand that when you have seen so many hopes crushed, so many bright futures ruined, it was hard to believe that hope would ever win out over despair, that success would ever triumph utterly over failure. I understand how it is hard, when you have seen over and over again the randomness of fate, to believe in a benevolent and sustaining cosmic order. I understand that when you have lived with physical, emotional, or economic pain for so long, it is hard to believe that you will ever draw an easy and free breath again. I understand that when you have been rejected and ostracized for so long because of your appearance or accent or intelligence or poverty, it is hard to believe that someday you will stand in a glorious place where everybody knows your name. I understand that when you have seen wars, many wars, it is hard to believe in a time when every day will be Shabbat and when nation shall not lift up sword against nation, nor will they study war anymore. I understand that when you have lived a life of fear, it is hard to believe that someday you will never be afraid of anything.

And I will then sing you a song. (That's one of the sure ways you will be able to know that it is the world-to-come—I will be able to sing.) This song comes from an old hasidic saying from Rabbi Nachman of Bratslav. The words are: *"Kol ha-olam kulo gesher tzar me'od, gesher tzar me'od. Ve-ha'ikar, lo le-fahed clal."*—"The whole world is a narrow bridge, a very narrow bridge, and the main thing is not to be afraid."

The Here and the Hereafter

Dow Marmur

THE DIAMOND PLUCKERS

Levi Isaac Horowitz is the first American-born hasidic leader. He is known as the Bostoner Rebbe. A recent book by Joshua Haberman, *The God I Believe In,* contains an interview with him. Rabbi Haberman describes this Hasid as "unique among Orthodox leaders in his openness and outreach to all sorts of Jews" and writes that "his warm personality and practical outlook make him a much sought-after counselor." Let us look at some of the rebbe's counsel.

In the interview, he was asked about his views on life after death. In characteristic fashion he began his response with a parable: Once upon a time there was a king who wanted to give a treat to the workers in his diamond mine. He told them that, for three hours only, they could keep for themselves all the diamonds they could pluck from the ground. Some got so excited that, as soon as they found a stone, they would polish it and fantasize what they would do with it once the three hours were over. Others just tried to collect as many diamonds as possible, leaving the polishing and the fantasizing to later. Needless to say, these collected much more than the others. "Why?" asks the rebbe, and answers: "Because they used the time for what was meant to be."

Having made his point, Rabbi Horowitz was ready to generalize. I quote from the interview: "Life is not meant to investigate what is going to happen afterwards. If you spend time on that which happens afterwards, you'll miss the opportunities that are here in life. There is so much to do while you are alive that while thinking about what is going to happen afterwards, you will be missing great opportunities of what is happening here at the moment." And the rebbe added: "The greatest moments are the moments that a person is alive. Concentrate on what you can take here; pluck as many diamonds as you can."

TRUTH, NOT CERTAINTY

Let these words be the message to us all. Few people facing death have not asked questions about the hereafter. We all want to know what will be beyond the grave. We are curious for the sake of those who died as well as for ourselves. We want to speculate about what will happen with the diamond we call life once the three hours are up.

As moderns, products of the age of science, we also want certainty. We are not satisfied with vague speculations and alternative theories; we want precision—and we want it now. Therefore, many of us may be irritated by the kind of story told by the Bostoner Rebbe. In the absence of exact answers, we may even be tempted to conclude that Judaism does not believe in life after death. You hear that kind of nonsense from a lot of Jews who should know better.

Some are so desperate that they seek out other religions or go to spiritualist séances in the hope of finding certainty. And, needless to say, in our consumerist society there will always be those who, usually in the guise of mysticism, package the message according to customer demand, whether it is true or not, thus pretending to provide definite answers to impossible questions.

We must not fall into that trap. We must not confuse certainty with truth. Though the rebbe, as an authentic exponent of Judaism, seems to be less precise than many would want him to be, he speaks the truth; his words are rooted in the Torah. He speaks on behalf of our tradition, which affirms that truth is often ambiguous. In fact, one way of defining Judaism would be to say that it is a way of living with ambiguity.

No responsible exponent of Judaism would say that there is

nothing beyond the grave. Life would be pretty meaningless if it were only an episode between birth and death. But Judaism is saying that we cannot know what came before birth and what will be after death. Speculating about it only mars our enjoyment of life and prevents us from taking the opportunities that life provides.

To be "otherworldly" may be considered "religious" by some, but it is viewed as an evasion of responsibility by our teachers and sages, for whom human responsibility means responding to the "here," not speculating about the hereafter. Our tradition impresses upon us that ours is the task to pluck as many diamonds as possible in the few hours allotted to us, and to worry about what to do with them once we no longer can work the mine.

We will not be helped if we spend all our time speculating about what we cannot know. It is not right for us to give assurances that no human being who has integrity and insight can dare to offer. It is far better for us to accept responsibility in life and to focus on what we can do here and now to make this world as rich and livable as possible.

Not that there is nothing beyond this life, for our tradition is replete with references to *olam habah,* the world-to-come. But it insists that there is nothing you or I or any other human being can know about that world; all we can do is yearn and hope for it, not speculate about what it's like. To be responsible means to recognize our limitations as humans and accept our inability to see beyond the grave, and do the best we can now—in spite of the uncertainty.

This is not as easy as it sounds. It is particularly difficult for those who have just lost someone near and dear. Life seems empty and meaningless without the one whom we have loved. Collecting rough diamonds to be polished at a later date seems futile to the point of being delusionary. We ask impatiently: if we are not able to discern purpose and meaning here and now; if we cannot see what the diamond is to be used for—is it not a ploy? To be told to await illumination at some unspecified later time, and get on with mundane matters in the meantime—is this not a fraud?

My answer is no to both questions. For the purpose of the rebbe's parable is to suggest that life has intrinsic meaning and that all you and I have some control over is to find some of that meaning now. That is how our tradition understands religion. By speculating about what is beyond, the meaning of *this* life will elude us and we'll be none the wiser about the next.

And grieving will become virtually impossible. For the purpose of mourning is not to find answers about the afterlife, but to help mourners find their way back to this life. By affirming life as we experience it now, we can also build memorials for the dead. By carrying on where they left off, we can bestow meaning on their unfinished work and give purpose to ours—in the hope that those who follow us will, in turn, give meaning to our endeavor.

This is the most important message Judaism has for us in the face of the mystery of life and death. Our teachers are adamant that the mark of true religiosity is to be found in the seemingly mundane. We are called upon to transform the profane into the sacred, not to break the barriers that time and space impose on us.

Therefore our teachers urge us to dirty our hands by plucking the diamonds from the ground, even though what we find is not as perfect as we would like it to be. Authentic exponents of Judaism of every denomination urge us to reflect on the lives of those whom we have lost not by speculating about where they are now but by remembering them as they were then, when they used their time on earth "for what was meant to be," as the rebbe put it. Let us use the time we have on earth to better the world and thus hallow both God and the memory of the dead.

The Fate of the Soul

Zalman M. Schachter-Shalomi

A PERSONAL MEMORY

The fate of the soul after death has deeply concerned me ever since I awakened to my own thinking.

In 1939 I was fourteen and a half, and we were refugees in Belgium. Hitler had just taken over Austria, where I grew up. I felt as if all of my roots were cut from under me. The specter of not being left to live out all my allotted years because of Hitler was in the foreground of my mind. I was angry with God. I wanted to have some people in God's place so I could vent my frustration and anger on them. One Shabbat afternoon I decided to visit an Orthodox youth fellowship, Pirchei Agudat Yisrael, where I could count on them to study a text of the Mishnah, *Pirkei Avot,* the Ethics of the Fathers.

The lesson always begins with "All of Israel has a share in the world-to-come." I think to myself: Oy, will I give it to them! I go there prepared with all my ammunition, and sure enough, sitting opposite me at the head of the table is a young man with a Talmud folio before him; he begins to read this Mishnah. Before long, after he translates the first part, I jump into the conversation and I put out all of my denial: "The world-to-come! Pie in the sky! Nobody has ever come back from there! Baloney! Opiate of the masses! This is only to enslave and deceive people! You rob them in this world but promise that they'll get something in the next world." And as I start to pour my pent-up anger, the people around the table are getting furious, ready to tear me apart. But the signal from their leader at the head of the table is to stay calm and let me finish.

When I finish, he says to me, "Would you like to hear from someone who agrees with you?" I say, "Sure enough!" At this point, I can't back out of it. He begins to read for me Maimonides' Mishnah commentary on the section he has just read, which deals with the issue of the afterlife. Maimonides debunks the popular gross ideas of the folktales arising from a naive understanding of Torah and Talmud, and then proceeds to refine them to a most sophisticated subtlety.

Hearing this reading touched me in a deep way, and at that moment I began to make my deep commitment to Judaism. I now had a sense that there exists this spirituality beyond what I saw as the fairy-tale language used in the Talmud. And with the debunking came the affirmation that there really was something there. But this something was much more subtle and much more spiritual than what I had heard up to that time. With this affirmation, the issues about God and soul took on greater clarity for me.

We are dealing here with material that seems to scandalize the rational, everyday mind. If it were not described by those seers endowed with a "fantastic" vision, we would not be able to approach this issue at all. We cannot and must not approach the subject with the attitude of nineteenth-century scientism, asking, "Who has ever come back from there?" This is not material that has hard, laboratory-repeatable, empirical data behind it. But given that one looks at the prima facie anecdotal reports on our own and other traditions, one meets countless reports that rivet one's attention and demand that one look into them for the paramount patterns they share.

There are people who have been researching in what we may call borderline sciences, studying psychic phenomena, parapsychology, and near-death and out-of-body experiences. Often in their studies they quote Hindu and Tibetan Buddhist texts and compare them with the reported phenomena. Whenever I as a Jew read that material, I felt that tradition and the teachings I received about the afterlife were confirmed by these outside sources. And yet I also experienced a very deep frustration and regret that our Jewish sources were not part and parcel of their conversations.

In the 1950s, when I was searching for this type of information for myself, I began by looking in the library's subject catalog. I got to know names of authors who had written about postmortem survival. One day, I ventured into the stacks and discovered an entire section in the Dewey decimal system filed under number 133. I still remember it well! There, facing me on the library shelves— far beyond anything I ever imagined—were all kinds of studies of what the philosophers and the religious writers had to say about the world beyond death.

To my delight, one day I discovered thirty volumes of *Arcana Celestia,* written by the Swedish mystic Emanuel Swedenborg, and I opened one to see what was inside. How surprised I was to see an amazing midrash on the Torah interspersed with observations that Swedenborg, trained as a scientist, made when in one of his altered states. He was able to visit realms that compare with our *M'tivta D'rakia,* the Academy on High. Swedenborg knew these worlds as the realms of good and of truth. In the Jewish mystical tradition of Kabbalah, one would speak of similar worlds described by Swedenborg—the worlds of Yetzirah, and of Briyah, and the Gan Eden below and the Gan Eden above. Here I had found Jewish Kabbalah, in a different cultural garb.

To my surprise, another author I found was Sir Arthur Conan Doyle. He had been for me just the creator of the Sherlock Holmes mysteries until I discovered, also in those 133 stacks, how he and Sir Oliver Crookes had worked together in the British Societies for Psychical Research, applying their intellectual acumen to the question "What happens to us after we die?" The Societies for Psychical Research, in this country and in England, produced many works concerning communing with the departed, mediumship, and other psychic phenomena, and studies of the near-death experience and life after death. It became very clear to me that the literature on this subject was enormous.

About the time I was reading about the afterlife, I also started to pay attention to spiritualism. I visited people working as mediums and settings in which spirits of the dead purportedly came through. I discovered that these kinds of encounters brought about a deeply surprising experience of authentic and truthful material being communicated. This also gave me an understanding of what I read in the writings of the psychic Edgar Casey and in the kabbalistic text *Shaar Ha-Gilgulim,* a medieval text on the reincarnation of souls.

And yet, as I read through all these kinds of studies, I realized that what we Jews had to say about such topics never entered into the discourse. It was no wonder! The first translations of Jewish classics from the Hebrew were done by rationalists. They were ashamed to make available texts that would expose the kinds of mystical writings that the Jewish historian Heinrich Graetz rejected as irrational superstition. They did not translate works dealing with otherworldly matters such as soul and afterlife, so these sources did not get to be known in German or English translations. Sure enough, the Yiddish author Y. L. Peretz could tell stories about *Yenne Velt*—"the other world"—but that was safe enough for translation since it was seen as folklore. As long as it did not philosophically contradict the *Religion der Vernunft*—"Religion of Reason"—as Judaism was understood to be, the rationalists felt safe. In this way, our teachings on the afterlife remained unknown to the world at large. For many Jews, the thirst for knowing something about our teachings regarding the mystical journey of the soul was not quenched.

For me personally, the matter became crucial about 1950 when the Lubavitcher Rebbe, Rabbi Yossef Yitzchak Schneersohn, passed on. Suddenly, without access to the master's guidance, we were bereft. I often pondered, How can I contact the rebbe? At one point, I even offered his son-in-law and successor to train as a medium so that the Hasidim would be able to consult the late rebbe and continue to receive his guidance. In the first year after his father-in-law's demise, Rabbi Menachem Mendel Schneerson insisted that he was not the rebbe but that he was merely the chief of operations for the late rebbe. "The rebbe, Rabbi Yossef Yitzchak, is the leader of the generation. What difference does it make if he is in this world or the other world?" was how he put it.

"Medium?" he said. "If the rebbe wants to come through, he'll find his ways to come through. We don't have to provide jumping tables. Let him go direct to each individual Hasid in visions, apparitions, or dreams. The rebbe knows how to move around the narrow limits." And, in truth, for a while I received his guidance in dreams. In this way, my concerns about and interests in the issue of the afterlife were sharpened by the loss of my master's physical guidance and reinforced by the dream apparitions. As a result of these experiences, I began to look at the classical doctrines on postmortem survival with a fresh eye.

DOCTRINE AND EXPERIENCE

Classical Jewish belief is very clear: there is this world, *olam hazeh,* and there is the world-to-come, *olam habah.* At birth the soul enters the body, and at death it leaves it and continues to survive. This belief is referred to in Jewish sources as *hash'arat ha-nefesh*— literally, "the survival of the soul." There is judgment and reward and punishment in the afterlife. According to the Ethics of the Fathers, we are to give our report or reckoning, our *din va-heshbon*, before God for a lifetime lived and expect that we will be judged by God after death. Additionally, there is Gan Eden—paradise— and Gehinnom—purgatory. All these beliefs are articles of faith in the Orthodox world, where they are read about in traditional sources and taken seriously. However, for most people these worlds beyond death are seen as some supernal reality that is not directly accessible to human experience within this world. There is an unbridgeable reality gap between what is believed, because one has to believe it, and what one actually experiences.

Even among those who, as a matter of doctrine, affirm a belief in divine postmortem reward and retribution, there is very little awareness of the specific teachings found in the tradition. If you were to say, "Do I have to believe that?" people would say, "Yes, that's what you have to believe." If I were to retort, "Can you show me where in Jewish literature such teachings can be found?" only a few could cite chapter and verse. They will affirm existence of a life after death as part of their creedal commitments, but believe that it is a reality of another kind, not accessible to us here.

It is this type of thinking that divides the *mitnagged* from the Hasid, the rationalist from the mystic. For the mystically inclined, the underlying question is always: When I perform a commandment, does it have a certain psychospiritual effect on my connection with God? How does the fulfillment of a commandment impact upon my being, my soul, my consciousness? For the rationally thinking *mitnagged,* on the other hand, there is an unbridgeable chasm between the transcendent reality and personal human experience. In other words, it doesn't matter if one has a direct experience of some deeper level of consciousness. What is important to the rationalist is that God's will is fulfilled on this plane. There is no notion about what a mitzvah, or commandment, is beyond that. Clearly, this dividing line between two types of mind, rationalist and mystic, affects the way people think about these questions.

If you read, you will discover just how much mystical literature is available and how, over the course of millennia, Judaism has traditionally accepted the existence of an ontological or ultimate reality in the life after death. Only in the last one hundred years has the rationalist mindset hidden this mystical point of view in the closet.

As human beings, we have deep hunches about the afterlife. But there has been much denial about death in general and about one's own mortality. The reason this conversation does not come out of the closet is that although we have deep hunches about it, we do not have socially acceptable means to talk about it. A tradition provides a person with a socially acceptable means to enter the conversation. By hearkening back to the tradition, I can go back to these intuitive feelings, the hunch that there exists an afterlife.

A MEDITATION ON THE EVOLUTION OF IDEAS AND SOULS

What I have learned in my encounter with the question about life after death leads me to the following meditation. The early parts of the Bible know not of an afterlife above or in heaven. There is a region known as Sheol, the netherworld—Hades. In that region all souls, righteous and wicked, abide (including the patriarch Jacob, who says that he shall surely "go down to Sheol," and Samuel, the prophet, who is raised from Sheol by the Medium of Ein Dor). Scripturally, the dead sleep in the dust and await the time they will be raised from their grave.

Apparently, at that time there had not yet taken hold a belief in a heavenly afterlife in which the blessed and vindicated souls abide. We find in the "intertestamental period" the extracanonical texts of the Apocrypha, and in them there are already other beliefs about the afterlife that in the talmudic period become distinct visions of heavens and hells. In the Middle Ages and Renaissance, especially after the publication of the Zohar, there are complete geographies of the seven levels of Gehinnom and the many mansions of the heavens. Around this time, teachings on reincarnation make their appearance, after having been denied in earlier times. What is one to believe today, in the welter of seemingly conflicting notions of afterlife found throughout history? Are these beliefs really in conflict, each one contradicting the other? Or, perhaps are they philosophical ideas that reflect various stages in the evolution of both the ideas of soul and the soul matter of the world?

As I started looking through history, I saw a growth in the history of ideas. In my meditations I often contemplate the cycles, the patterns, as they unfold. Patterns, rather than specific details, give us the deeper insights. For me, the deepest midrashic process is to discover patterns that are embedded in the ancient texts. As we wrestle with the meaning of these texts, they begin to issue forth new insights and patterns that we then apply to our readings of other texts.

When I bring together what I have learned from the study of psychology and from my own introspection, I discover the existence of similar developmental patterns. I frequently ask myself if the development of the stages of the afterlife deals only with ideas or if there is a deeper pattern that reflects the evolution of the soul itself. I see in the variety of teachings on the afterlife a parallel to the long evolutionary process in which consciousness arises from single cells to sexual reproduction in animals and at last reaches that of human beings. After many millennia of evolution, human souls emerge out of, and at death return to, a primordial pool. Thus, for instance, in Judges 2:10 we find the statement that "an entire generation was gathered into its ancestors." As a soul discarnate, one returns to the "ancestors" after a lifetime. This is to be taken as an ontological reality and not as a mere figure of speech.

Through the process of evolution, more and more consciousness emerges with each life cycle. The experience of each lifetime creates a deeper and stronger imprint of specific personality molded on the spiritual substance of the individual soul. Through her evolving biology, the earth produced the now-enhanced matrix of the human soul. That soul matrix proceeded so far that it reached that level where it could even think about the process of thought, thus reaching the sophistication in which it would turn its thought to the meaning of life and to what happens after death.

With the close of the biblical period, we are talking about judgment before God, purgatory, and a heavenly life after death. But at that time and at that level of evolution, we see only one individual life cycle. Then, centuries later, there is the introduction of the possibility of multiple lifetimes, many cycles. Notions of reincarnation appear in religious texts all over the world. So, too, people report déjà-vu phenomena and relate their experiences of recalling past lives. These testimonies enter the stream of popular culture, again suggesting that the ontological reality of people's lives, as well as the inner consciousness, reflects what is found in the text, and vice versa.

AFTER-DEATH CARE

Another important consideration is: how are we to help those who die and those who have died? I think often about those dying now who are making their way through to the other side and the problems they are likely to encounter. I pray that they are getting help from those who come to meet them on the other side.

From Jewish texts, we know of states of the after-death experience in which the soul is disoriented and confused. Our sources speak of *Hibbut Ha-Kever*, the pangs of the grave, and *Olam Ha-Tohu*, the world of confusion. How do we understand the reality of these states for people who are now dying or who are recently deceased? Are there any traditional models of care for the souls of the dead? From the legacy of Hasidism, we know that the Baal Shem Tov used to talk about *Tikkun Ha-Neshamot*, "the fixing or mending of souls." Before Shabbat he would help all those souls that had passed during the week to make their reconciled entry into the world beyond. It was known that on Friday afternoons he would say a long Minhah Amidah, afternoon silent prayer, and, using deeply concentrated prayer, would act as a guide on behalf of the souls of the dead. Similarly, in the premodern Jewish world there were lay societies—the Hevra Tehillim and Hevra Mishnayot—who took upon themselves to provide after-death care by reciting psalms, the Kaddish prayer, and selected texts of the Mishnah.

Even now in this age of the epidemics of cancer, AIDS, and

other ravaging diseases, we need adepts to do this type of sacred rescue work. Members of the Jewish burial society, the Hevra Kaddisha, could learn to offer such help to those who have died; ideally, each Hevra Kaddisha group could have its own set of hospice workers to help people make the transition from life to what lies beyond. These and other possibilities are a natural outgrowth of the research on Jewish ideas of the hereafter. With a deeper knowledge of Judaism's afterlife traditions, individuals and communities can be more adequately equipped and motivated to create cooperative institutions dedicated to postmortem care of the soul.

THE RESURRECTION

Finally, in reflecting on ideas about the afterlife, I turn to the question of the meaning of *Tehiyyat Ha-Metim,* the resurrection of the dead. Each day I recite several times the traditional Jewish formula "Blessed are You who revives the dead." In what way can one affirm this ancient principle of the faith the sages and Maimonides teach as an essential component to being a believing Jew?

I do not believe that the crypts will open up in cemeteries and corpses will crawl out of them. Do I believe that at some time at the end of days the individual cells of my remains will be reconstituted? How many bodies have I worn out in only one lifetime already? We keep on changing. I cannot claim that this body will rise at the time of the resurrection. Which one of my various bodies, from which incarnation, which time in history? So I ask myself: How can I say I believe in the resurrection of the dead and mean it?

I believe that the resurrection occurs when dead matter proceeds to become a conscious, living being. This resurrection seems to be happening to the totality of this planet right now, at this very moment. On the cusp of the twenty-first century, this planet is waking up, being raised from being merely dead matter to becoming aware, conscious, alive. In paying attention to the emerging conscious ecology, we are part of this miraculous process of the rising from the dead. As human beings, we are becoming part of the planet's consciousness. In the language of the Lovelock-Margolis

"Gaia hypothesis," we serve as the cells of the global brain. We are hearing the message of the planet Earth saying to us: "You can no longer do what you are doing to me. You have to change your ways. You have to collaborate with me." As we begin to awaken and hear this message, we begin to collaborate with earth's awakening and healing.

I believe *Tehiyyat Ha-Metim* is the resurrection of matter. In the past we used to think of matter dead and unconscious. Today, in this age of nuclear technology, genetic engineering, and supercomputers, matter is becoming alive to us. We speak of atoms, molecules, and cells as strings of information. Biologists have discovered genetic consciousness as encoded in DNA and RNA. With the advent of the computer, we now think of the memory as resident in silicon, a stone chip. Our thinking about matter and the physical world has undergone a shift from death to life.

Tehiyyat Ha-Metim, the resurrection of the dead, can then mean the coming to total awareness of the planet as a living organism with which we are connected. As beings in connection with the holographic planet mind, we will be augmented in consciousness and enriched by all other conscious beings.

This meditation on the evolution of the soul follows the way of the evolution. In this flow of thought, the disparate statements regarding the fate of the soul become of one piece. We meet the treasured pearls not separately but as part of a whole string, one in succeeding connection with the other. The teachings of Jewish tradition on the soul and its afterlife destiny can in this way be seen in a unified-field theory, as a part of the greater whole.

Love As Strong As Death

Bonny V. Fetterman

"Love is strong as death," says the Song of Songs. Not stronger, but as strong. My father died sixteen years ago. There is a hole in my life, as there is an empty place at our table. Neither can be filled. And yet, he is with me every day and we are closer now than we have ever been.

Dad had had a stroke, after which he sank into a deep coma. He awakened once and asked me what had happened to him. I told him that he had had a heart attack and that the doctors said he would recover. He closed his eyes and became comatose once more. After a few weeks, with him still in the hospital, I returned to my apartment in Boston.

One morning, I woke up extra early. I felt my father die. I felt a gust of wind shoot by me, and I knew it was my father's soul escaping from his tortured body. I packed a suitcase and went to the airport. When I arrived at my parents' home in New York, my sister told me they had tried calling me all morning. But I had already known my father died. I felt he had tried to say goodbye.

He died two days before Passover, on the 12th of Nisan, so we had to end sitting shivah as the holiday commenced. Silently we assembled at my sister's house for the first seder. I was never so relieved to have a text and a tradition tell me what to do. We got through the seder. Dad would have been proud of us, and we were together. The unstructured hours of the long days that followed were unbearable.

In the days and weeks that followed, I felt a stranger in my own life. I quit my job and moved back into my mother's house. Nothing felt normal, until one night I had a dream unlike any I had ever had before. It was a visit from my father. I could feel his big, bear-like hug and hear the sound of his voice. He told me not to worry, everything would be okay. After that, it was. I made a life for myself in New York and tried to give what comfort I could to my mother.

Eleven months after he died, I had another dream visit from my father. This time I could only hear, not see, him. He told me I would no longer see him because his soul was leaving his body, but not to doubt that he was always there. I believed him, as I always had. Years later, a friend who studies Kabbalah told me that Jewish mystics believe the soul takes leave of the body after eleven months.

I visit his grave before his yahrzeit. It is always a visit with Dad for me. I feel his presence there and talk to him. Seeing the headstone with his name always stabs my heart, but I leave comforted after leaning against the monument for a hug. Over the years, I feel more and more that he never left me. When I do something particularly mature, I feel his approval shining on me. When I miss the mark, I feel his reassurance that I will grow up. Nobody does it all at once, he used to say. His love echoes in my ears.

This strong attachment that I feel strikes me as strange. We were not particularly close during his life. Our relationship was friendly, easy, not intense. We were so different in temperament: he, patient and stoical; I, restless and quick-tempered. I think with pain about my own adolescence, a time when children assume parents don't know anything, which in my case coincided with a coming of age in the turbulent sixties. My mother tells me stories of Dad's own conflicted relationship with his parents. I recall that I came into my father's life when he was at the seasoned age of forty-five. I am forty-five now, and I understand his acceptance of many things, opting for grace instead of struggle.

In his last years, my father aged far too quickly; he aged before I knew how to make life easier for an ailing person. My attempts to care for him were clumsy and probably annoying. At any rate, I was sucked into the family's generalized panic at an illness that would not go away. I'm sorry to say that we were constantly pressing him "to try to get better" when he alone realized that this was not a matter of choice.

I think of my father's life as sad in many ways: so many gifts and talents unused, so many ambitions disappointed. He was a plumber, a job he hated. Not that he didn't respect the profession—he frequently told us how civilization as we know it rests on plumbing—but he hated the hard, dirty, manual work and its lack of status. He dreamed of being a writer, a poet, an actor, an inventor, a millionaire—all dreams thwarted by family exigencies. Every time I turn my back on a road not taken, I think of the choices he made and the reasons why he made them. Sometimes, when I can bear to, I reread his letters to me at college, his stories, the columns he wrote for a plumbing magazine in which he had a regular advice column—and I think of my own work as an editor. No doubt genes run true. Often, when I pick up his tools for a household repair and do it smart and neat, I thank him for these gifts.

I am not the sole inheritor. I think of his genes as marbles, and I got the blue ones, steadfast and loyal. My brother the scientist, with his indefatigable curiosity, got the red ones. My artistic sister, the sunny yellow ones. But we all share the tutelage of his consistent example and unique personality.

When we were young, and other families made Sunday outings to parks and beaches, we just as often would go to what was then called Idlewild Airport. There, one building, encased in glass, was devoted to the boiler room, and every pipe was painted a different color, like a gigantic Mondrian painting. Dad was fascinated by this building, and we would all trek out to admire it. Sometimes I remind myself to appreciate the beauty to be found in unexpected places, a gift that came so naturally to him.

My father spent every day doing mitzvot—not mitzvot in a religious sense, but good deeds and acts of kindness that he felt commanded to do. I remember him rising early every Sunday morning to buy fresh rolls and deliver them to various people he knew who were shut-ins or alone, people he felt could use a visit and a treat from a good kosher bakery. We called these excursions "Dad's bread route." He understood loneliness, and he also knew how to overcome it. In the course of my days, I try not to let an opportunity to do good get by me, and then, like him, take it one step further. I think of him whenever I push myself to reach beyond myself.

My father lives in me, in my memory of his personality intact, vital, and inspiring. To whom will I leave my legacy? I have no children to whom I can bequeath these genes or my memories of a life lived. And yet, like my father, I have faith in the cosmic economy. Who knows what lives we touch and how? In keeping alive the memory of the person that he was, I wonder if he would ever guess it would be me—the youngest and most rebellious of his offspring. Knowing him, I guess he would have been amused, and maybe a little happy. I have no doubt I'll find out one day. The fact that love is strong as death gives me reason to hope.

Where Does It End?

Ben Zion Bokser

I look out upon the far horizon. Where does it end? The line drawn by my eye is only imaginary. It will recede as I come near it. Space, like time, is continuous, and there are no sharp interruptions to differentiate one thing from another.

And is it not likewise with my life? I look back into my past. I cannot tell where it began. I am familiar with some of my ancestors, but my life did not begin with them. It stretches far back into time beyond my reckoning. A long line of generations labored to produce me.

The peculiarity of my walk, of my smile, may go back to one, and the bent of my mind to another. The sound of my voice may carry an echo of some unknown benefactor who passed something of himself on to me. The seed that develops in me was planted in a faraway past, and as I reap the harvest I know that other hands made it possible.

Equally long is the line of my spiritual ancestors. The love of life and the sense of kinship I feel for my fellow man are but simple expressions of my spirit, but men achieved it after groping and suffering. The first man who rubbed two stones to produce fire is my ancestor, and so is the first man who discovered the glow of friendship in the clasp of two hands. The men who explored the seas and the mountains and who brought up the hidden riches of the earth are my ancestors. They enriched me with the fruit of their discoveries, as well as with the spirit of their daring.

I am what I am because of the first amoeba that developed into a more complex form, impelled by the divine imperative to grow. A thousand sunsets have shaped my sense of beauty, and a thousand soft voices have taught me to be kind. Waters from a thousand springs have quenched my thirst. I look out upon my world and act in it with all that is mine, with every past experience, and with everything that entered into it.

As I think of the long line stretching far into the past, I also cast my glance forward. The line into the future is just as unbroken. It moves through me into generations yet unborn. And as I think of this, I am comforted. For I am a point in that line, and the course of existence travels through me. I have inherited from all the past and I will bequeath to all the future. In the movement of that line lies the secret of immortality, and I am a part of it.

Chapter Twelve

What Do We Need Death For?

Jack Riemer

I had a daydream. In my reverie, I argued with God. I told God that I was angry, for I had just lost my sister-in-law, who was like a sister to me. It is true that she brought her life to a close in a wonderful way. When she learned what her illness was, she made the rounds visiting and saying goodbye to all the people whom she loved. And then she was ready. She died peacefully and gently. But I was angry. So I said to God in my dream: Why did such a good person have to die? And while I'm at it, God, why did my brother, who was such a wonderful person, have to die, years before her? And why did my parents, who were such good people, have to die?

That is what I said to God with all the pent-up anger in my heart. And God said to me: Do you not understand the place of death in the divine economy? Would you rather have it your way? And I said impetuously: Yes!

So God granted my request. And then, for a while, in my dream, it was wonderful. I ran and skipped and danced with pleasure at what I had persuaded God to do. But only for a while. Summer came and went, fall came and went . . . and I could not tell the difference. They were exactly the same. Not a leaf withered. Not a flower faded. And soon the flower that looked so beautiful began to look boring. And the tree that looked so lovely became dull. And everything on earth seemed vapid, boring, stale. No one died, but no one was ever born either.

Eventually I came back to God and said: You are right and I was wrong. And I said the blessing that you are supposed to say when you have a loss, the blessing that acknowledges that God is the one true judge.

The Jewish religion celebrates life, sure it does. If there is one word that every single Jew in the world knows, it is *l'chaim,* which means "To life!" If there is one blessing that every Jew can recite by heart, it is the *Sheheheyanu,* the blessing that thanks God for the gift of life. If there is one commandment that every Jew takes seriously, it is *'uvecharta b'chaim*—Thou shalt choose life. We are a life-affirming people.

On the one hand, we are a people whose central prayer on the Days of Awe is: "Remember us for *life,* O king who delights in *life,* and write us in the book of *life,* for Your sake, O God of *life.*"

But this same religion that so celebrates life also recognizes, and forces us to recognize, the reality and the ever-presentness of death. One way it does so is by means of the Day of Atonement. Yom Kippur has many meanings, but surely one of them—and perhaps the main one—is that it is an annual confrontation with our own mortality.

The tradition makes us say the Yizkor, the memorial prayer, on this day. It locates this prayer at the center of the day, at high noon, so that we cannot avoid or escape its message. And the tradition makes us say on this day the *Unitane Tokef* prayer, the most awesome prayer of the year, which says, "Who will live, and who will die, who by fire, and who by storm, who by thirst, and who by hunger, who by earthquake, and who by plague?"

So which is it? is Judaism a religion that celebrates life or is it a religion that focuses on death? Or is it a religion that strives somehow to hold the two—life and death—in a strange, inseparable, inextricable balance, because it believes that we cannot apprehend one without the other?

There is a strange comment found in rabbinic literature. The Torah says that when the creation was completed, "God saw all that He had made, and behold, it was very good." Says Rabbi Meir, "What does 'very good' mean?" It means "including death." How could Rabbi Meir have said that? How could he, who was surely an authentic Jewish teacher, say that death is very good? Doesn't that go against the love of life that we have been taught is central to Judaism? The implication is that life would be ultimately incomplete without death. Is that what Rabbi Meir meant?

There is a children's story called *Tuck Everlasting,* written by Natalie Babbitt. It tells about a girl named Winnie who accidentally discovers the secret of the Tuck family. It seems that many years before, they drank from a certain hidden spring that gave them eternal life. As a result, they never age. They can never die, not from injury, not from disease, not from old age.

The two sons, Jesse and Miles, will always be seventeen and twenty-two. The father of the family, who is called Tuck, explains to Winnie why this is not as wonderful as it seems at first. They are floating down a stream in a rowboat, and he says to her:

"Know what that is all around us, Winnie? . . . That's life, moving, growing, changing, never the same two minutes in a row. This water . . . you look out at it every morning and it looks the same, but it ain't. All night long it's been moving, coming in through the stream back there to the west, slipping out through the stream down east here, always quiet, always new, always moving on, and someday, after a long while, it comes to the ocean.

"D'ya know what happens then," says Tuck, "to the water? The sun sucks some of it right out of the ocean and carries it back in clouds and then it rains and the rain falls into the stream and the stream keeps moving on, taking it all back again. It's a wheel, Winnie, everything's a wheel, turning and turning, never stopping. The frogs are part of it, and the bugs and the fish and the woodthrush too. And people . . . but never the same ones. Always coming in new, always growing and changing and then moving on. That's the way it's supposed to be. That's the way it is."

The rowboat bumps into the branches of a fallen tree and stops. Tuck continues: "It goes on to the ocean . . . but this rowboat now, it's stuck. If we didn't move it out ourselves, it would stay here forever, trying to get loose but stuck. That's what we Tucks are, Winnie, stuck so's we can't move on. We ain't part of the wheel no more. Dropped off, Winnie, left behind. And everywhere around us things is moving and growing and changing. You, for instance, a child now, but someday a woman, and after that, moving on to make room for the new children."

Winnie is overwhelmed with understanding and she blurts out: "I don't want to die." "No," says Tuck calmly, "not now. Your time's not now. But dying's a part of the wheel, right there next to being born. You can't pick out the pieces you like and leave the rest. Being part of the whole thing, that's the blessing. But it's passing by us Tucks. Living's heavy work, for off to one side, the way we are, it's useless. It don't make sense. If I knew how to climb back on the wheel, I'd do it in a minute. You can't have living without dying. So you can't call it living, what we got. We just *are*, we just *be*, like rocks beside the road."

The story is saying that without death you don't really have life, you have only existence. It is only the fact that life has an end that makes each day precious. That is what Rabbi Meir meant when he said, "Very good"——that is death.

There is a family in my congregation who taught me this truth. In November, they got a death notice. The doctor told them that the father of the family had only six months to live. His children decided to pack those six months with as much living as they possibly could. So they came to visit him frequently, one from California, one from Virginia. They brought him to visit them. They took him to Israel to celebrate his eighty-second birthday. And they managed to get to all the places in this country that he wanted to see.

The six months turned out to be ten. Those ten months were filled to the brim with all kinds of wonderful experiences. After the father died, the son said: "If we had thought that we had an endless amount of time, we may never have gotten around to doing all those things we did with him and for him this year. We would have put them off and said we'll do them 'one of these days.' But precisely because we knew that we had a deadline, precisely because we knew that we wouldn't have him for much longer, we put him first on our list and made him our priority. We filled each day of his life and our lives with precious shared experiences that we will never forget."

That son was saying in his way what Rabbi Meir said: "God saw all that He had made and it was very good . . . including death." It is precisely the knowledge that our lives are limited that drives us to make the most of them while we have them.

My friend and colleague Danny Pressman tells me that he knows some people—not many, but a few—who live life so well and who feel so connected to the wheel, to the past and to the future, that they are not afraid to die. He says that he was once at a wedding and was standing next to the grandfather, watching the dancing. The man said to him, with a smile on his face so bright it could light up the room: "Rabbi, if I were to die tonight, I'd have no complaints."

What did he mean by that? I think he meant that he could see with his own eyes the continuity of his family, and he could see with his own eyes the continuity of his values, so he was able to say: If I were to die today, who I am—who I really am—would continue to live.

That's the choice, the real choice, that every one of us has to make in this world. If you put your trust in things, and those things wear out, as all things inevitably will, who are you? If you put your trust in your body, in your good looks, or in your youth, and they disappear, as they inexorably will, then who are you? And where are you?

But if you see yourself as part of the wheel, as Tuck says, if you see yourself as part of a great, never-ending cycle, and if you see that who you are and what you stand for will continue, then you can let go of life with confidence, with trust, and with faith.

I went to visit one of my congregants in the hospital the day before he died. I was tongue-tied, squeamish, nearly mute. I didn't know what to say, but he did. He said very simply: "I've had a good life, and this last year has been the best."

If you can say that about the last year of your life—that it has been the best—how rich, how very fortunate you are. And how able to let go.

What is it, then, that we must learn each time we confront mortality? Each time we remember those we have lost, we weep, for we miss them so much. Their deaths have left a rip, a gash, a tear in our lives. There is no denying it. And each time we remember those we have lost, I suspect that we also mourn for our future losses and for the eventual loss of our own life. This encounter with our own mortality ought to be a moment in which we come to terms with the reality that our life is both precious and precarious, precious *because* it is precarious.

If there were no death, how pointless and meaningless and endless our lives would be! But because there is death, how pressured and how precious, how challenging and how sacred, and how brief and how beautiful our lives can be. The psalmist had it right: "Teach us, O God, to number our days—and teach us how to appreciate our lives, whether they be short or long—so that we may thereby acquire a heart of wisdom."

Contributors

Bradley Shavit Artson is the rabbi of Temple Eilat, Mission Viejo, California. He is the author of *Pursue Peace* and *It's a Mitsvoh: Jewish Living Step by Step*. He is now researching a book about Judaism and the environment.

Patricia Z. Barry is a member of the faculty of the School of Public Health, University of North Carolina, Chapel Hill.

Rookie Billet works in Jewish education, student guidance, and college teaching. She is an administrator of the Yeshiva University High School for Girls and is active in the Young Israel of Woodmere, New York.

Debra Reed Blank was ordained by the Jewish Theological Seminary in 1989. She is now a doctoral candidate in the field of liturgy there.

Ben Zion Bokser was the rabbi of the Forest Hills Jewish Center in Queens for fifty-two years. He served as professor at the Jewish Theological Seminary and at Queens College. He is the author of twelve books of Jewish thought and liturgy.

Ruth Brin has published books of poetry and liturgy for children, as well as texts for Jewish composers. Her work appears in a number of modern Jewish prayerbooks.

Arlene Rossen Cardozo, Ph.D., is the author of *Sequencing, Jewish Family Celebrations, Woman at Home,* and other books, essays, and reviews. She teaches and lectures throughout the country.

Barry D. Cytron is the senior rabbi of Adath Jeshuran Congregation in Minneapolis. He teaches Jewish studies at the University of Saint Thomas and at Macalester College.

Amy Eilberg is the director of Kol Haneshamah, the Jewish Hospice Program of the Bay Shore Jewish Healing Center. She was the first woman ordained by the Jewish Theological Seminary. She writes frequently on Judaism and healing for many journals.

Sharon S. Epstein is a social worker in Stony Brook, New York.

Bonny V. Fetterman is the senior editor of Schocken Books.

Nancy Flam is the West Coast director of the Jewish Healing Center. She was ordained by the Hebrew Union College–Jewish Institute of Religion. She has written about Judaism and healing for many publications, such as *Reform Judaism* and *Sh'ma*.

Chava Freud is a freelance writer in New York.

Barry Freundel is the rabbi of Congregation Kosher Israel in Washington, D.C., and adjunct professor of law at Georgetown University. He is the chair of the ethics committee of the Rabbinical Council of America.

Debbie Friedman is a composer and folksinger. Her songs have become part of the liturgy of many synagogues throughout the country.

Jeff Friedman is a therapist, bereavement counselor, and guitarist. He lives in Jerusalem.

Yaffe Ganz is the author of stories, articles, and books. In 1990 she was awarded the Sydney Taylor Body-of-Work Award from the Association of Jewish Libraries for her contributions to Jewish juvenile literature. Her latest book is *Cinnamon and Myrhh*. She lives in Jerusalem.

Stanley J. Garfein is the rabbi of Temple Israel in Tallahassee, Florida.

Marc Gellman is the rabbi of Temple Beth Torah in Melville, New

York. He is the author of *Does God Have a Big Toe?* and coauthor of *Where Does God Live?*

Marvin Goodman is the rabbi of the Peninsula Sinai Congregation in Foster City, California. He is the former director of the Far West Region of the United Synagogue of America.

Blu Greenberg is an author, lecturer, and former college instructor. She is the author of *On Women and Judaism* and *How to Run a Traditional Jewish Household.* Her articles have appeared in *Hadassah Magazine, Moment, Lilith,* and many other journals.

Hayim Greenberg was the editor of the *Jewish Frontier* and the *Yiddish Kempfer* and the head of the Education Department of the Jewish Agency. His essays in Hebrew, Yiddish, and English were collected after his death. The English volumes are entitled *The Inner Eye.*

Agnes G. Herman is a retired social worker and freelance writer. Together with her husband, Rabbi Erwin Herman, she serves as the administrator of the National Association of Retired Reform Rabbis. She is also an advocate on behalf of AIDS Awareness and gay and lesbian rights.

Marcie Hershman is the author of the novels *Safe in America* and *Tales of the Master Race.* She teaches writing at Tufts University.

Abraham Joshua Heschel was professor of Jewish ethics and mysticism at the Jewish Theological Seminary and an activist on behalf of Soviet Jewry, civil rights, and other causes. He is the author of numerous books, including *The Earth Is the Lord's, The Sabbath,* and *Man Is Not Alone.*

Milton Himmelfarb is the retired director of the Department of Jewish Information of the American Jewish Committee. He is the author of *The Jews of Modernity* and the editor of many volumes of the *American Jewish Yearbook.*

Margaret Holub is the rabbi of the Mendocino Coast Jewish Community, a rural alternative *shtetl* on the northern California coast.

Yoel H. Kahn was ordained at the Hebrew Union College—Jewish Institute of Religion. He is the rabbi of Congregation Shaar Zahav in San Francisco.

Shamai Kanter is the rabbi of Temple Beth El in Rochester, New York. He is the former editor of *Conservative Judaism*.

Leon R. Kass, M.D., teaches classic texts in the College and the Committee on Social Thought of the University of Chicago. He is the author of *The Hungry Soul* and *Eating and the Perfecting of Our Nature*.

Gail Katz teaches writing and literature at the Edward R. Murrow High School and at Kingsborough College in Brooklyn, New York.

Alan Kay is professor of English at the New York City Technical College of the City University of New York and is a rabbinical school student at the Academy for Jewish Religion in Manhattan. He is the author of *A Teacher's Guide to My Generations: A Course in Jewish Family History*. He is the founding editor of *Shofar: A Magazine for Jewish Children*.

Anne-Lynne Keplar is the pen name of a devoted wife and mother, who is active in the Gordon Day School of Congregation Beth David in Miami. She is a well-known businesswoman who assists and counsels those coping with pregnancy loss and neonatal death.

Samuel Klagsbrun is the executive director of the Four Winds Hospital in Katonah, New York. He is the chair of the Department of Pastoral Psychiatry at the Jewish Theological Seminary and is a consultant to Saint Christopher's Hospice in London.

Susan Knightly is a writer who lives in Brooklyn, New York.

Abba Kovner was a resistance fighter during the Holocaust and then migrated to Israel. He organized the Vilna ghetto revolt and was a partisan fighter after the ghetto fell. He helped bring thousands of Jews to Israel after the war. He was a member of Kibbutz Ein Horesh. In 1970 he was awarded the Israel Prize. He died in 1992. His last book of poems about facing cancer is called *Sloan-Kettering*.

Janet Roth Krupnick is a graduate of the Cantorial School of the Jewish Theological Seminary and has occupied pulpits in New Jersey and elsewhere.

Alisa Rubin Kurshan is a Wexner Fellow and doctoral candidate in Jewish education at the Jewish Theological Seminary.

Lawrence Kushner is the rabbi of Beth El Congregation in Sudbury, Massachusetts. He is the author of many books, including *The Book of Words, The Book of Letters,* and *The Book of Miracles.*

Herbert J. Levine is the editor of *The Reconstructionist.* He is the author of *Sing Unto God a New Song: A Contemporary Reading of the Psalms,* which is to be published by Indiana University Press this year.

Joseph Levine is the Jewish chaplain at the Clinical Center of the National Institutes of Health in Bethesda, Maryland, and at St. Elizabeth Hospital in Washington, D.C.

Bernard Lipnick is the Rabbi Emeritus of B'nai Amoona Congregation in Saint Louis, Missouri. He is the author of *An Experiment That Worked,* which describes a pilot program in Jewish education that he designed for his congregation.

David (Mickey) Marcus was a graduate of West Point and a colonel in the United States Army, who served in World War II. He went to Israel to help train the new army that was being formed during the War of Independence. He was killed in an accident there.

Dow Marmur is the senior rabbi of the Holy Blossom Temple in Toronto, Canada. He is the author of several books of Jewish thought.

Marshall Meyer was the rabbi of B'nai Jeshuran Congregation in New York City. He was a leader of Latin American Jewry for twenty-five years. He founded the Seminario Rabbinico, Congregation Bet El in Argentina, and Camp Ramah of Latin America. He died in 1994.

Marcia Moskowitz is a member of the English department of

Parkway West High School in Ballwin, Missouri, and a devoted member of Shaare Emeth Congregation in Saint Louis.

Marian Henriquez Neudel is a lawyer, who practices in Chicago.

Joseph Ozarowski is the rabbi of the Elmont Jewish Center on Long Island. He is the author of *To Walk in God's Ways: Jewish Pastoral Perspectives on Illness and Bereavement*.

Linda Pastan, poet laureate of Maryland, has received fellowships from the National Endowment for the Arts and the Maryland Arts Council. She won the Dylan Thomas Prize in Poetry and many other awards. She is the author of *The Imperfect Paradise* and other books of poetry.

Rex D. Perlmeter is the rabbi of Temple Israel in Miami, Florida. He was ordained at the Hebrew Union College–Jewish Institute of Religion and was graduated from Princeton. He is active in interfaith and inner-city causes and in Jewish community affairs.

Rachel (Blawstein) was a part of the Second Aliyah group of pioneers that came to Palestine in the 1920s. She lived on Kibbutz Kinneret. She died of tuberculosis in 1930 at a young age.

Nessa Rapoport is the author of a novel, *Preparing for Sabbath*, and of a *Woman's Book of Grieving*. She is the coeditor of *Writing Our Way Home: Contemporary Stories by American Jewish Writers*. Her short stories and essays have been widely published.

Philip Roth was born in Newark, New Jersey. He began his career with *Goodbye, Columbus,* winner of the National Book Award for Fiction in 1960; in 1987 he won the National Book Critics Circle Award for his novel *The Counterlife* and again in 1992 won the National Book Critics Circle Award for his autobiographical memoir, *Patrimony*. He has published nineteen books.

Steven Saltzman is the rabbi of Adath Israel Synagogue in Toronto, Canada. He is at work on a book about the stories of Genesis.

Zalman M. Schachter-Shalomi is one of the major teachers of the

Jewish Renewal movement. He is the author of *The Paradigm Shift*, *Spiritual Counselling*, *Fragments of a Future Scroll*, and *The First Step*. He is at work on a new book about spiritual aging.

Arthur Gross Schaefer teaches at Loyola University in Los Angeles. He was ordained by the Hebrew Union College–Jewish Institute of Religion. He served as rabbi of Congregation B'nai Brith in Santa Barbara. He does mediation and counseling and has studied the ethics of the workplace.

Harold M. Schulweis is the rabbi of Valley Beth Shalom in Encino, California. He is the author of *For Those Who Can't Believe* and other books and is the founding chairman of the Jewish Foundation for Christian Rescuers.

Rami M. Shapiro is the rabbi of Temple Beth Ohr in Miami, Florida. He is the author of many books, the most recent of which is *The Wisdom of the Jewish Sages*.

Joyce Slochower is associate professor of psychology at Hunter College in New York City and a psychoanalyst in private practice.

Elie Spitz is the rabbi of Congregation B'nai Israel in Tustin, California. He is a student of meditation and of interactive study of the biblical tales.

Ira F. Stone is the rabbi of Temple Beth Zion–Beth Israel in Philadelphia, Pennsylvania. He wrote *Seeking the Path to Life*.

Lawrence Troster is the rabbi of Oheb Shalom Congregation in South Orange, New Jersey.

Daniel E. Troy is an attorney with Wiley, Rein and Fielding in Washington, D.C.

Y. M. Tuckachinsky is the author of *Gesher Chayim,* a compendium of the Jewish Laws of Mourning.

David Vorspan is the executive director of Shomrei Torah Congregation in Woodland Hills, California, and the founder/director of the STS Institute of Jewish Culture. He was the rabbi of Temple Beth Ami of Reseda, California.

Elli Wohlgelernter is a journalist living in Jerusalem, where he is the deputy foreign editor at the *Jerusalem Post*. He is a former managing editor of the Jewish Telegraphic Agency.

Ron Wolfson is the director of the Whizin Institute for Jewish Education and Vice Chancellor of the University of Judaism. His books include the *Shabbat Seder*, the *Passover Seder*, *Hanukkah*, and *A Time to Mourn, A Time to Comfort*.

David Wolpe teaches at the University of Judaism. He is the author of several books including *The Healing of Shattered Hearts* and *In Speech and In Silence*.

Permissions Acknowledgments

Stanley J. Garfein: "An Ethical Will" by Stanley J. Garfein, copyright © 1990 by Stanley J. Garfein. Reprinted by permission of Stanley J. Garfein.

Marc Gellman: "Permission to Believe" by Marc Gellman, copyright © 1993 by Marc Gellman. Reprinted by permission of Marc Gellman.

Blu Greenberg: "Is There Life After Death?" by Blu Greenberg, from *What Happens After I Die?,* edited by Rifat Sonsino and Daniel B. Syme (U.A.H.C. Press, New York, 1990). Reprinted by permission of Blu Greenberg.

HarperCollins Publishers, Inc.: Excerpt from *Love Poems* by Yehudah Amichai, copyright © 1981 by Yehudah Amichai; "Going to Shul" from *The Jews of Modernity* by Milton Himmelfarb, copyright © 1973 by Basic Books, Inc. Reprinted by permission of Basic Books, a division of HarperCollins Publishers, Inc.

Barbara and Benjamin Harshav: "Prelude" by Abba Kovner and "To Wake Up in the Hospital Early in the Morning" by Rachel, translated from the Hebrew by Barbara and Benjamin Harshav. First published in *Orim, A Jewish Journal at Yale* 3:2, Spring 1988. Reprinted by permission of Barbara and Benjamin Harshav.

Agnes G. Herman: "Firepower in Mitzvot" by Agnes G. Herman (*Hadassah* Magazine, February 1994). Reprinted by permission of Agnes G. Herman.

Margaret Holub: "How Tradition Brought One Community to Life" by Margaret Holub. Reprinted by permission of Margaret Holub.

Jason Aronson Inc. and Alan Kay: "Shloshim: the First Thirty Days After Burial," from *A Jewish Book of Comfort* by Alan Kay, copyright © 1993 by Alan A. Kay (Jason Aronson Inc., Northvale, New Jersey). Reprinted by permission of Jason Aronson Inc. and Alan Kay.

Jason Aronson Inc. and Joseph Ozarowski: "Keri'ah: the Tearing of the Garment" from *To Walk in God's Ways* by Joseph Ozarowski, copyright © 1995 by Joseph Ozarowski (Jason Aronson Inc., Northvale, New Jersey). Reprinted by permission of Jason Aronson Inc. and Joseph Ozarowski.

The Jerusalem Post and Elli Wohlgelernter: "Ha-Makom Yenahem: The Place Gives Comfort," previously titled "The Dead Come Home" by Elli Wohlgelernter. Reprinted by permission of *The Jerusalem Post* and Elli Wohlgelernter.

The Jewish Calendar: "A Way to Mark Shloshim," previously titled "A Tree of Memory" by Arthur Gross Schaefer (Chanukah, 1993). Reprinted by permission of *The Jewish Calendar.*

Jewish Frontier Association: "The Funeral of Franz Josef" from *The Inner Eye 2,*

Parenting Inc. Reprinted by permission of *South Florida Parenting* Magazine and Anne-Lynne Keplar.

Elie Spitz: "Why Bury?" by Elie Spitz, copyright © 1994 by Elie Spitz. Reprinted by permission of Elie Spitz.

Ira F. Stone: "A Yizkor Prayer for Stillborn and Infant Deaths" by Ira F. Stone (*Kerem: Creative Explorations in Judaism,* Winter 1994), copyright © 1994 by Ira F. Stone. Reprinted by permission of Ira F. Stone.

Tikkun: "The Therapeutic Function of Shivah" by Joyce Slochower. Reprinted by permission of *Tikkun* Magazine, a Bi-monthly Jewish Critique of Politics, Culture, and Society.

University Press of America: "Coronary Connections" by Harold M. Schulweis, from *Jewish Values in Health and Medicine,* edited by Levi Meier, copyright © 1991 by University Press of America. Reprinted by permission of the University Press of America.

David Vorspan: "Instructions to Those Who Plan My Funeral" by David Vorspan, copyright © 1994 by David Vorspan. Reprinted by permission of David Vorspan.

David J. Wolpe: "Why Stones—Not Flowers?" by David J. Wolpe, copyright © 1994 by David J. Wolpe (*The Jewish Week,* New York, 1994). Reprinted by permission of David J. Wolpe.

Women's League Outlook: "Three Responses to Miscarriage" by Debra Reed Blank, Amy Eilberg, and Marvin Goodman (*Women's League Outlook* 62:3, Spring 1992), copyright © 1992 by the *Women's League Outlook.* Reprinted by permission of *Women's League Outlook,* published by the Women's League for Conservative Judaism.

Women's League Outlook and Ron Wolfson: "The Art of Making a Shivah Call" by Ron Wolfson (*Women's League Outlook,* Fall 1993). Reprinted by permission of the *Women's League Outlook,* published by the Women's League for Conservative Judaism and Ron Wolfson.

Wylie, Aitken & Stone: Excerpt from *Patrimony* by Philip Roth (Simon and Schuster, 1991), copyright © 1991 by Philip Roth. Reprinted by permission of Wylie, Aitken & Stone.

OTHER SCHOCKEN BOOKS OF RELATED INTEREST

The Mystic Quest: An Introduction to Jewish Mysticism
by David S. Ariel
0-8052-1003-2

What Do Jews Believe?
The Spiritual Foundations of Judaism
by David S. Ariel
0-8052-1059-8

On Judaism
by Martin Buber
Foreword by Rodger Kamenetz
0-8052-1050-4

Entering Jewish Prayer
A Guide to Personal Devotion and the Worship Service
by Reuven Hammer
0-8052-1022-9

Jewish Meditation
by Aryeh Kaplan
0-8052-1037-7

When Bad Things Happen to Good People
by Harold S. Kushner
0-8052-4089-6

When Children Ask About God
A Guide for Parents Who Don't Always Have All the
Answers
by Harold S. Kushner
0-8052-1033-4

The Trial of God
by Elie Wiesel
Introduction by Robert McAfee Brown
Afterword by Matthew Fox
0-8052-1053-9

Available at your local bookstore
or call toll-free: 1-800-733-3000 (credit cards only).